SURVIVAL & REVIVAL

SURVIVAL AND REVIVAL

Stroud during the war and recovery years

Joy Thacker

First published in the United Kingdom in 1995
by Joy Thacker, Fairhaven, Whiteway, nr Miserden, Stroud, Glos.

ISBN 0 9521760 1 7

Cover design: Katrina Thacker and Martin Latham

Produced by Alan Sutton Publishing Ltd., Stroud, Glos.
Printed in Great Britain by Alden Press, Oxford and Northampton

CONTENTS

Dedicated to the worthy people of Stroud

ACKNOWLEDGEMENTS

My gratitude to all those enthusiastic Stroud people who have welcomed me (often as a stranger) into their homes, endured hours of interrogation, and then entrusted me with precious family photographs. Although I have implied somewhere that community friendliness ceased when war ended, I am pleased to admit I was wrong. Instead, my research became a pleasurable time among friends, with chuckles later as I wrote up my notes. Thank you to *The Stroud Journal*, and *Stroud News* whose weekly reports available through the Stroud Library Newspaper Reading machine set me on the right tracks, and turned me into a newspaper addict. Also to my family: Vicky for her proof reading, Katrina for her inspired cover, Keith and Kevin for their forebearance and teasing, and mother who recounted numerous episodes from her life. Many thanks to Sue Everson from Alan Sutton Publishing (how can I ever repay her for her enormous support?) and to Fiona Latham, who shouldered the entire enterprise thereafter to bring the book, which is positively bursting with all your personalities, to fruition.

INTRODUCTION

People who have experienced the dreadful blitz in London and other targeted cities during wartime, and witnessed the aftermath and revival throughout the fifties and sixties might laugh wryly if anyone suggested sleepy old Stroud had anything much to offer. To most, Stroud was 'country', 'safety', and perhaps 'boring'. A place where nothing much happened.

They, of course, were right. Nothing too dreadful did happen here. People usually had a home still standing to which to return following a day's work. There were no horrific mass injuries as those encountered nightly in those danger zones, no scurrying to the underground to yet another sleepless night, worrying your home might not be there when you emerged. Country districts did not encounter too much change or death. People did not really expect to be the victim next time. They naturally did worry, but not on the same scale.

Having said all that, Stroud took no risks, preparing itself regardless for every eventuality, welding in consequence, a fondly remembered bond throughout the entire district which endured throughout the following decade.

I was born in 1944, in the midst of it all, unaware of the impact of war or its later influences until I visited Stroud Library to read about the year of my birth on their newspaper reading machine. A few enjoyable hours discovering the local events that surrounded the birth of this new baby named Joy. The celebration of Victory in Europe, a glimpse of who married whom, how much things cost, and what was going on generally.

Within the hour I was completely hooked. Rationing took on a new meaning and made me feel ashamed of any attempts at slimming. The Home Guard television comedy programme with decrepit old people made more sense, and the lists of men lost fighting for their country made me feel sad.

Memories were triggered of childhood days. Comments by father such as 'best butter'. His disgust when we went over to soft margarine for the 'sake of our health'. The tin of salmon opened for a special treat, half a banana, the two squares of chocolate produced for mid-morning break at school, and mother announcing the fruit cake had three eggs in it, 'so it must be good'.

Investigating one year was not enough; it stretched into two, three, several more until twenty had undergone scrutiny and the sixties had been reached. I learned what Stroud did to prepare itself for the impending war; how it coped when the war was over; what people did for fun, and how all this affected our lives during the consumer years of the fifties and sixties.

I soon realised that far from sloping into dormancy as I once thought, Stroud had made a vital contribution a vital part to the war effort and our country's recovery, working prolifically at setting the country straight by getting the exports out. What's more Stroud had fun.

To understand the area in which we live, an insight into international and national affairs is essential. The Second World War brought a change to British social life, altering its structure and attitudes for ever.

Britain's men and women rallied to fight for their country on the battle front, their jobs left to be filled by people not only unskilled and unacquainted with their new role, but prepared after only brief instruction to step in and undertake responsibilities never before dreamed of. Women, who had fought and gained the vote in 1918, had freedom forced upon them almost overnight whether they wanted it or not. Some joined the one-hundred-thousand-strong Women's Land Army, others worked in factories or entered the male domains of construction, engineering and welding. Strange new roles, but essential to Britain's survival and ones which benefited many working-class participants during successive years. Many admitted they enjoyed it! Some resented and rebelled against returning to their narrow lives when victory was announced, and their menfolk returned to claim back their livelihoods.

So began a gradual social change, which throughout the fifties and sixties accelerated dramatically to touch, in some way, all classes of people throughout the British Isles.

In 1945, with imminent danger dispelled, Britain picked itself up and proceeded to rebuild itself at home and abroad. Technological advances, developed in defence projects, were now to benefit commercial and civilian life.

Post-war motor-car production, having suffered fuel, material and labour shortages, increased dramatically, resulting in the need for adequate roads. Aviation had made remarkable progress with the introduction of radar and the jet engine, and long distance travel became much easier.

But Britain's oldest form of travel, shipping suffered greatly, unable to compete with the speed and versatility of its rival in the air. Efforts to expand trade introduced oil supertankers, and luxury cruisers, but the age of speed was upon us, and ships were just too slow. Ports declined along with the number of dockers.

All these factors cannot be ignored when looking at Stroud: although far away, they influence us all. Only by combining them into our district appraisal can we understand why shortages remained for many years, how local efforts combated them and our subsequent change in lifestyle during succeeding years.

This account does not wish to infringe on cherished private thoughts, or diminish them in any way. It merely aims to remind the reader of occasions (often humorous) Stroud encountered at work and at leisure throughout twenty odd years, which have been gleaned through personal childhood memories, numerous newspaper articles, and enjoyable meetings with a host of people who have graced me with their memories and photographs so *Survival and Revival* could appear.

A CHRONOLOGY TO THE BOOK

1934
Hitler became both President and Chancellor to assume complete rule over Germany. Every German male served a year's conscription.

1935
9 July. A Government White Paper ensuring civilian protection during wartime was issued to Local Authorities.
Housing Act. Subsidies introduced to deal with overcrowding. Local Authorities now required to operate a Housing Revenue Account. Rent and Subsidy 'Pooling' to ensure a roughly uniform level of rents across any one local authority. National Government control.

1936
May. Insurance scheme for persons in agriculture, horticulture and forestry began.
2 October. A meeting at Shire Hall, Gloucester, set up an Organisation Committee to provide a precautionary protection scheme against attack from the air.

1937
The Air Raid Precautions Act was passed, and a badge approved by King George VI.

1938
10 March. Regulations augmented for ARP (General Schemes and Fire Schemes).
14 March. Peace Week during which the Home Secretary asked for Civil Defence Volunteers .
22 March. The County ARP Organiser, Capt. Shakeshaft, addressed a crowded Premier Hall at Stroud.
Lectures began on first aid, anti gas, air raid warning procedure.
The Women's Voluntary Service for ARP was approved. A flurry of civil defence activity began throughout Stroud district.
Housing Act. Slum Clearance and Overcrowding subsidy introduced at single rate under a National Government.

1939

Rent and Mortgage Interest Restrictions Act. Re-introduced rent control. National Government.

January. Investigation of housing accomodation for evacuees and emergency workers.

May. Recruitment for Women's Land Army.

3 May. A meeting at Shire Hall determined county councils should assume direct responsibility for their district's ARP, and its personnel recruiting.

July. Every household received the first of five public information leaflets, entitled *Some Things You Should Know If War Should Come*.

8 July. The first of several 'Black-out Exercises' in Stroud.

August. Local Fuel Overseers were appointed.

August. Stroud Ritz opened.

August. Arrangements for sudden evacuation were implemented.

Local War Instructions (of which there were twenty) were issued to Local Authorities from the Central Authority ARP at Gloucester.

27 August. Stroud's first consignment of evacuees arrive.

31 August. Stroud on Stand-by. Many plans were in operation by 7 p.m. Evacuees arrived, the Black-out enforced, and reserves mobilized.

1 September. German Troops invade Poland.

3 September. Britain proclaims war on Germany.

7 September. Bedford Street Canteen opens.

September. The Fuel and Lighting Order and Retail Prices Order, together with a Fuel Advisory Service, was introduced. The first Schedule of Prices in Stroud became operational on 20 October.

29 September. National Registration Day.

1940

January. Food rationing was introduced.

Further evacuees arrived from March until September when those from Eastbourne arrived.

April. Introduction of Compulsory Military Training.

14 May. The Local Defence Volunteer force was formed.

June. Salvage schemes introduced.

26 June. Bombing began in Stroud district.

8 August. The Battle of Britain commenced.

26 August. Berlin bombed for the first time.

28 August. Stroud district suffered its first bomb damage at Cranham Mill.

7 September. The London Blitz began.

10 September. Dig for Victory Scheme began.

13 September. Evacuees from Eastbourne arrived in Stroud.

15 September. The Battle of Britain.

14 November. Coventry bombed.
December. Bristol bombed.

1941
June. Clothes rationing began. The Utility Scheme was introduced.
Continued incendiary bombing led to the formation of a Fire Watching Scheme.
6 August. The announcement of the formation of the Fire Guard.
14 September. Stroud's Fire Guard Registration.
23 December. The Control Room in the Stroud Rural District Garage came into operation.

1942
Publication of the Beveridge Report.
Star Lighting introduced in Stroud.

1944
The Education Act.
6 June. D Day. The Allies land in Normandy.
Masses of Americans left Stroud overnight.
September. Fire Guard duties and other Civil Defence Services began to wind down.

1945
2 May. The Civil Defence for war ended.
July. The General Election.
Tuesday 8 May. VE Day. (Victory in Europe).
6 August. Hiroshima destroyed by US Bomb.
14 August. Nagasaki destroyed by US Bomb.
14 August. VJ Day. Japan surrenders.

1946
Housing Act. (The Financial and Miscellaneous Provision) increased subsidy levels and Local Authority contribution levels, under Labour control. Sunnyhill built at Cashes Green.

1947
An atrocious winter.
January. Bisley Old Road prefabs erected.

1948
The National Health Act.
Stroud's Water Plan.
Stroud's Joint Sewerage Scheme

1949

Housing Act. Removed statutory restriction limiting local authority housing to 'the Working Classes'. Improvement grants introduced, under Labour control.

1950

February. General Election.

1951

Festival of Britain.
October. General Election.

1952

Housing Act. Subsidies increased under Conservative control.

1953

February. Sweets eventually off ration.
2 June. Queen Elizabeth's II Coronation Day.

1954

Wartime rationing ended.
Housing Repairs and Rents Act. Slum clearance re-introduced. Private sector improvement and housing introduced under Conservative control.

1955

'Teenagers' were invented.

1956

Housing Subsidies Act. General housing needs subsidies reduced. Local authority rate fund contributions no longer compulsory. High rise building encouraged under Conservative control.

1957

Housing Act. Consolidating Act. Rent Act. Re-introduced the de-control of rents. Under Conservative control.

1960

National Service ended.

1961

General needs subsidy re-introduced. The Right to Buy introduced by 1980, together with abandonment of large scale building by Local Authorities.
Ritz Cinema fire.

CHAPTER ONE

LOOKING AHEAD TO WAR

With the imminent inevitability of war with Germany, Britain endeavoured to prepare mentally and practically for its arrival. The chief difference between this war and the First World War, or indeed any in history, when conflict was confined principally to the battle zone, was its widespread impact. This time, twenty years on, attack from the air would replace face-to-face combat, with an anticipated world-wide destruction of homes and industrial premises, ports and cities, far from the centre of battle. Before this war and the introduction of fighter aircraft, men could expect to return from war to a country more or less intact, but now their homeland, along with their families, was the target. This war was to affect everyone, no one was entirely safe.

During the second half of the 1930s, Britain had increased aircraft production, trained and equipped her Navy and Army, and radar, radio, and surveillance technology was advancing. However on home ground it was apparent that Britain's ordinary men and women would be Britain's protectors. A situation which prompted the government to assume complete responsibility for the entire country, encompassing every aspect of life – eating, sleeping, working and leisure. The government made the decisions, the local councils implemented them.

Food was a major issue so stock piles were accumulated and surplus buildings in the district commandeered for storage. The country became split into divisions and Home Office Food Departments were formed to deal with numerous aspects of food-related matters. A range of food-related tests and menus were designed to encourage nutrition as even in 1938 many children were still suffering from malnutrition, and people were ignorant of food values. Information pamphlets were produced and distributed throughout schools and clinics, and to parents.

As early as 1935 an Air Raid Precautions system was in operation. The dread of large-scale bombing and gas attack which had cast such fear since the First World War prompted its appearance. In 1938 it was revised under Sir John Anderson, the Lord Privy Seal, to include twenty regulations. Booklets were produced giving information and advice. One entitled *What Everyone Should*

*Wartime welfare 'goodies' ensured the
author ' filled her pram'.*

Know, explained that enemy air attacks were designed to cripple normal life
and work and that an adequate civil defence system, through thinking and
planning ahead, should allow life to proceed as normal.

Eight points were covered; air raid warnings, which allowed a seven minute
interval between the siren and the raid; light screening, to enable dawn until
dusk precautions – it was advised that food, everyone should keep a week's
supply in store; fire, the clearance of attics was suggested, as the top of the
house was the most dangerous part; and evacuation, which advocated keeping
newly evacuated children in the house and amused.

Volunteers were required for a whole range of duties. Men for stretcher
bearers, rescue workers, and firemen, and women to join the Women's
Voluntary Services, the ARP and countless other things.

Some of the first civil defence posts were filled by wardens, who were
chosen from 'level-headed men over thirty', of which eight hundred thought
they qualified and enrolled by October 1938, while the remaining two million
filled one or another of the long list of positions. First aid, clearing, ambulance
services, decontamination and debris removal squads, highway and public
building repair, the removal of citizens from dangerous zones, or the
Emergency Fire Brigade Service.

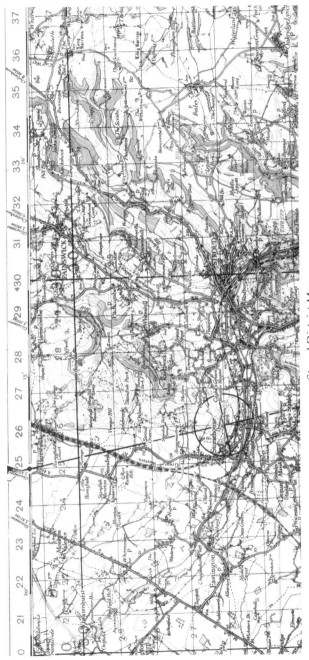

Stroud District Map.

Ernest Dickenson 'Special Constable'.

When choosing special constables, men with experience of the First World War were preferred. Reg Tomlinson was the special constable sergeant at Slad, and Jim Dickenson's father, Ernest, along with Mr Davis, Mr Edmunds and Jack Haliday were among others. During the first part of the war, a constable had to be on duty all night, walking around the village to see if everything was alright.

Nothing exciting happened in Slad, even the incendiary bomb which was dropped behind the church was not discovered until later on and caused no fire.

Tact between the special constables and offenders was generally the order of the day, after all they had to live with one another when the war was over. Instead positive action was pursued, as a young chap who persistently revved his motorbike up outside The Woolpack at eleven o'clock each night found out. When requested to stop, he responded with further revving before roaring off with a farewell, 'How's that, then!'. The failure of his machine to start, despite the energy he pumped into it the following night stopped any further late-night noise.

Soon anti-gas and first aid classes sprang up. Trenches and anti-invasion devices appeared in parks, on commons, and in school fields. Gas masks were

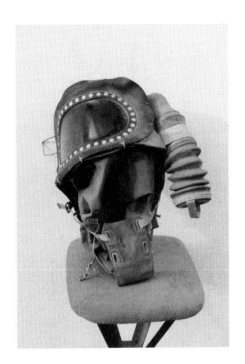

Baby Helmet.

produced and assembled in varying sizes, the first sign of war promoting their immediate issue. Mothers were bothered when baby helmets, which were red affairs with a pump, blue filter and a large window, failed to appear. In the new year when they did arrive, mothers were even more dismayed. A young mother sums up their feelings, 'They were a claustrophobic affair, only really suitable for slim babies. Every mother dreaded the thought of having to put her baby into such a thing.'

Advice was given on testing and cleaning of respirators, and Stroud's first class held on Thursday 19 September 1939 at The Board Room, John Street. People were advised to wipe masks out with toilet soap and a damp cloth after each wearing, and instructed to carry them at all times, because they would be useless if left at home. Once people had one in their possession they practised wearing them, at work, at school, and in the home. Stroud's telephonists wore theirs for an hour while operating their switchboard, and children found they could make rude noises with their Mickey Mouse ones. Min Browne remembers wearing hers while doing Physical Education (which must have been hot) and pupils wore them at practices in school trenches. George Webb at Frampton-on-Severn Church of England School remembers, 'There was always a good deal of fumbling to get them in the right position, and it was hard to see out when the windows became fogged up by steam. There were always tears when we had to wear them. They had a rubbery smell and made us want to retch. We were told not to be sick in our masks.'

Early days saw gas mask boxes everywhere, some of which were brightened up with oil cloth by school children. On the very Sunday war was declared, a member of a church congregation who had her new acquisition beside her on the pew nervously whispered in a fellow worshipper's ear, 'If a raid comes now, I'll have to put my mask on in church, won't I dear?' while a civil servant confessed he took his dinner to work in his.

Air raid warning practices were arranged so everyone would know the drill. The first was on Monday 4 December at 1 p.m., and thereafter every month. It consisted of a steady note (Raiders Past Signal) for thirty seconds, followed by the Action Warning, which was a warbling sound, and finished with a steady note for one minute. The Air Raid Warning Red was a two minute warbling accompanied by short whistle blasts, while bells and hand rattles indicated gas.

Cynthia Shaw, a telephonist at the RDC in John Street, Stroud in 1941, took ARP daytime calls during the early years. She remembers only one Warning Red in her short time in council employment before she moved onto a farm to milk cows. She remembers the Stroud Report and Control Centre was (in her words) 'a glassed-in affair in the Rural District Council car park'.

The government's decision to evacuate people living in danger zones to the comparative safety of the countryside resulted in the biggest mass movement of people ever known, and was certainly the first time so many homes were shared with complete strangers. When it became known Stroud was to be a reception town, a spate of meetings took place to sort the matter out. In time, the public received a letter signed by the Chairman of Stroud District Council, Mr P.E. Hayward, who requested billeting cooperation. He wrote,

> The Council have been requested by the government to cooperate in plans which are being made for the protection of civilian life in the event of war. . . . This protection can only be given with the cooperation of those like ourselves who live in less congested towns or villages. . . . I feel I can rely on the people of Stroud to offer all help they possibly can in this important branch of civil defence.

Subsequently all suitable household space in the Stroud district was commandeered, on the basis of one person per room, which ultimately revealed 26,746 rooms available for billets.

Suggestions of who should go where were many and varied. One idea was to billet all the children together in large camps where friends could remain together, or place them with families near the schools and Stroud centre so the need for transport might be reduced. In the event most areas shared the accommodation problem, welcoming the young strangers into their homes and schools alongside their own children.

As the anticipation of war increased, a well-publicised voluntary National Service Scheme appeared, which asked for volunteers but touched upon a responsibility and duty to one's country.

Its aim was two fold. To show up any gaps in military, civil, and defence positions while ensuring that essential home industries and services were protected. To assist in assessing who would do what, and who should go where, HM Stationery Office with the Post Office Stores Department produced a National Service Guide which included simple basic information on all the available services, along with a table and index. The entire distribution of this was completed within three days of issue, on 15 January, through head postmasters, local post offices and posts.

There were tasks for every age group. Some were suited to the academic, scientific and technically adept, while others catered for the unskilled worker. It soon became clear that every able-bodied person, male or female, was a potential candidate for something.

Two forms were supplied for application. Stroud's Employment Exchange remained open from 5–7 p.m. on Monday, Wednesday, and Friday to assist with the form filling. 'Sluggish' was the initial report on enrolment, but the figures had soon picked up by the end of April. From perusal of the forms, it was certain Tom, Dick, Harry and Mary too, given the incentive, could step through the diversity of wartime work from their limited pre-war circles into spheres hitherto unknown.

Most training was brief and concise, offering a taster of the real skills which were mainly learned on the job. Special constables normally received just twelve hours annual training, divided between lectures and practical on-the-spot experience such as beat work with another officer or traffic control. During wartime they became supplementary to the regular police force or if they chose or applied for police reserve work, which was originally intended to be temporary, could end up being full-time with more interesting work.

As war organizations demanded so many voluntary workers many Stroud firms began to reimburse their employees for their training session time; Listers of Dursley being among the first.

Stroud Volunteer Fire Brigade was formed in 1938, consisting of six separate brigades. These were Stroud Urban, Stroud Volunteers, Nailsworth Urban, Nailsworth and Woodchester Valley Volunteers, Brimscombe Volunteers and Painswick Volunteers. During the war 'fit men over twenty-five' were eligible for the Auxiliary Fire Service, and assumed a number of auxiliary stations, training and working with the regulars.

In 1941 the National Fire Service was formed and Mr Gough became Company Officer in charge of Stroud, Nailsworth, and Painswick. The service was denationalized in April 1948.

Armed with information gleaned from the earlier form filling, a promotional recruiting drive was launched on Monday 1 May entitled 'National Service, An Effort For Peace'. Sir John Anderson, head of the ARP said in his speech, 'Men and women today all over the country are eager to fit themselves voluntarily for National Service . . . the call is to peace and not war. We have no thought of aggression, our one wish is to live at peace with all nations.'

Stroud's main campaign day was Thursday 4 May and commenced with a short address at the Gaumont Palace followed by a grand procession throughout the town by the services. The Brimscombe and Thrupp British Legion Band headed the parade and two tanks, the Royal Gloucestershire Hussars of the 5th Battalion of the Gloucester Regiment, Stroud and Cirencester Sea Cadets, the Red Cross, VAD and ARP workers, and various representatives from the National Service followed on, to congregate at the Subscription Rooms. Following community singing, Major Sir Frederick Cripps, the chairman of the ARP, and presider of the meeting spoke,

> A good many people think that as soon as the present difficulties are gone that all this will disappear. I wish myself I could think that. . . . The civil defence and ARP know they are necessary to safeguard the populate of this country. . . . The people must realize that the arrangements for war made twenty years ago had no relation at all to the civil defence that was absolutely necessary today. To see that their volunteers were thoroughly trained was the greatest safeguard that any nation could have against attack from another.

The following week recruiting and propaganda work took place every day except Sunday, and there was an evening procession composed of a variety of defence and care bodies headed by a loud speaker van intent on enrolling a minimum of three hundred volunteers into one or other organisation. Many did join something during that week, no doubt thinking that by enrolling as a volunteer they had a choice, which they might not have should call-up time arrive. Local firms, acting upon the government's request to encourage their employees to assist in National Service, helped in any way they could. War demands resulted in auxiliary reserves and back-up groups, with newspaper advertisements jostling side by side for people's support.

An organization that had no difficulty in obtaining members was the Territorial Army, which was established in 1908. They began their training regime early in 1938, and became so popular that by the time war was declared, two regiments were formed instead of one, to become the 1st and 2nd Royal Gloucester Hussars. Territorial Army recruits trained in peacetime with the unit with whom they worked in war.

During the two week training course they camped under canvas, and learned track vehicle driving, foot drill and other skills, followed by Sunday and evening weekly exercises. While only ten drills a year were compulsory, many recruits involved themselves in more.

Ted Hewer joined the Royal Gloucester Hussars Ex-Cavalry Regiment as a

The Royal Hussars.

volunteer at its Gloucester Headquarters in 'A' Squadron in 1938, 'when things were hotting up'. His swearing in followed in May 1939. His training was foot drill on Sunday mornings, which progressed to driving army vehicles, gunnery, wireless procedure, and maintenance. There was a weekend camp at Kenilworth Castle, a stint on Salisbury Plain, and invasion training off Scotland in 1943. As a volunteer he was paid £5 at camp, but when mobilization came on 1 September 1939, and full-time employment, he donned 'his natty khaki suit', to receive 2s a day, rising to 3s 9d on promotion to Lance Corporal.

The 1st Regiment of the Royal Gloucester Hussars was comprised of 'A' Squadron Gloucester, 'B' Cirencester, and 'D' Bristol, while the 2nd combined the Squadrons of 'F' Gloucester, 'H' Cheltenham and 'G' Stroud and Tetbury. There was no 'C', as that unit was wiped out long ago.

Ted recalls chaotic accommodation arrangements on mobilization. Sleeping on the floor of the Domestic Science School in Gloucester and in the bitterly cold Tote buildings, which had no windows, at Cheltenham Racecourse. There, his shaving brush froze even though it was wrapped in his haversack which doubled as his pillow. Night and day, intensive training followed, with

9

Ted Hewer with the Corporal in charge of Squadron cooking near Hanover. Ted forgets his name but remembers he was one of the original Sherwood Rangers and came from Nottingham.

Dunkirk in 1940 and the formation of Yeomanry Armoured Detachment (YAD) which guarded the shores in case of invasion. Eventually Ted left the regiment to join the Sherwood Rangers in Europe, becoming one of the first to cross the German border. 'Yeomen of England', said Ted, was the name attributed to the voluntary services, while PBIs (Poor Bloody Infantry) were the foot soldiers!

Jack Hatherall, in The Stroud and Tetbury 'G' Squadron, and member of the 2nd Royal Gloucester Hussars, fared better than Ted on his mobilization. His unit slept on straw-filled mattresses in empty houses, and went to the yard of the Ormans Head Pub in Long Street, Tetbury for English breakfasts prepared by the Cookhouse. Within several days his unit moved to barracks in the Cirencester Road, and thence to Ilfracombe, where they stayed in hotels before reverting back to private house accommodation at Bristol Airport. On Old Year's Night in 1941 they were off to Warsop in Nottinghamshire, again in private house lodgings and also a church hall. Finally in 1941 they went to Westbury and then travelled overnight to Africa.

In 1936, Alec Alder, keen to join the 5th Gloucesters in Stroud, put his age up by a year in order to be accepted and went on an annual two-week training course at Ludgershal, Pawthcawl in 1937 and again in 1938. In those days, Stroud's TA Drill Hall was at Merrywalks on the site of the future bus station and the .22 rifle range was where the bus company's offices now are.

At the outbreak of war, Alec was working at Parnels in Yate, riding his pushbike there and back daily, even on a Saturday morning, so that he could save money with which to get married. On 21 August, about a fortnight before war was officially declared, rumours abounded that call-up was imminent and when Alec's papers arrived, he went straight home and reported to the rank sergeant at the Drill Hall. 'We were sent off to various locations such as Wickwar Tunnel where I went, Badminton Tunnel, or Aston Down, and were told we were looking for IRA terrorists.'

Soon the real truth was known by everyone and following regrouping, the 5th Gloucesters went to France to suffer losses at Dunkirk.

Women were not left out. As war drew near, women were included in the Auxiliary Territorial Service, in a non-combatant and unarmed capacity, to work as drivers or in clerical positions such as bookeepers, store-keepers or cooks. When in full-time employment, a whole new world became their oyster, for they received not only payment, but as Generals a chance to serve overseas, or if a Local the choice to remain at home.

CHAPTER TWO

PREPARING TO BE PREPARED

As war drew closer, demolition and decontamination training was given and buildings were commandeered for storage, their contents comparatively safe in the peaceful Gloucestershire countryside.

Stroud's numerous mills were especially useful, some having been empty before the war, with a few more becoming so as a result of wartime cut backs. At Dunkirk Mill near Nailsworth, part of Walker's Stick Factory, a large building was used to store sugar, and Kimmins Mill, Woodlands and the New Mills at Slad housed other bulk foods. Hillier's Bacon Factory, Stroud Brewery, Woodchester Mills (home of the piano works), Davis Silk Mills, Lansdown Garage and Painswick Road Car Mart, all became buffer depots. 24 C, K, B, P, HH, BB, KK and X, being their numbers in sequence.

As a young man Philip Sawer worked at the Kimmins Mill at Dudbridge, before his call-up. He said the food arrived, usually by rail at Stroud Station and loads were dropped off at Kimmins to await collection by the Army, the RAF Seas of local firms. Philip's working hours fluctuated, but he always worked Saturdays, and often Sundays.

All the floors in Kimmins were filled to capacity, the mill lift from former flour milling days enabling the heavy bulk containers access to the sixth (top) floor. Philip remembers the day a barrel of milk powder from floor six came adrift and plummeted to the ground where it exploded. 'There was powdered milk everywhere,' he said. Kimmins was deregulated in 1947. Dudbridge was also home for Stroud's Equipment Depot at the OK Works, where forty thousand gas masks were stocked, a third of which were assembled ready for use by Copeland Chatterson, the wholesale clothiers Holloways, from Brick Row, and the Stonehouse Paper and Bag Company.

All towns and industrial premises provided air raid shelters. There were also temporary static water tanks, with netting over the top and large pipes leading to them, which were painted with black and white stripes. In cities they were large concrete constructions obviously placed along streets, but locally they were smaller, and more diverse. The underground in London created one vast

```
Buffer Depot 24 P. Hilliers Bacon Factory, Nailsworth.
-----------------------------------------------------

2500 c/s C.Milk    48/16oz.  Nestles
9000 c/s C.Milk    48/16oz.  Nestles.
2314 c/s C.Milk    48/16oz.  W.U.Dairies.


Buffer Depot 24 JJ. Davis' Silk Mills, Nailsworth, Glos.
--------------------------------------------------------

  49 c/s  8 tins C.C. Pork  12/6's.
5000 c/s C. Milk   48/16oz.  C.W.S.
1982 c/s C.Milk    48/16oz.  C.W.S.  (Cartons)


Buffer Depot 24 BB. Woodchester Mills, Woodchester.
---------------------------------------------------

4032 c'tons Tomato Puree 6/10's.
2899 c/s  6 tins Canned Beans 24/16oz.
2658 bags Dried Barley.
  48 bags Flour  Canadian x 1½ cwt.   Old Ship.
1680 bags Canadian Flour x 1¼ cwt.   (NEW SHIP)


Buffer Depot 24 X. Painswick Road Car Mart, Stroud.
---------------------------------------------------

  56 c'tons C.Milk 48/14½oz.
3999 c/s C.Milk   48/16oz.  W.U.Dairies.
1972 c/s Pork & Veg.  48/16oz.


Buffer Depot 24 HH. Stroud Brewery, Stroud.
305 c'tons FCU Milk 48/2 pts  Nestles.

  66 c'tons Beef Hash  48/15oz.
  86 c/s  Meat Roll    48/12oz.
159 c'tons Pea Soup    24/2½.
  38 c'tons Rice Puddings 24/1.

Buffer Depot 24 KK. Lansdown Garage, Stroud.
--------------------------------------------

5000 c/s C.Milk  48/16oz.  C.W.S.
2000 Cartons "        "        "
```

Buffer Depot orders in the Stroud area.

shelter, each platform crammed to the limit with bodies seeking security and impossible comfort.

Stroud's most prominent shelter was on the forecourt of the Subscription Rooms. It was impressive and central, but smelled so no one used it much except to wait for buses. There were thirty-six more dotted around the district: at the Ritz underground garage; the Co-operative Cellars in Slad road; Wood and Rowe's garage at Wallbridge; the Drill Hall or the Old Brewery at

13

Nailsworth; at Chalford and Thrupp; and at Lower Spillmans, Rodborough, which was a 'distinctive one with a zig-zag roof'.

Stroud was rather complacent about sheltering. One resident of Horn's Road remembers the night the raids on Bath drew practically all Horn's Road residents out into the street to watch. The reflection of the fire and searchlights were clearly visible on that lovely moonlit night, and sheltering did not enter anyone's mind. The youngsters were particularly excited as they shouted 'Look, there he is', as the German planes droned overhead.

Workplaces treated air raids differently. Everyone stopped work during an air raid and went to the works' shelter, most having their own fire fighting scheme ready to cope with any blaze.

Visiting a devastatingly bombed city like Bristol made one think. One look was proof enough a war was raging. The constant raiding there held little in the way of excitement as Pat Hawker from Horsley discovered on a trip to Bristol. On hearing the warning she dashed into a nearby Woolworths for cover. Later she heard a bomb had hit 'Woollies', and death to her seemed very near!

Even though Stroud was country area everyone was still urged to construct a shelter, financial help being available if it was needed. People with cellars simply used them, while others constructed something in their garden. Town dwellers could use Street Cabinets, which cost £8 and accommodated four people, but country dwellers probably preferred the Andersons, which had steel arches and were embedded in the ground, before being covered with soil.

Some Andersons leaked and were damp, so the Morrison shelter which arrived in 1941 and was designed for indoor use was preferred. It arrived in kit form, and comprised a wire encased framework with a solid top, and a sprung base to sleep in. It was usually placed in the sitting room, where it could be used as a low table. Stroud's gardens were ideal for individually designed shelters, constructed of whatever came to hand and costing little.

Ours at home cost nothing and would have been a total disaster if put to the test, constructed where it was in the narrow path between the back of the house and a bank. We never used it, no sensible person would leave a warm fire to huddle in darkness beneath its corrugated tin roof. However it did remain long after the war, even to the extent of surviving as a children's den, until rust not bombing caused its demise.

Some shops sold provisions sealed in gas-proof tins for use in shelters. The Cotswold Stores stocked a Peek Freen's six-and-three-quarter pound tin of Vita Wheat crispbread biscuits for 8s 9d, and Wheaten Crisp by Macfarlane Lang for 3s 7d, which could replace bread. Restricted space popularized bunk beds, which could easily be used in shelters. Listers of Gloucester sold one version which was six foot long, had a steel frame with a canvas cover and came in three tiers. The single cost 30s and the complete set was only 98s, the whole thing could be ready to sleep in in two minutes.

Molly Stephens smart in uniform.

Transport was a matter that received consideration, even before petrol rationing was introduced, after it was revealed five million vehicles were using Stroud's roads, two million of which were from local businesses. As priority would be given to government and services transport it was suggested that local firms reliant on transport should form groups of between fifty to a hundred vehicles to assist each other in time of need.

Two local businesses, the Stroud Brewery and Burtons the tailor's, were the first to take this kind of precaution, with eight groups ultimately formed in Stroud, and about the same number again in the surrounding district. In the event, Stroud did not need to resort to the above measures, as Vick Evans, who supplied the coupons for business petrol, ensured there was never a shortage.

Training in civil defence was encouraged by the factories and much was already underway. A report states Holloway's had several of their employees in territorial training camps, ninety girls in gas mask assembly and forty more in first aid instruction. There were several in the ARP from Strachans and Daniels' Iron Works at Lightpill had eighteen Wardens and fourteen members of St Johns Ambulance Brigade and the Red Cross among their ranks.

Recruitment for the Women's Land Army, a worthy female band who had proved themselves so ably during the First World War, began in May 1939. The criteria for joining were age, which had to be between eighteen and forty and 'able-bodied', the simplicity of which encouraged many town girls, lured perhaps by the glamorous advertisements, to leave office jobs for the real life backaching work amid muck.

Molly Stephens lived in London and worked in a factory. When the time came to 'do her bit for her country', she was advised to enter the Forces, because 'she was just the kind of girl the Forces need!'. Molly, adamant her need was not for the Forces life, being regimented and controlled by all and sundry, refused, preferring 'life in the country away from the bombing, with just one boss'.

'Perhaps you would like to think it over', they suggested, 'come back in a month and let us know!'.

'Have you changed your mind?' they inquired on her return. 'No', said Molly, 'I still want the Land Army'. Therefore, Molly and her friend ended up threshing on a Bisley farm, long hours, dirty work, comparative freedom, and just one boss!

Land Army recruits expected to receive a short period of training, although Molly received none at all. 'We learned on the farm', she said. Those fortunate to have training usually had between two and four weeks attending Cirencester Agricultural College learning tractor driving and milking. Some training centres paid 10s a week pocket money, but when girls were employed the wages could be 25s a week, with perhaps a 14s board and lodging allowance, a week's holiday and uniform made up of two sets of brown breeches, shirts, green pullovers and a coat, hat. Sometimes a bicycle was provided.

Farms were needed for training so farmers and market gardeners were asked if their facilities could be used. Many were not keen, but eventually gave in. William Stephens of Bisley did not want the four girls he was offered, saying he would never be able to control them, but eventually agreed on two. One of those remained permanently when she married him. A total of one thousand women undertook the agricultural work vacated by men serving away.

Girls who had come from bombed cities were accustomed to air raids night and day, and were not bothered by an occasional raid over quiet old Stroud. Molly said she heard a warning just once, when hoeing in the fields with her friend. Hearing one at all in the peace of the countryside was something of a shock. It was so small and insignificant after their experiences in London that they ignored it and kept working. The fuss in the district the following day surprised Molly beyond belief. She explained 'I could never believe one alert could cause so much fuss, and we weren't even bombed!'.

Doolie had no official training either, having learned hand milking when a friend of Juliet Palmer at Hilltop Farm at Whiteway. At sixteen, she began work

Will Stephens threshing at Rectory Farm Bisley. Down Farm Slad also benefitted from Will's services.

as a Land Girl at Long's Farm near Miserden, riding her own bike there and working a seven day week, with only half a day off at a time, except on Christmas Day. The cows had to be in for milking by 5.15 a.m., following which she had her breakfast and later her lunch. The farm supplied milk to Cranham Sanatorium and the bottling was done straight from the cooler.

Once when feeding the bull, of whom she was petrified, she could not get out of his pen because his rear end was blocking the way. Panic caused her to shoot under his stomach instead to escape. Although only eight stone when she began as a Land Girl, she was ten stone when she left two-and-a-half years later, to undertake the gentler occupation of nursery nursing on a six-month wartime crash scheme.

Farmers, formerly underestimated and overlooked, assumed importance as war approached. 'Britain's Future, Britain's Farms' was the slogan. 'Today the farms of Britain are the front line of freedom', said the prime minister.

Advice was offered from all angles. One dissuaded overstocking and to continue as normal, while another suggested continuing without waiting for the decisions of the War Agricultural Committee but to go ahead and plough as much land as possible, using every tractor and man they possessed. Eventually an extra ten per cent at £2 an acre was decided as recompense by the committee, and a deadline set for December. 'If all do their part', said the authorities, 'one-and-a-half million acres of land will go under the plough'. But the atrocious weather delayed the December ploughing target, so 15 May was fixed instead, whereon through black-out concessions, and day and night ploughing, much newly cultivated land was planted with potatoes, oats, barley, rye, and mixed corn in a grand attempt to boost home production.

The reversal of the farmer's traditional role as the producer of a quality product to one of great quantity, whether through arable or livestock, must have been difficult. Many farmers had spent years specializing in perhaps pigs or poultry, or growing a worthwhile crop with a sizeable yield. Now under the new sweeping government plan, quantity was demanded, and land once deemed unsuitable for arable crops, was ploughed and drained with the aid of a fifty per cent drainage grant.

Their role in wartime became so vital that when the rule to conscript twenty-year olds was introduced, the call-up for farm workers was postponed, to enable the nation to stay alive through stomachs, instead of arms. The average person in the street was probably astounded to learn Britain depended to such an extent on imported foods, that of every sixteen ounces of wheat consumed, thirteen ounces came from overseas as did seven-eighths of butter, cheese, tea, cocoa, coffee, tinned foods, wool, timber, rubber, and iron ore.

Industry too changed dramatically, especially in Stroud district which was rich in engineering. This was not fully realized then as wartime security measures prevented the full extent of Stroud's involvement being known, but everyone found out eventually. Here, if production was not beneficial to the country it ceased entirely or changed to government work, machinery was removed elsewhere or converted for a new use.

Pat Hawker worked at Chamberlain's, the leather board manufacturers at Meadow Mills in Nailsworth, gluing pieces of leather on sheets of board with hot glue and earning 8s 10d for a six-and-a-half day week. 'Just like a patchwork', she said. When war broke out everybody was laid off. Pat went along to the Labour Exchange and was sent to Newman and Henders. 'You went where you were sent', she says. Newman Henders manufactured shells in a variety of sizes for guns and ships. The shells were brass and painted green and Pat said she painted most of the time she was there, working days and being eighteen years of age, night shifts as well.

From 1941, Gladys Vick also worked at Newman Henders. She examined bullets for Oirlikon Guns on a micrometer. 'They had to be 'five thou' above, or five thou' below' she said. 'If they weren't just right they were thrown out and remade'. Her former employment had been at Bonds Carpets in Ham Mill, where Gladys wove complex patterns on a six foot loom. (One she wove had peacocks at three foot intervals). Bonds had been operating forty-eight looms in 1939, but when in 1941 the mill was commandeered by the Gloucester Aircraft Company for Admiralty and Army war work the carpet weaving, which had already reduced to part-time production, ceased entirely and moved out.

One event stands out more clearly in Gladys' memory than any other during the war. In 1943 Queen Mary, who was staying at Badminton, paid a visit to the factory. Following her tour, she joined the company's workforce which were lined up outside in readiness for the photograph. The photographer requested Her Majesty to 'move back a step please' and a well-heeled shoe landed right onto Gladys' foot, where it remained until the photographer had finished. A memory Gladys recalls with feeling. Factories were visited by royalty to keep up morale. Queen Mary visited Hoffmans at Stonehouse, and her bouquet of flowers was presented by Mrs Whale, who was the oldest lady there and landlady of the Woolpack at Butterrow.

Lodgemore Mills, while retaining their cloth manufacturing machinery, were required to change their production for war. Ada Webb left school at fourteen to work on quilling there, earning 11s a week. Her day was spent dashing to and fro filling the empty bobbins for the weavers who were on piece work, and to whom loss of production meant loss of pay. After her marriage to Leslie in 1937, she was summoned to the office to see which job she would like to do next. She requested weaving, which was colourful, patterned, and interesting, and she looked forward to running her own loom following her training. When war broke out, all colours and patterns ceased as all the cloth produced went either to the Navy, Army or Air Force.

After failing to get her own loom she left Lodgemore Mill and went to Hoffmans instead where she worked on munition, making ball bearings for aeroplanes. While there she trapped her finger in a machine, but because of the urgency of the work was allowed no time off for recuperation. So Ada carried on, her bandaged finger (she indicated visually), 'was stuck in the air'. Shortly afterwards she left there also, but this time for different reasons. Her baby was on the way.

Wartime shift work turned normal family routine completely upside down. While Leslie worked days at Newman Henders, Ada did nights at Hoffmans.

'We hardly saw each other at all during the week', said Ada. 'We passed in the hallway, Leslie coming in and me going out; we only met on Sundays. The bed though was always warm, there was always one of us in it, although rarely together'. A comment which caused laughter.

With so many positions to be filled, it seems remarkable any people remained free to join the Local Defence Volunteers (LDV) launched in May

Queen Mary visiting Strachans on November 5th 1941. Ada Webb was somewhere in the workforce. Courtesy of Milliken.

Fromehall Mills. By courtesy of Milliken, Woollen Speciality Products, Lodgemore Mills, Stroud.

1940. The response following Mr Eden's radio appeal so overwhelmed the Stroud Police station at Merrywalks that enrolment papers ran out, and more had to be sent. All villages offered tremendous support and Captain P.R. Symonds, the Coordinating Officer for the ARP, was able to report that every eligible man in his parish had signed up.

The success of the LDV may have been because older people were included, who were barred from the regular services by the fifty-year limit. Every type of person was involved, and terrific community bonding resulted, as night patrols and exercises united all classes together. The Home Guard, as it became known, operated with ranks, uniforms, arm bands and weaponry as an army might. Through divisions and ward groups, head wardens and wardens, and

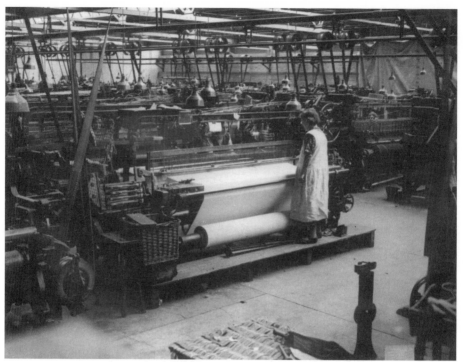

Weaving at Lodgemore Mill in 1937. Courtesy of Milliken.

volunteers who undertook various duties within the vicinity of their homes, 711 people underwent warden training, although only 258 were originally estimated. Classes were held to cover everything from first aid to 'What to do if attacked by gas'.

The main training establishment for the Home Guard in Stroud was at the Board of Guardians' Room in John Street, while Swifts Hill was the location for Sunday morning exercises, when local boys gathered to collect their empty cases. Otherwise villages chose their own meeting places. The Jovial Foresters at Forest Green, run by Daisy and Alma Smith, was deemed suitable by Dudley Vines and Harry Burford of the Nailsworth ARP Warden. The Bisley Home Guard used the Snooker Hall above Bisley Reading Room in the High Street, and the draughty old Isolation Hospital at the Wittan Tree as their look-out post.

In April 1930 compulsory military training, which had been abolished following the First World War, was reintroduced by the Conservative Party. It

Stroud Home Guard used to march down the High Street and veer into the Bedford Street Restaurant. When Mike and Kay Samson who contributed this photograph investigated its contents, they discovered both their fathers were sitting within a few yards of each other.

Band of the 7th Home Guard, BN Glos Regt, 1944.

was an unpopular peacetime move, and much talked of by the opposition party, the public expressing their views for all to see in the papers. In reality its effect was minimal, as it applied only to twenty-year-old men, and only for a six month period. It was a preparatory measure for times ahead, although by September the National Service Act was embracing the wider age range of 18–41, followed in 1941 with a call-up for women, many of whom chose the Forces and a chance of travel and independence in preference to industrial work at home.

CHAPTER THREE

1939. LOOKING ON THE BLACK SIDE

From September 1938, the ARP began a succession of mock air raids, with 'enemy bombers' to add a touch of realism to the tests. Trenches were dug, redundant buildings set alight, and people commandeered as casualties. The experience and atmosphere of bomb and fire impact was a test of people's ability to cope should raiding occur.

Stroud's early black-out came on 8 July 1939, one of many throughout Gloucestershire. It was costly, took tremendous organization, and involved only civil defence personnel. The general public were only requested to cooperate with an indoor black-out, along with reassurance that as this was a preliminary trial, no prosecution would result, as it would in real war.

Light exclusion was essential. People were told how the smallest chink of light could be seen from the air. Simply lighting up a cigarette in the street could be seen from an aeroplane three thousand feet up, information rightly or wrongly which aimed to discourage any smoker who dared try. Noise was confronted too. Hooters, horns, bells, and whistles were silenced, their future use confined to wartime warnings.

Safety was paramount. Lofts were cleared of debris and windows were taped with brown paper strips to stop them shattering. 'All the windows had kisses in them', said George Webb.

People dealt with the black-out in a variety of ways. There was black-out material which was matt black one side and shiny on the other, and was hung as normal curtains were. Some people stretched it onto frames and lifted those into place. Curtaining a complete house was expensive so an assortment of other methods such as blankets, black paint, and Sisalcraft paper were used. Many people treated just the downstairs windows, feeling it a waste of money to black out a room like a bedroom used just for sleep. Gladys Vick said a piece of cloth wrapped around their bedroom lampshade reduced their need for a bedroom black-out.

Our house did not use any of the above methods. Father erected shutters instead which were fixed to the outside wall and held back by hooks. It was a simple matter to close them at night. The shutters were brown during the early years, but I remember them blue and permanently hitched back after the war was over. Eventually when despite several layers of paint, rot set in, they were taken down and burnt.

According to *The Stroud News* the first trial black-out caused an eerie stillness as the area was plunged into darkness. It lasted for four hours during which time the district was examined for light. Special constables walked miles informing inhabitants if light was showing. Chalford showed no lights, Nailsworth one, while Minchinhampton showed seven.

On 9–10 August a second exercise took place. This was a larger affair, involving four hundred volunteers, falling bombs, casualties, and atrociously wet weather. Special constables guarded the bridges, roads, and important buildings, and the telephone department was split into two sections, so one part could receive instructions from the county authorities at Gloucester, while the other dispatched instructions to areas and units.

The report states that the greatest shock of the evening was the total demolition of Stroud Police Station at Merrywalks with all its personnel. Ironically it seems the weather was the winner when the exercise finished at 2 a.m., allowing the 'injured and dead' to return home to dry off.

These exercises, including another one on 26 November, were largescale and supremely organized, but other more modest affairs were arranged locally between villages. In these, one village might fiercely protect its pub or post office from their neighbouring enemy, who were determined on razing it to the ground.

Bisley versus Miserden carefully blocked their entrance roads when The George Inn was targeted during their inter-village practice. Bisley emerged triumphant and relieved as their pub was still intact. However disappointment followed when Miserden claimed they had won, and proved it by pointing to the 'bomb' on The George's window sill.

During 1942 and 1943, Nailsworth, Forest Green, New Market, Horsley, Woodchester, Amberley, Cainscross, and Stonehouse all combined in civil defence and Home Guard manoeuvres, most of which occurred during daylight when headgear was the distinguishing mark between the enemy and the defending troops. Field service caps might be worn by the invaders, while 'we' sported steel helmets, and the umpires wore white armbands. Usually the public played their part, by offering picks, shovels or ladders to 'us' and by unmercifully denying all help to the enemy.

'The Battle of Stroud', the Home Guards' invasion test on the weekend of 14–15 March 1942, was a large combined military and civilian effort involving ARPs, fire patrols, regular and Special police, the National Fire Service, and every Home Guard in the district. All aspects of defence were involved, even to the extent of tear-gas bombs which were still feared by many.

High Street, Stroud in the 1950s.

It ran from 3 p.m. until dusk on Saturday and then from daybreak until midday on Sunday. During the action, relays of 'bombers' dropped incendiary and tear-gas bombs, and many fires were started. The main services were seriously affected, and there were sixty-nine 'casualties', and seven hundred people made 'homeless'.

The first real black-out came on 1 September 1939, taking many by surprise. Ada Webb, returning from work that Friday evening to her converted grocery shop home which still retained its large shop window, was unaware of any black-out. Though she found out within minutes of stepping inside. She says, 'Two Special constables were on the doorstep asking why my light was on, "Don't you know your light can be seen over at Woodchester?". Before he could finish talking my light was out and Leslie and I spent the night by a candle'.

The following day Ada, along with others caught on the hop, visited Bells, the High Street Drapers, where she purchased black-out material at 7s 6d a yard before the stocks ran out, from which she made curtains, putting coloured bias binding along the hems to brighten up their gloom. Following the war she converted them into several aprons.

As a first offender Ada got away lightly with only a ticking off, but from

Friday 1 September when the black-out began, a private interior war against escaping light persisted throughout the land. 'Anyone who fails to shield his windows is guilty of an offence against the neighbourhood in which he lives,' was the general feeling. But while offenders offered all manner of excuses, fines of anything between 5s and £1 were generally enforced with offenders' names printed weekly in the papers.

One lady received a fine of 10s for simply shining her torch at a photograph in a shop window, while a man paid 15s for a second offence when he allowed a light to show through his glass panelled door. Even in the depths of the country a man merely visiting his woodshed was fined for allowing a torch beam to show. Everyone in the district read of it in the paper the following week.

The black-out had many drawbacks, petty thieving being an obvious one. Cigarettes, chocolates, and clothes were favoured by the light-fingered, although one more adventurous thief removed a sawn-up tree and paid a 10s fine for his efforts. Black-out crimes were generally petty, non-violent affairs. A survey proves petty crime actually fell in Gloucestershire during the war years, from 197,089 in 1939 to 161,671 by 1945, whereas the number of serious crimes rose from 60,104 in 1939 to 86,750 by the war's end.

Much petty crime was vehicle-related. The failure to screen lights adequately received fines of 5s, whereas driving without a licence was only 4s. Car theft reduced dramatically during wartime too. There is one report of a person trying who gave up when the petrol ran out a few yards up the road.

I asked one lady if she was ever frightened in the black-out, but she laughed and said she liked it as it gave her a privacy unattainable in her large family at home. One effect of total blackness was the dramatic increase of home-based accidents, a hundred-fold during the first six months. Hylda Griffin cracked her head and needed six stitches after slipping off the pavement and falling into a lamp-post, and there were countless others.

Precautions were taken to combat the problem. People going out were advised to carry a newspaper or something white. The arduous task of painting white lines along kerbs, pedestrian crossings, and the middle of roads began, the last proving so effective that drivers tended to drive astride them, until reminded they marked a divisional boundary over which no car should pass.

Pedestrians were asked to walk to meet the oncoming traffic, so they could see the car before it saw them, but fifty people were still killed in Stroud district by January 1940, as against twenty-nine over a similar period in 1938. In December alone there were 266 injuries and 15 deaths, 13 of which occurred during black-out and involved people aged over fifty. A 20 mph speed limit was enforced which, combined with limited petrol and less travel, reduced accidents.

The war prompted immediate unlit and unsignposted roads. Hylda said it was terrible when working late everything was totally black by six o'clock, as most of Stroud's shops closed by five. Sometimes even natives found themselves lost.

A particularly tragic accident occurred at Stroud's railway station, which certainly everyone reading of it in the Stroud Journal at the time, will not have forgotten. The Chief Rural Officer of the National Council of Social Services arrived at Stroud one evening, on a train of many carriages and great length. In the gloom he alighted onto what he thought was the railway's platform, but in fact was the four foot parapet of the viaduct approaching the station. His fall to a glass roof below was thirty-seven feet, and fatal.

Blacking out vehicles was a complicated affair, involving shielding here and blacking off there. A whole range of specified dimming regulations were issued, which required implementation before taking to the road. In the early days, only side and rear lights were allowed, a filter of light struggling for survival through their two inch aperture. Eventually headlights, just one at the start, were allowed as long as they were encased in a slitted mask with a thirty-six watt bulb. Red stop lights and reflectors also received the shielding treatment, although indicators could have a tiny arrow showing. Number plates were unlit and projections such as bumpers and running boards were supposed to be highlighted with white paint, though I suspect father's prized Standard Ten escaped this fate.

It must have been difficult acclimatizing to wartime regulations which contrasted so greatly with normal road practice. During peacetime a Stroud traffic offender was fined 10s for driving without lights, and a cyclist fined 2s 6d for riding 'a lightless cycle', but wartime procedure dictated 'all lights out', and hefty fines for not complying.

Drivers faced with black-out driving for the first time found their journey full of hazards. Nurse Pockett, a district nurse, was called out to a baby delivery in the depths of the country. She missed her turn on a dark country lane, and caused her Austin Seven to end in the ditch. There followed a muddy trek through fields to her patient's home 'where worried relatives were out in the garden with torches'. The next morning, having delivered the baby safely, and now equipped with dried shoes and washed stockings she hesitatingly retraced her steps to where she had left her car. Delight awaited her when she discovered it 'hauled out and hosed down by a kind soul who had recognized the nurse's car, and so set it ready for her return'.

Cyclists suffered battery problems. The law specifying red rear lights caused bicycle owners to suffer agonies trying to get the batteries with which to power them. In Stroud, a lightless cyclist was fined 10s. Soon the battery battle encompassed everyone, as torches which offered the easiest and most adaptable form of light became widely used. Flashing to preserve power for indoor use, such as shelters, and purchase of larger batteries was advised. The

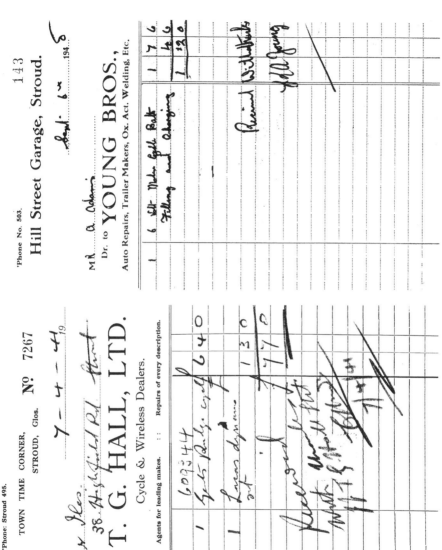

T.G. Hall cycle receipt. Battery receipt. All receipts courtesy of Dorothy Iles, who began her 'receipt spike' on her marriage to Edgar in 1935.

31

Corn Stooks at Down Barn Slad. Part of a five year rotation plan.

Ernest Dickenson with his waggon. Down Farm still used horses during wartime.

9*d* ones gave twelve to fifteen hours of light, whereas the 3¹/₂*d* ones only gave two. At all times light, whether from car, bicycle or torch, was veered downwards; any waving up to the skies was emphatically condemned.

But old habits die hard and my mother recalls an example. Her weekly treat was the cinema: a romantic film, a sweet or two, and peace. Half-way home up Rodborough Hill one Friday night folowing the performance she was awakened to reality as a hand suddenly grabbed her wrist in the darkness and a voice commanded, 'Get that torch down, they'll think you're a bike. You might get run into'. Her assailant was only a Special constable doing his duty but he terrified mother. 'I was all on my own and I had to walk round that lonely top road after that in the pitch black'.

Battery shortages continued throughout the remainder of the war, but several attempts were made to remedy the situation. Curry's had a scheme for High Tension (HT) batteries, which guaranteed 'a new factory fresh battery worth 17*s* 6*d* for a payment of 1*s* down, and weekly instalments', and other firms followed suit.

The arrival of summer-time lessened the black-out substantially. It shortened to forty-five minutes after sunrise and before sunset, instead of the thirty minutes in operation previously. In 1941, because the extra British Summer-time hour had operated continuously throughout the winter of 1940–41, another hour was added when spring arrived. This was effective from 4 May until 8 August, and became Double Summer-time. Almost everyone complied with this new elongated time-scale, except for the dairy business and agriculture who, because of the cows' inability to understand war or tell the time, remained in single time. All their milking and collections continued as before.

CHAPTER FOUR

TESTING THE TESTS

The announcement at 11 a.m. on Sunday 3 September by Neville Chamberlain of Britain's entry into war with Germany was not unexpected. Much activity had already been seen over the weekend. Since Friday, Stroud had waved farewell to the RAF Reserve and Anti-Aircraft Units, witnessed preparation for the mobilization of the 7th Battalion of the Gloucestershire Regiment of the Territorial Army, been informed of stand-by by the ARP, and experienced the effects of total black-out. Stroud and Stonehouse railway stations had bustled both with outgoing servicemen and also incoming evacuees. Here were thousands of confused strangers, suddenly faced with unknown people in a strange new town.

The Stroud News recorded 'an outward calmness', but some people did show a more immediate response. Mike Hawkes, coming home through the Vatch on his way to the Riflemans, remembers Mrs Herne calling frantically to her three children to come in at once as 'the war has started', and one vicar stopped his sermon midway, deciding rousing hymns were more appropriate in times of disaster.

Wilf Merrett, on hearing the news of the sinking of the *Athenia* on a wireless in town felt, 'Oh dear, they've already sunk a ship', and rushed home to tell his father, who decided there and then to buy a wireless.

Min Browne's mother's main worry was, 'Would all my five sons have to go to war?', while Min's future husband, Keith, who was but five years old and living at Lower Spillmans in Rodborough Hill, only remembered a lot of excited talking.

Father, as was his way, showed no emotion when mother greeted him with the news, but simply stated 'I'm not surprised' as he continued with some important Sunday morning task. Bryan Durn, whose sixth birthday it was that very day, could not understand why neighbours at Summer Street were crying on his birthday.

Suddenly, soldiers came on duty to guard roads and public buildings everywhere, while Stroud's telephone lines were immediately swamped with calls, those by the public quickly giving way to official more urgent ones. Despite it being a Sunday, the Post Office was open all day, to deal with urgent telegraphic messages and bulletin issues arriving from the County Authority. Gas mask distribution began. Over two-and-a-half thousand were distributed from Cainscross between 6 and 10 p.m., with accompanying warnings that 'you will be sent home' if workers and children turned up the next day without one.

Some people began to hoard. The urgency of the occasion prompted the most honest people to flock to the shops for tinned and imperishable goods, although they had been requested by the government not to do so. Intent on stocking up, they circulated several retailers, buying a packet here and a tin there. Any feelings of guilt were ignored in their anxiety for the future. In 1939, 1s 3d would buy a tin of corned beef, 7d one of Deva beef, 10d a small tongue, and 6½d, a tin of pilchards.

The black-out caused a candle shortage. Users of gas and electricity were asked to leave the candles and oil for people living in rural areas. Those who had no mains relied on candles and oil gas to light and heat their homes.

All planned events changed. Some were delayed, while others were brought forward, and many were cancelled indefinitely. Marling School, faced with inflated numbers due to the evacuees, delayed their commencement of the autumn term for a fortnight to organize their schedule. The number of weddings increased, some say by fifty per cent, and many were brought forward. Loans were not made including those by The Public Works Loan Board. Existing council housing contracts in Stroud were not affected however, as the authorities feared they might be. 'Stroud has an influx so can continue for a time'.

Even funeral arrangements were affected, although not to the drastic extent of cancellation. To many the living came first now. Consequently, the weekly *Stroud News* funeral flower list was omitted in favour of war reporting (unless there was a special request and payment of 3d a line).

The Stroud News itself eventually had to change. The publishing time was changed to 10.30 a.m. on a Friday, instead of the customary 6 a.m., to avoid night work, and the pages were reduced to eight because of the paper shortage.

The car owners, worried about petrol shortages, rushed to fill their petrol tanks, and emptied the pumps. When it was announced that petrol rationing was postponed for a week, the whole procedure was repeated causing shortages where before there were none.

The black-out dramatically affected people's ability to go shopping. Unlit streets, blacked-out shop windows, and dimly-lit interiors caused difficulty in deciding which shops were open and which were closed. Customers were disinclined to shop when they bumped into things, and could not see what they were buying. As a result, emergency shopping hours were introduced. A meeting at the Premier Hall in Bath Street agreed to earlier closing (at 6.30 p.m.)

The Shambles during the 50s.

for the first three days of the week, and 7 p.m. on Fridays and Saturdays. Thursday was early closing day and unaffected.

A few shopkeepers were unhappy with this compromise. One wanted the hours to remain as they were, saying that he could sell several pairs of socks during the last half-hour. However, the traders generally agreed upon the revised times and the railways adjusted their deliveries accordingly. Soon the majority of shops took to closing as early as 5 p.m., or even 4.30 p.m. if there were no customers. British Summer-time, which was extended until the middle of November and brought forward to February, eased the shopping problem for everyone.

Churches, an oasis of calmness amidst all the activity, prayed for Peace. The subject of the Parish Church address was 'Shall I not drink this cup?', and soon Sunday evening services changed to an afternoon timetable.

In the garden, an army of caterpillars, which had devastated vegetable plots throughout the district, were intent on working their way indoors. When it became known that they had worked their way through the vegetables in Stroud Hospital garden, a 'Caterpillar Fund' was set up to replace the patients' greens. This was possibly the first of many war funds, although totally unconnected with Germany, a furry creature being the enemy on this occasion.

The newly-formed 7th Battalion of The Gloucester Regiment (TA) received

Wilf with his red Singer 9 Roadster in 1951 for which he paid £300. During frosty weather it was necessary to place a small paraffin heater underneath the radiator when parking, because it could not retain antifreeze. A beer crate was required to support the passenger seat.

their call-up papers early on Monday morning, and were on the move and gone completely by Tuesday afternoon, leaving their employers with a suddenly-depleted workforce.

'Reserved occupation' enabled survival at home during wartime. People whose work was beneficial to the war effort remained in their line of work, and stayed to keep the country running. They were dissuaded from enlisting, and some men resented this, especially when they saw their friends go keenly off to some romantic notion of war. Some who felt strongly applied to the Forces regardless. When accepted, they presented their papers to their unsuspecting employers at the last minute, before rushing off to join their unit.

Bernard King, on escaping from his reserved employment in engineering, wanted very much to work with wireless. When told he could not do this work, he enlisted for radar, in which he gained full training, before finally swapping over to wireless, his original choice. A move which benefitted his interest as a radio amateur.

Changing employment was not easy as permission had to be granted, requiring a letter with a sound reason, to the Ministry of Labour. When Wilf Merrett wished to leave Newman Henders, he chose the direct approach to the question, 'Why do you want to leave?', and replied with the positive, 'I think I can serve my country better!' (a phrase guaranteed to open any military door). His first position was at Aston Down in aircraft publications, before moving to semi-skilled assistant Rigger, 'patching up planes'. This physically harder work afforded him an extra daily half pint of milk, and starting pay of 30s a week,

Whiteshill School in 1939. Originally Whiteshill boasted two schools, one each for boys and girls, but by 1939 the boys' one housed both sexes. However when the evacuees arrived the former girls' school was re-opened especially to house them.

L–R. Back row. Miss Hutt (teacher), Marshall Snell, Colin Quest, Graham Hogg, Adrian Asher, ? Bill Foxwell, Alan Green, Ralph Hancock?

2nd Row. ? Fletcher, Eddie Hughes, Margaret Steele, Mirrium Neale, Audrey Gay, Betty Horton, Margaret Payne, Doreen Durn, Royland Chandler?

3rd Row. Avril Woodham, Pam White, Diane Pitfiel, Jean Beard, Mary Smith, Pam Payne, Greta Cleaver, Margaret Jones, Iris Cave.

Front Row. Tony Whitaker, ? Raymond Green, Peter Mills?, David Hill.

which rose to £4 later. Horsa Gliders came next, which Wilf 'screwed together and covered up the joins'.

'Not fancying the Guards', Wilf volunteered for the newly formed Royal Electrical Mechanical Engineers (REME),travelling there on the Dudbridge Donkey and thence to Derby. Three lorries and an RSO awaited the new boys, who, conspicuous in civilian clothes, tasted real service life as 'leering old hands called "Oh, you lucky people!", as we drove through the gates'. Food compensated for the initial impact. 'At home, food was rationed and of poor standard, here it was better quality and plenty of it!', said Wilf. Normandy beckoned on 4 July 1944, but Wilf was pleased he joined. 'You felt you were doing something', he said.

Teachers were particularly requested by the County War Emergency Committee to refrain from volunteering, unless they were asked through the

Military Services, because of their need in wartime education. On 24 August every teacher was needed, and many were recalled from their summer holidays to cope with the evacuation arrangements.

Stroud district was designated to accept around two thousand evacuees, and arrangements to receive, billet and school them had been in progress for many months. Households were visited (Doreen Ireland remembers Mrs Fisher from Castle House coming to see them at Middle Hill), and promises of accommodation pledged. Compensation was fixed at 10s 6d a child, or 8s a week if a mother provided for her child herself. With war upon us, the people who had pledged a room were reminded of the fact, so compulsory measures could be avoided.

The evacuation procedure went admirably smoothly. Masses of children, mothers, and teachers, with only necessities and a few treasures, arrived at Stroud's LMS railway station where they were met by billeting officers and welcoming parties.

The first consignment for Stroud was Edgbaston High School for Girls, who arrived early, on 27 August, to avoid the weekend crush. This, when it arrived, consisted of 242 children, the British School of Commerce, and 366 Handsworth Grammar School boys. On Saturday even more came to Stroud, along with 79 children, 14 teachers, 8 babies, 7 mothers, and many helpers who arrived at Stonehouse.

Because of the 'phoney war' (and no bombs), many mothers and youngsters drifted back home at Christmas, leaving their places to be filled by eight hundred children from the South and East coast towns of Frinton, Clacton, Walton, and Eastbourne a few months later.

In the book *They Met in a Barn* by Molly and Alfred Hoy, published in 1987, there is a copy of the notes made by the Reverend F.H. Dixon, Minister of Bedford Street Congregational Church, describing the arrival of the evacuees from Eastbourne in 1940.

They arrived about 5 p.m. on Friday – trainloads of them. Platforms were piled high with parcels and baggage; the station yard was crowded with weary men and women, crying children, and perambulators. The Bedford Street contingent was conducted from the station to the Church by Messrs Knight and Dixon, and on arrival was provided with tea by the Canteen. Those who wished then went out to inspect Stroud, while the remainder prepared to settle down for the night. As many of them had had little sleep for weeks, and had spent 8 to 10 hours in the train, they were past complaining at the scanty comfort we could provide. A number of lady members of the Church came to assist in making these poor folk as comfortable as possible, using pews as beds, cushions as mattresses, clothing, blankets, curtains and rugs, and anything else available, for covering. The men had to lie on the bare floor of the Red Cross Room, (above the Lounge) with no covering save their coat. (They said afterwards that they had to walk about most of the night to keep warm. Sleep was out of the question.) The Canteen provided hot milk for the numerous babies, and throughout the night rendered noble service in taking round glasses of water, helping to soothe noisy infants, and generally bringing comfort wherever possible. Messrs Knight and Dixon spent the night on watch, using the vestry as headquarters. Few could have slept that night. Coughs were prevalent, and continually woke the babies, who proceeded at once to wake everyone else who had succeeded in dropping off. By morning the atmosphere was beyond description.

Breakfast was provided by the Canteen, and then began the task of billeting. This was terribly slow, owing to the extent to which Stroud was already crowded, and it soon became evident that many would have to spend a second night on the premises. During the day, however, a band of willing workers drawn from the ranks of Church members, 'spring-cleaned' the Church as thoroughly as possible. The Lounge was in constant use as a rest room, and was crowded throughout the day. All meals were served free in the Canteen.

As there were fewer to be accommodated the second night, it was possible to make them more comfortable, though the improvement was but slight. Messrs Scott and Wyatt kept vigil. Early on Sunday morning, other helpers prepared the Church for morning worship, the evacuees being moved to the Lounge again for their day quarters. Morning service and afternoon School were held as usual, but word having come through that another train-load was expected at tea-time, evening worship was reluctantly cancelled, and preparation made once more for the reception of the homeless. Through the day, billeting had gone on, but at evening there were still some unfortunates left on the premises. The extra train-load did not arrive, so once more it was possible to improve the conditions of those who remained.

On Monday, the premises were officially closed as a reception depot by the billeting officer, so no more were allowed to sleep there, but throughout the week, the Lounge was open as a restroom.

However, despite the reception closure, the Bedford Street schoolroom canteen facilities which had opened on 7 September 1938 originally to provide midday meals for evacuee children, continued to remain open throughout the war years under the enduring management of Miss Jessie Payne (an eventual MBE for her efforts), and her willing supporters.

Initially, the evacuee accommodation was well supported. Anyone having the slightest space was approached and persuaded. It was new and everyone did their part; even Stroud's children seemed to take it in their stride. Keith Browne's parents took on eight-year-old Francis Sutton who, unlike most other evacuees who arrived by train, came in a large car with his parents. He did not stay long, and Keith thinks he left when the Browne's new baby, Keith's brother, was born.

On another occasion, an evacuee family of a father, mother, and daughter

Betty Jameson and Josephine Dickenson from London with Jim Dickenson. During their six-month stay they boarded at The Birches School, Uplands, but their weekends were spent at Down Farm.

spent some time at the Brownes'. Their sudden arrival was occasioned when Keith's father spotted them in Russell Street, following a train journey down. Keith thinks they were probably bombed out. Their stay was short too, due to the fact that the father was a skilled carpenter who was employed quite soon at Tylers (who made Mosquito parts for the Ministry of Aviation), and they then found a home of their own.

Min Browne remembers some evacuees had glamorous names. One which sticks in her mind was Zelda Morris. She remembers living in the accommodation over the shops (which was incidentally reserved for evacuees) and there seemed to be lots of foreigners around, who she now thinks might have been Poles.

The Hawkes family took in Joan Barber, who was an evacuee from Glasgow High School, and had been staying with Doctor Green, the County School doctor. She and Nancy Hawkes became like sisters, attending together every available dance in the district, and having a whale of a time. It was war duties which eventually split them up, when Joan left her job in the Cost Office at

Recreation House and Well Cottage (left) at Slad in 1963, when the snow was five feet deep.

Wallers for service training at RAF Credenhill in Hereford, while Nancy remained behind in reserved occupation to work for Admiral Bommingham.

Other people left bombed cities to settle in Stroud, staying with relatives as Doreen Ireland's sister-in-law did from London. 'They were always terrified when they heard a plane coming', she recalls. Some others came because their work was transferred. The Nippers had already moved from their home in Fishponds, before a bomb 'dropped over their heads' at Parnels at Winterbourne Down and Mr Nipper was transferred to a branch of Parnels at Slad Road. Their final move here was decided for them when their daily transportation by coach to Stroud ceased to run. Mrs Nipper found herself a job, and they settled in a rented room at Recreation House, Slad, living there for six years before they were moved across the road to their own cottage. Recreation House, according to Mike Hawkes, is haunted. A nun-like apparition is thought to appear when a death is imminent, but no one has lived to tell the tale.

As incoming workers and more evacuees continued to arrive, the billeting

Sheepscombe evacuees performing The Princess and the Swineherd *at Briar Cottage in 1941.*

officers found their work increasingly difficult. People's responses to taking in visitors were less enthusiastic. Some having tried it once were not too sure they wanted to again. Soon the question was asked, 'Could the district take any more?' and when the answer was 'no', evacuee rehabilitation began.

Some were sent home, while others were transferred. Handsworth School went to Barnstable, and Eastbourne left for Bournemouth. Free railway travel was provided, and the people who chose to remain forfeited their billeting allowance.

Soon a Lodging Restrictions Order, issued through the Ministry of Health, was introduced. This investigated rooms and numbers of people, and recorded who slept where on 15 April. If anyone stayed more than three nights, permission was required from The District Billeting Officer. Extra hostel accommodation was provided; many large houses such as Brick House in London Road (where Waitrose is now), Field House, and West Grange were used, as well as accommodation above the shops, but Stroud's authorities were still pushed to the limit. The arrival of unofficial evacuees, who hoped to find

Sheepscombe evacuees and village children. Among those pictured are Back Row L–R: Stella Rand, ?, ?, Evelyn Statham, ?, Maureen Skinner; Front Row: Joy Sollars, Margeurite Statham, ? John Everleigh.

solace in over-packed Stroud, added a strain on resources. An incredible nine thousand extra people inhabited Stroud during the war years.

One lady clearly remembers her mother taking in a married Eastbourne couple, because she gave up her bedroom for them, and shared with her mother during their stay. The evacuees arrived on an autumn Saturday, the day before Harvest Festival, but within a day or so it was plain all was not well with their marriage; one or the other was found sleeping on the settee downstairs. The husband's employment as a night watchman resolved the situation.

The reduction of the local bus service by half on 6 September brought the effects of war straight to the heart of Stroud. Due to fuel and labour worries, all unnecessary buses were cut out, and the late night service reduced. Immediately there was overcrowding, people were left at bus-stops, and bus companies appealed for places to be left for passengers living further afield. (A typical example were the workers from Chalford unable to get home because of Brimscombe passengers filling the bus). To help alleviate the problem, the Red

Red & White Services Ltd.

The following service will be operated jointly with the **Western National Omnibus Company Ltd.**

War Emergency Restricted Time Table No. 1

Commencing 17th September 1939.

No guarantee can be given, but every effort will be made to operate the schedules set out.

Changes may be made at very short notice.

DURSLEY—STROUD—BIRDLIP

Weekdays.

	a.m.	a.m.	a.m.	a.m.	a.m.	noon	p.m.	p.m.	p.m.	p.m.	p.m.	p.m.	p.m.	p.m
DURSLEY (Market Square)	7.20	8. 0	9. 0	10. 0	11. 0		12.30	1. 0	1.30	2.30	3.30	4.30	5.10	5.30
Uley (Kings Head)	7.28	8. 8	9. 8	10. 8	11. 8		12.38	1. 8	1.38	2.38	3.38	4.38	5.18	5.38
Uley (Old Crown)	7.30	8.10	9.10	10 10	11.10	12.10	12.40	1.10	1.40	2.40	3.40	4.40	5.20	5.40
Nymphsfield					11.20				1.50		3.50			5.50
Selsley (New Inn)	Stop	Stop	Stop		11.30				2. 0		4. 0			
Selsley (Bell Inn)					11.32				2. 2		4. 2			
Dudbridge					11.35				2. 5		4. 5			
Golden Cross					11.37				2. 7		4. 7			
Stroud (King Street)					11.40				2.10		4.10			
Stroud (King Street)	7.15	7.35	8.35						2.10		4.30			
Slad Church	7.25	7 45	8.45						2.20		4.40			
Bulls Cross		7.46	8.49						2.24		4.44			
Sheepscombe		7.50	8.53						2.28		4.48			
Camp Cross Roads		7.55	8.59						2.34		4.54			
Miserden		8. 0	9. 7						2.42		5. 2			
Whiteway														
Fostons Ash														
BIRDLIP (George Hotel)														

Weekdays. / **Sundays.**

	p.m.	p.m.	p.m.	p.m.	p.m.	p.m.	p.m.	p.m.	p.m.	p.m.
DURSLEY (Market Square)	6.10	6.30	7.25	8.15	8.45	10.15			3.15	7.45
Uley (Kings Head)	6.18	6.38	7.33	8.23	8.53	10.23			3.23	7.53
Uley (Old Crown)	6.20	6.40	7.35	8.25	8.55	10.25			3.25	7.55
Nymphsfield		6.50			9.15	10.35			3.35	8. 5
Selsley (New Inn)	Stop	7. 0			9.25	10.45			3.45	8.15
Selsley (Bell Inn)		7. 2			9.27	10.47			3.47	8.17
Dudbridge		7. 5			9.30	10.50			3.50	8.20
Golden Cross		7. 7			9.32	10.52			3.52	8.22
Stroud (King Street)		7.10			9.35	10.55			3.55	8.25
Stroud (King Street)	6. 0	7.10				11. 7	1.30	2. 0		8.30
Slad Church	6.10	7.20					1.40	2.10		8.40
Bulls Cross		7.24						2.14		8.44
Sheepscombe		7.28						2.18		8.48
Camp Cross Roads		7.34						2.24		8.54
Miserden		7.42						2.32		9. 2
Whiteway										
Fostons Ash										
BIRDLIP (George Hotel)										

Short journeys between Stroud and Slad will start and terminate at Slad War-Memorial.

Weekdays.

	a.m.	a.m.	a.m.	a.m.	a.m.	a.m.	p.m.	p.m.	p.m.	p.m.	p.m.	p.m.	p.m.
BIRDLIP (George Hotel)	—												
Fostons Ash													
Whiteway													
Miserden			8 10			9.48						3.18	
Camp Cross Roads			8.15			9.56						3.26	
Sheepscombe			8.20			10. 2						3.32	
Bulls Cross			8.24			10. 6						3.36	
Slad Church	7.25		8.27			10.10						3.40	
Stroud (King Street)	7.35		8.35			10.20						3.50	
Stroud (King Street)						10.45				1.45		3.50	
Golden Cross	Stop		Stop			10.48				1.48		3.53	
Dudbridge						10.50				1.50		3.55	
Selsley (Bell Inn)						10.55				1.55		4. 0	
Selsley (New Inn)						10.57				1.57		4. 2	
Nymphsfield	6.52					11. 7						4.12	
Uley (Old Crown)	7. 5	7.35	8.30	9.15	10.15	11.15	12.15	12.45	1.20	2.15	2.45	4.20	4.45	5.20
Uley (Kings Head)	7. 7	7.37	8.32	9.17	10.17	11.17	12.17	12.47	1.22	2.17	2.47	4.22	4.47	5.22
DURSLEY (Market Square)	7.15	7.45	8.40	9.25	10.25	11.25	12.25	12.55	1.30	2.25	2.55	4.30	4.55	5.30

Weekdays / **Sundays.**

	p.m.	p.m.	p.m.	p.m.	p.m.	p.m.	p.m.	p.m.	p.m.
BIRDLIP (George Hotel)									
Fostons Ash									
Whiteway									
Miserden		5.23				8.18	3.18		9. 5
Camp Cross Roads		5.31				8.26	3.26		9.13
Sheepscombe		5.37				8.32	3.32		9.19
Bulls Cross		5.41				8.36	3.36		9.21
Slad Church		5.45	6.15			8.40	1.45	3.40	9.27
Stroud (King Street)		5.55	6.25			8.50	1.55	3.50	9.37
Stroud (King Street)			6.30			8.50	2.30	5.55	—
Golden Cross		Stop	6.33				2.33	5.58	
Dudbridge			6.35				2.35	6. 0	
Selsley (Bell Inn)			6.40				2.40	6. 5	
Selsley (New Inn)			6.42				2.42	6. 7	
Nymphsfield	5.50		6.52				2.52	6.17	
Uley (Old Crown)	6. 0	6.20	7. 0	7.35	8.30		3. 0	6.25	
Uley (Kings Head)	6. 2	6.22	7. 2	7.37	8.32		3. 2	6 27	
DURSLEY (Market Square)	6.10	6.30	7.10	7.45	8.40		3.10	6.35	

Short journeys between Stroud and Slad will start and terminate at Slad War Memorial.

Wartime Emergency Bus Timetable.

and White Bus Service issued 'Workers' Tickets', which had to be used before 9 a.m. and after 3.30 p.m, and gave workers preference, but these became a target for abuse and did not prevent the overcrowding. When too many people were standing for safety, the extras were asked to get off, and schoolchildren, who had once offered their seats to their elders, abandoned all their previous manners for fear of 'turfing off' and having to walk home!

In an attempt to rectify this, a change in the seating was organized, whereby some seats were placed lengthways instead of in rows. This enabled two dozen standing places instead of the customary eight. The paper reported a spate of minor accidents, caused through the crush to get on board. One old lady was reported to have acquired a black eye, while another had her glasses smashed. Therefore, to avoid the mad scramble and potential for injury some passengers abandoned it all, preferring to walk home!

Fridays and Saturdays, the main shopping days, were always the worst days for buses as housewives bought their perishable goods at the last minute to see them over the weekend. Mother went shopping on both days, not bothered if her bus was full, as she could always walk. Her meat came from Mr Cove in the Co-op at The Cross, and 'boughton cake', a treat for us who thrived on home-made, from Dick Tucks in Lower Street.

Mercifully, a 'theatre service' remained in operation on most nights. These buses left from Kings Street, The Subscription Rooms, and Rocks Cafe in London Road, at 10.15 p.m., or whenever the film finished.

As no interior light was allowed on buses, an employee of the National Western invented an electric device which resembled a cocoa tin. This was hung from a wooden rail, so that it could be moved along to wherever illumination was needed, in order to enable the conductor to see what he was being paid. However, it could not show up the difference between foreign and English coins, which was unfortunate as the conductor was required to reimburse the bus company for any shortfall. Eventually, the Red and White Service attempted to alleviate the problem by installing lamps above the luggage racks which focused on the ceiling and reduced the glare.

As this situation persisted, with belated starts and occasional cancellations, unspecified bus stops and haphazard pick-ups, passengers began to use the conductor's 'stop and start' button. This habit was frowned upon by drivers and conductors alike, since most passengers did not use the coded rings, (one ring to stop and two to go, and several in an emergency).

In 1940 the situation was eased a little when lady bus conductresses (clippies) arrived on the scene, on both the Red and White, and Western National services. A few were imported from Weymouth and Plymouth where people were not so crowded any more.

Jack Ireland, who was involved with Stroud's public transport for the better part of his working life, remembers the variety of bus stops around the

Jack Ireland with a National Western Bus.

town. The Whiteshill bus left from Badbrook, the Nailsworth one from Lewis and Godfrey's, the Painswick, Randwick, and Kingscourt from the Station Yard. All these were single deckers. There were also the Stonehouse and Gloucester (which went via Quedgeley) from Stroud post office, the Cirencester from the Subscription Rooms, and the Minchinhampton from the Rocks Cafe.

The fare from Stroud to The Prince Albert and Dudbridge was 2*d*, to Kingscourt and Woodchester 3*d*, to Beards Lane it was 1*d*, to Newman and Henders 4*d*, and Nailsworth 5*d*. The return to Cheltenham was 2*s* 6*d*. Some buses were timed to run to and from the work place, although the ordinary public could use them too. Listers had one at 6.15 a.m. to get the workers there for a 7 a.m. start.

The trains did not escape criticism, as they were being used by the government for bulk goods transportation, and at the same time endeavouring to keep passenger services running.

Inevitably, passenger services became disorganized amid the continual manoeuvring of troops at short notice. Food and ammunition transportation meant varied routes, so destinations often took longer to reach. Once it took two hours to travel from Stroud to Cheltenham, an occasion causing one frustrated passenger to announce, 'It would have been quicker to have walked across the fields!'

Coal shortages were another worry, as factories increased their fuel consumption for war work, or to produce electricity. An older, and smaller, work-force remained in the mines, struggling to keep up production after many of the younger miners had left for the services, or been lured through better pay and conditions into munitions factories.

All coal prices were governed by the Retail Coal Prices Order, and coal merchants were required to register through the Local Coal Overseer. They could only supply customers who were on their books, or people holding a certificate from the Local Overseer. Although domestic rationing of coal was considered, and many thought it was rationed, it was never actually enforced. A Controlled Premises Register was adopted instead, where allocation 'according to supply' operated. A schedule of Prices was introduced, based on the average price of all grades as they stood before the Order. There were nineteen in all, the first becoming operational on 20 October 1939 when 'best coal' was 56s 6d a ton. For the Stroud locality, *The Stroud News* printed a list of the fuels available, as quality and quantity plummeted. As the situation worsened and restrictions tightened, the stockpiles which were stored on the wharves at Stroud and Ryeford, were occasionally used, and wood was allowed to be burned if unsuitable for any other purpose.

Fuel economy in transport was controlled by speed limits, and horse power determined petrol allocation. Assessment based on a 20 h.p. car averaging 10 to 12 miles per gallon allowed the owner 10 gallons a month, which was gauged to be enough for about 150 or 200 miles. Proportionately, a vehicle of 7 h.p. received 4 gallons of petrol, and a motor cycle, 2 gallons. Each gallon claimed one unit in the ration book. As a result, cars were left at home and public transport became even more crowded.

The changes on Stroud's roads were summed up by one Stroud councillor when he said, 'Hitler has done something that the County Council, the District Council, and the Chamber of Trade could not do. He has solved Stroud's traffic problem.'

The darker side of war was also unavoidable. Coffins were set aside, hospital beds increased (sixty at Stroud General), and buildings were allocated for future mortuaries. Appeals for blood donors went out, and a spate of 'will making' hit the nation. The Midland Bank Executor and Trustee Company regularly advertised the 'Wisdom of Making a Will' in the newspapers.

CHAPTER FIVE

REACTING TO RATIONING

National Registration Day took place on 29 September 1939. Every householder throughout the nation was obliged to fill in a form providing information on the people in their home on that day. Identification cards were received by everyone within days, closely followed by the Ration Book, which was the government's control over the allocation of all basic commodities. The books were issued by post in November, but not operational until 8 January 1940. They were the first of many such issues over fourteen years, and were all prized like gold.

The main ration books were fawn (general RBI) and green (children RB2), with additional booklets for a host of special requirements and occasions. 'Schemes' and 'points' coupons covered a range of food and household commodities, and more items were added to the list as supplies dwindled. A page lasted for one month, holders being supplied by their nominated retailer. In addition, a weekly survey governed prices, and two monthly updates kept customers informed.

Supplies were issued through Food Offices, and permits were allocated to retailers enabling them to receive their relevant supplies from the wholesaler. 'Points' offered the freedom to buy what you wanted, where you wanted, and 'schemes' supplied welfare items such as milk and vitamins. There were special authorities to deal with an assortment of commodities, while permits and coupons could be used to obtain all manner of goods, such as extra bedding, and animal foodstuffs (which came through the War Agricultural Committee). Little escaped the rationing procedure.

There was much paperwork involved. Changes of address had to be recorded, as well as births and deaths (following which the deceased's book had to be returned to the authorities). Certainly Stroud's Food Office was very busy, dealing as it did with a fluctuating community of evacuees, war workers, servicemen, and visitors.

Hylda Griffin remembers the ration at one time was two ounces of butter or a quarter-of-a-pound of margarine for which the shop keeper cut out four coupons. Her mother could not eat margarine, so they swapped mother's margarine for butter from a friend with a large family who was short of cash. Sometimes they exchanged part of their rations for tea or sugar plus a shilling or two. 'That is how one got by', she explained.

She continues, 'On a Friday the word would go around, "Balls' Fruit Shop will have a box of bananas." You were allowed two on a book but you had to get there by 8 a.m., for 9 o'clock opening. All the bananas were sold out in fifteen minutes, and then it was "No More", and the doors would be shut for another week.'

Ada Webb remembers a similar incident, when potatoes were in short supply and she joined a 'potato queue' (there were queues for everything in wartime). She was there early, but not early enough. This day, as often happened, the stocks ran out, but they were told, 'More will arrive later'. Ada having waited once, did not want to risk missing out again, so she 'stayed put', receiving as her reward the first of the new stock.

Food Offices received frequent complaints as inevitably problems arose when everyone was controlled so tightly. Ada recalls being unhappy with her designated grocer, whom she felt was giving her a raw deal. Through living only twenty minutes walk away from the shop, she invariably found the 'extras' had been claimed before she arrived, causing her to miss out on special offers like cake which disappeared before she had the chance to buy any. After a while she decided to change her shop. Once she had satisfied herself that the Co-op at Cainscross would take her on, she visited her shopkeeper. Marching boldly in she said, 'I realize you have your favourites, so I'll have my book back if you don't mind please'. This, when safely in her possession, accompanied her to the Co-op, and a fairer deal.

A reference leaf, an identity card, a permanent address (with block capitals but no stamp), were the means of obtaining a ration book. This required early application as the first ration books only lasted six months. However, by book five a twelve-month span was operating, along with additional milk, vitamins, eggs, orange juice, and cod liver oil. Babies fared better in wartime than ever before. I should know, as my family claimed I filled my pram! By book four, a 'points' system was in operation, and special points for sweets were in book five. Points offered a choice of goods and a chance to visit other stores, whereas units were only accepted at registered outlets.

People approached their reduced provisions in different ways. Some, when faced with their tiny portion of butter, cheese or whatever, carefully marked it into seven, carefully using only one part each day, while others wolfed it down in a moment of indulgence, with none for the rest of the week. Father would have missed his cheese had not the extra manual allowance allowed a little more.

The invitation to, 'Come to tea' in wartime became a communal effort, as visitors arrived clutching their individual portions of tea, milk, sugar and cake. Although the combined tea portions produced a stronger brew, the sugar could not match it. 'You couldn't ask for more than one cup, because there wasn't enough sugar', said Ada. Meat was allocated by money, not by weight. Adults received 1s 2d worth a week during the early rationing days, and each child 7d worth, but dogs had none at all! However, it was the quality of the meat, not the quantity, which generally disappointed them. As the war progressed, whale meat, calves' heads, offal, and horse flesh, which required no coupons, were introduced. No one liked this, but tried it just once.

One story tells of a woman who found her meat so tough she was unable to eat it, so she gave it to the dog. He could not manage it either, so it had to be cut up for him. The butcher, who bore the brunt of all complaints, suggested mincing!

Meat was rationed from three days into the war, suffering several reductions as the years passed by. By 1950 it had dropped to 8d, with a supplementary 2d for corned beef. Meat finally came off ration in 1954.

In case of invasion, a list of Emergency Food Rations was published, with details of where to obtain them locally. A basket or pillow case was required to transport them home in and the allowance weighed 9lb. Soup, tinned milk, beans, biscuits, sugar, margarine, and tea were included.

People saved up small amount of fruit, sugar, and butter for special occasions. Once again, people with children fared better than those without. My Aunty Kitty had no children, and was therefore restricted in her choice. Through mother's efforts our Christmas cake was fairly bursting with accumulated goodies; but poor Aunty's, 'Well you could have counted the sultanas in hers. It was a pity, she thought she had done wonders'.

Christmas did present a challenge. Ruth Morgan's 'Wartime Cookery Page' suggested 'thrilling little savouries to make a not particularly large bird or joint go further'. These included potato stuffing, which consisted of mainly mashed potato with a rasher of fat bacon; haricot bean stuffing; and economical sausage meat made mostly of bread and herbs. Chocolate fingers graced the tea table, potato powder took the place of some of the flour, and wartime marzipan covered the cake. This was a mixture of stale cake crumbs with liberal doses of almond essence. Christmas cakes were unlikely to be iced, and many war brides had to be content with plain Dundee cake after 1940, when icing on wedding cakes was banned.

Women's Institutes encouraged improvisation schemes. Sheepscombe WI commenced their 1941 programme with a talk on 'Thrift', a theme which was incorporated in every talk thereafter. Cookery demonstrations of Wartime Recipes tackled bread making, in case the village bread supply was cut off, eggless cake, and soda bread and jam. A talk given on 'How to make the most of your sugar ration' possibly benefited The Fruit Preservation Committee, and

Aladdin Re-visited *performance by the Sheepscombe WI in 1959.*
L–R: Mrs K French, Mrs Cole, Mrs A Beacham, Mrs J Brough, Mrs H Cowdry, Miss Gainey,
Mrs C Hopcraft, Mrs Williams, Mrs Workman, Mrs Morgan, Mrs Wray, Mrs Oakley.
Horse: Miss Robinson and Mrs White.

inspired members to compile a recipe booklet from their own tried and tested favourites. The profits from the sale of these purchased coupon-free knitting wool from the Army Comforts Depot, and members of the weekly knitting party produced helmets and mittens for the 'boys in khaki and blue'. Their efforts produced a total of 161 garments in a little over twelve months. During the spring, nettle collections were made, and in the summer, several tons of herbs. Blackberries and rose-hips were the autumn's assignment, which realized 4s profit from 28lb of the 56lb collected.

Each week the pie and pastry group produced 120 pies to sell through the WVS, and regular first aid and home nursing classes were held. A Rabbit Club was formed as a result of a talk on rabbits, and the Garden Club collected leek seed. There was a talk on renovation, a scheme for egg distribution was set up, the subjects of the need for extra buses, water, and sewerage supplies were tackled, while the ever popular National Savings Stamps were on sale at every meeting. These positive meetings considerably lifted morale, to prove without doubt that limited resources do not restrict inventiveness.

Some people probably thought obtaining goods on the black market was being inventive. It seemed innocent enough, and Stroud, in common with most towns, 'was on the fiddle'. For most people it was simply a case of a favour done here deserves another. Sometimes a neighbour who had run out of money would sell her excess coupons, which were useless to her anyway; while practically a whole street could reap the benefits of a pig whose slaughtering had slipped through the net of officialdom. One beneficiary licked his lips as he recalled the tasty Sunday breakfast of bacon and eggs which resulted from some bacon acquired from a friend's cellar. 'The delicious smell wafting down our street must have made everyone wonder', he said.

However, as large scale black marketing was capable of wrecking a well-organized rationing system, the authorities regarded it with disdain, promising heavy fines and possible imprisonment for those who were caught.

Children probably only noticed rationing in 1942, when their sweet supplies were affected. Their eight ounce sweet or chocolate quota was required to last four weeks. When sweets were first derationed in April 1949, children were to receive preferential treatment for the first two days, and so the shopkeepers armed themselves with extra assistants ready for the rush. Most children on their first trip spent between five and seven shillings, their keenness overcrowding the shops, and emptying jars. One Stroud shopkeeper said he sold as much in two hours as in three weeks during rationing, while Eric Wood's Off Licence on the corner of Acre Street and Chapel Street, who opened on Sunday morning, was sold out by lunchtime. The extravagance caused shortages, and rationing returned until 1953, with half pound limits.

War children did not miss bananas because they had not ever eaten them. Bryan Durn says he used to look at the enamelled sign on the wall of Bradshaws' Fruit and Vegetable shop at the Cross, and wonder what they tasted like. Indeed, in 1946, when they were on our shores again, many toddlers treated them cautiously, not knowing what to do. Ada peeled and ate one in front of five-year-old Margaret to demonstrate how it was done, and mine was cut in half for years in case I wasted it. Everything capable of preservation was bottled, dried, salted or made into jam, a sugar allowance being made especially for this purpose.

It is said that whole eggs were available in tins, but I never saw them. Ours were either fresh from the hen, dried, or preserved in isinglass. Many people liked the dried egg powder as it was fine for anything requiring beaten eggs, but a boiled-egg lover complained it was 'no good for dipping your soldiers in'.

Bottling was quite difficult as it involved gentle oven heating to seal. There were a lot of failures, so 'The Campden Preserving Method' which sterilized with tablets was adopted by some bottlers. Salted foods necessitated meticulous soaking and rinsing, but the salt taste always crept through. The item best suited for salting was bacon, so many people with a bit of land kept pigs.

A Message from Canada

This package contains five ounces of Canadian Grade A dried eggs — approximately one dozen shell eggs.

They have been dried by a specially developed spray process, packaged to retain freshness and food value.

Nothing has been added, and only the shells and water have been removed.

Restore the water and you can use them as you would whole, fresh eggs for baking, in puddings and as scrambled eggs or omelettes, and other egg dishes.

How to RECONSTITUTE DRIED EGGS

A level tablespoon dried egg + 2 level tablespoons water = 1 fresh egg.

Add 1 tablespoon of water to the dried egg and blend to a smooth paste. Gradually beat in the other tablespoon of water.

When reconstituted, egg should be used at once. Do not reconstitute more than you are going to use.

How to USE DRIED EGGS

Dried eggs may be used in any recipe which calls for "beaten eggs".

For custards, milk puddings and other milk and egg dishes reconstitute the eggs and use in the same way as you would beaten fresh eggs.

For quick mixing and good texture in batter puddings and other cake mixtures, cream the dried egg with the fat and add the water necessary for reconstituting to the liquid called for in the recipe.

For light, tender scrambled eggs and omelettes, reconstitute the dried eggs and add a pinch of baking powder or bicarbonate of soda for each egg just before cooking.

How to KEEP DRIED EGGS

Egg leaflet.

54

Grandfather as I remember him in the early 50s. Every Thursday evening, Father, dirty and straight from work, shared a meal with him, shaved him with a cut throat razor, and trimmed his hair and moustache. At one time negotiating his cottage via the field was a precarious journey for me with short legs. Several times the dairy cow chased me down the field, head down like a bull, but Grandfather's gate saved me. Habitually the cockerel destined for Uncle Francis' Christmas Dinner raced towards me to flutter at my throat, despite frenzied stick waving to ward him off. I was very glad when he was hung, drawn and roasted with stuffing. Grandfather loved his garden, and his sizeable vegetable plot occupied a piece of the field. Once when there I put my foot in a wasps' nest, and when stung rushed up home crying for treatment with the 'blue bag'.

In my family, grandfather, uncle, and father kept a pig, and any kitchen scraps from the three families were divided between the chickens and the pig. When the piglets first arrived they were pink, plump, and squealing, unimaginable as future meals on plates. But a few months of swill soon transformed them into potential bacon breakfasts, roast joints, and crackling. Slaughter, which in pre-war days was performed by Grampy, was carried out during wartime by a Ministry commissioned slaughterer. He arrived around Christmastime and took half the pig for the nation, while claiming the equivalent meat tokens from the family. Grandfather, still had to deal with the singeing, jointing, curing, and ham cooking, before he could share the portions out between his large family.

Cider was plentiful on the farm at Down Farm, Slad. There, the men were allocated a quart of cider daily, which had been made on the farm by Jack Timbrell with apples from Peglers orchard. The old pensioner horse, Boxer, turned the cider mill. It was Jim Dickenson's job as a boy to fetch the cider from the cellar. He remembers his grandfather, who knew he would drink some if he had the chance, standing at the top of the cellar steps, saying, 'Let me hear you whistle, lad'.

The old Cider Mill at Down Farm.

Clothing coupons arrived on 1 June 1941, and people were anxious to use them. There were twenty-four coupons to a page, and the number needed depended on the size and worth of the garment. A dress required eleven coupons (plus the money), and a handkerchief just two. Hylda, who was in the NFS and required to wear a uniform, says a white blouse was sixteen coupons, and a tie and stockings were two each. 'I had to scout around for coupons, and I would often pay 10s for a page if I wanted clothes apart from my uniform'. However, by 1942 the point value had dropped to sixty over fifteen months instead of twelve, and to forty by 1945.

Remaining smart was difficult, but people made the effort. Women who were handy with a needle unpicked and turned, trimmed here and added there, to produce from apparently redundant clothes a 'new' garment worthy of admiration. Mother was armed with her pre-marriage skills in Court dressmaking and her oak Singer treadle sewing machine (purchased with football pontoon prize money). She converted her outdated coat into a coat and hat for my sister, with the saving on coupons going towards a pair of shoes. One of her acquisitions shortly after the war was a cream parachute, from which she made five dresses which 'washed lovely'.

Joseph Dickenson in his garden at Down Farm during the early days of war.

Mr Laichbury and Mr Hall shearing in the cattleyard at Down Farm. The sheep were fed on linseed, while 200 chickens benefitted from the oat crop. The potatoes, which farmers could sell wherever they wanted at market prices, grew better with a complete granular fertilizer of ICI no. 1.

Ingenious ready-made clothes appeared on the market, such as the reversible jacket, which by being plain one side and patterned the other, incorporated two outfits in one. Waistcoats were popular; being sleeveless and collarless they saved on cloth, and could be made from a whole range of fabrics for day and evening wear. Farm or factory wartime work made trousers socially acceptable for women, along with the public display of the turban which had hitherto only been seen at home – hats were generally worn when out. Generally, fashion became straighter and plainer, and this was enforced in 1942 by a government clothes' restriction which reduced pockets, buttons, straps, trouser turn-ups, pleats, and skirt lengths.

Some churches received clothes parcels from abroad. Ours had some from America. Mother chose a pretty dress for my sister, and I can remember wearing one resembling the Stars and Stripes. Included too were 'nice big bars of chocolate, which were out of this world'. Mother, in common with many women, used to wonder, 'Will I ever be able to go out and get what I want again?'.

Stockings are always associated with wartime. Margaret Turner remembers buying Miners Leg Make-up to compensate for their lack. This was applied with cotton wool to give a suntanned look, and an added pencil line gave the impression of seamed stockings. At the department store where she worked, no girl was allowed on the shop floor without stockings, so the girls employed there bought rayon stockings, which had to be turned inside out to expose the seam, with the fluffy bits around the heel trimmed off, to give the appearance of silk stockings.

When nylons appeared, the word spread and queues formed to buy them even though they were quite expensive. Margaret earned £1 10s. One pound went to her mother, 2s 4d paid the stamp, 2s 6d bought subsidized lunches, and the rest was her own, to be spent on stockings when her department's turn to buy them arrived. Of course you could buy them off 'spivs' in the streets, but you often found that the seams were crooked or one stocking was smaller than the other, or they had various other defects. There was a machine installed on the ground floor of our store where a lady invisibly mended them for 6d.

The Limitation of Supply Orders meant that retailers had supplies of basic hardware and household furnishings drastically reduced. This made replacing goods practically impossible, and what was produced was plain, all decoration having been banned. China was white, walls were painted, and floors were uncarpeted. Families who had been bombed or newly-weds could, with their allowance of sixty units per couple, get essentials such as bedding and utility furniture, but even this point allocation was reduced by half in 1944.

Petrol rationing operated differently in that it allowed a set monthly amount for private motoring, alongside supplements for business use, although a dye had to be added in 1948 to prevent people from using commercial petrol for

The Post man would have been sure of his petrol allowance. Here is Joe Coupland delivering the post around Sheepscombe in the early 1950s. His daughter's names – Julie Louise Coupland – were the same initials as those on his number plate.

their own private use. All journeys had to be necessary, and pleasure driving was a thing of the past. Petrol misuse fines of £10 were commonplace until petrol rationing finally ended in 1952 .

As a result, people walked more. Ada regularly walked with Leslie to Cheltenham. One day they had walked there singing, 'I'm Happy when I'm Hiking', as they looked forward with anticipation to their time in the shops, but they were disappointed when they arrived, because they had chosen early closing day. So they sat on a park bench to eat their dinner before setting off to walk back home.

CHAPTER SIX

BATTLING ON

As the war progressed, fearful reports of bombing in London, Coventry, Bristol, and many other cities and ports reached Stroud. Situated in the safety of the countryside, our town in comparison witnessed little destruction, yet remained physically and mentally prepared, lest any stray bombs come our way. Mother, living high on her hilltop, with panoramic Stroud stretched out below her, often stood in the darkness at her open door holding my older sister's hand, as German fighter planes droned nightly overhead on route to bomb Bristol. She felt little fear, only slight apprehension as she watched the sparking lights from our own anti-aircraft, although her heart beat a little quicker when a stray bomb landed on Selsley Common in December 1940, causing a crater, and rattling her window-panes.

Betty Morgan, living in rural Sudgrove, happily walked home through the trees, not bothered at all by the falling shrapnel on the leaves above her. However, following reminders of the danger, she resorted to wearing to a tin kitchen bowl on her head for her short walk's duration.

To combat any blasé feeling in Stroud, positive instructions were issued on 'What To Do In Case Of Invasion'. The main aims were 'Remaining Calm without Panic', 'Staying Put', and 'Thinking Before Acting', as well as 'Refraining from Gossip'. 'Keep Mum, Save Dad' was the current catchphrase. If invasion occurred, people were supposed to hide food, maps, petrol, bicycles, or anything which might help the enemy's progress, or hinder the work of our military. People were advised to remain indoors, 'not barricaded and bolted', but simply to stay off the streets to reduce chaos. 'The enemy would love to see hoards of frightened people blocking the roads', said the government instructions.

Guides on procedure were produced, and facilities made available for those bombed. There were centres and administrative offices which would deal with lost or destroyed documents, identity cards, ration books, bedding, clothes and respirators, and advice was offered on what to do with the dead. Rest centres would provide a good meal, and cars would provide transportation of the homeless to billets; or travel vouchers would be issued for people travelling elsewhere. An Emergency Repair Squad, formed from local volunteer tradesmen on continual twenty-four hour call-out, would ensure your home was weatherproof, and your movable property would be stored in one of the buildings in Stroud district commandeered for the purpose.

The authorities were responsible for war-damaged property. Casualties whose incomes were below £400 per annum, would receive compensation, and also some clothes, if their income was £250 or less. People who were injured, and unable to work for seven days, would be able to claim for lost income, and if unable to work at all, receive a pension.

Gloucestershire's first bombs came in June 1940, Stroud's self-confidence being shaken at the end of July. On Thursday 25 July at 2.25 p.m., a Jukers 88 Bomber came down at Oakridge Lynch, and its crew of four were captured, one by a member of the Home Guard in Oldhill Woods. Shortly afterwards, as a result of a collision with the above, P.O. Charles Bird and his Hurricane Fighter also came down. P.O. Bird was killed, only his unsigned driving licence remaining to prove his identity.

The Battle of Britain in August brought a flurry of warnings and indiscriminate bombings. Cranham endured several shocks before Christmas, starting on 28 August, when a bomb falling in the orchard of Brook Cottage in Mill Lane created an enormous crater. Another bomb, just missing Cranham Mill, landed in the lake behind, where it is said to lie unexploded today. Finally, on 11 December, fifteen incendiary bombs fell at Overton Farm, but only an outbuilding received any damage.

Over the next two years, numerous incendiary bombs littered Stroud's countryside. Harescombe, Painswick, Forest Green, Chalford, France Lynch, Selsley, Stonehouse, and Standish were all victims at one time or another.

Incendiaries were a nuisance, and obviously a fire hazard, but not so physically damaging as a devastating High Explosive (HE) Bomb. Painswick discovered the effect of one of these in 1941, having escaped previous incidents with minor damage. A stick of eight bombs on 15 June, possibly the most destructive in the Stroud District during the entire war, resulted in two direct hits on Poultry Court, damage to a house in Tibbiwell Lane, the death of two evacuees (one an elderly gentleman, and the other a lady from Eastbourne WVS), and three houses demolished. In addition there was extensive damage to six more homes, which resulted in later demolition, and minimal damage to thirty-five homes. Twenty-nine people were made homeless, and telephones, gas and electricity services were all put out of action, until reinstated by the recovery services later in the day.

Peggy Perrins who, with her husband, was living with her parents Herbert and Hesba Ireland in their paper shop, remembers all the chaos, the rubble and the stalwart determination by Painswick businessmen to carry on regardless.

William Simmonds was Head Warden for Oakridge and the surrounding hamlets of Bournes Green, Tunley, Waterlane, Far Oakridge and Oakridge Lynch during the war, of which he drew an ARP map. Although born in Constantinople, where his architect father supervised the rebuilding of the British Embassy, in 1912 William and his wife came to live in Far Oakridge, where until his death in 1968 at 92 he pursued a range of art skills, particularly animal carving. His renowned The Farm Team graced the 1967 Stroud Festival, and his designs and drawings were exhibited at The Royal Academy and the Tate Gallery. He also created puppets and marionettes, in accurate detail, and locally partook in amateur dramatics in which he acted, stage managed, and designed and built sets.

Amid the disorder, in the beautiful sunny weather that followed, the paper shop carried on, Mr Birt, the butcher, found alternative accommodation, and Mr Hopkins continued cobbling.

As she writes in her interesting account in the *Painswick Beacon*, 'The night bombs fell on Painswick',

'In true British fashion we picked ourselves up, dusted ourselves down and got on with living.

Mrs Whitting had just gone to bed, following a dance at the Institute, when the bombs struck the town. All the family got up at once, shocked such a thing could happen in quiet old Painswick. However all the village pulled together, Mrs Whitting's father, a special constable, digging out Mrs Hollister from her cottage in Tibbiwell lane, who along with shock, suffered injury to her back, when a beam of the house fell down.'

Other districts received their share of HE Bombs. These included Oakridge, Selsley, Minchinhampton, Tunley, and Wotton-under-Edge.

While there were bombs about, constant vigilance against fire was needed, but this was an unpopular duty. The Fire Prevention (Business Premises) Order, implemented by the Minister of Home Security, required that all industries employing thirty people or more should be fire-watched by employees. This created difficulties as many employees were already committed to other Civil Defence duties, and therefore could not included. Shops usually had a smaller workforce and no fire-watchers of their own.

However, some shops and most factories did have their own fire schemes up and running. Worth and Sons at Ham Mill, Thrupp, installed new fire fighting appliances in January 1940, and demonstrated their effects before the ARP and Fire Brigades. Ivy Lusty remembers crawling on all fours through a smoke-filled room at Holloway's clothing factory, and searching the building for a red glowing torch, which was intended to represent an incendiary bomb.

When Ivy and her workmate fire-watched at night, their shift finished at six a.m. They then went home for a short break before returning at nine, an hour later than normal, for their daytime work. Fire-watchers were not supposed to sleep on duty, but two rest rooms supplied with beds were provided, one for men, the other for women. These were next to each other. Ivy and her colleague knew the men with whom they shared their duty would take a nap when everything was quiet. So one night they hid some saucepan lids, tied together with string, in the mens' rest room, and threaded the cord through the gap in the wall where the pipes went through. During the night, as their fellow watchers slept, Ivy's friend pulled the string, and the lids crashed to the ground, 'just like an air-raid'. But Ivy missed the fun, because she had nodded off too!

Advice was issued on dealing with incendiary bombs. Speed was of the utmost importance. Several methods were used to extinguish the incendiaries, the most common being to sprinkle them with water or sand. But any high power water jet treatment was useless because this method generated oxygen, and consequent high combustion.

The continuing lack of volunteer fire-watchers eventually led to compulsory registration and enrolment, and the formation of The Fire Guard in August 1941. It became a regimented system involving officers, training, committees, posts, and teams, and premises initially at John Street and then as space ran out, the Old Billiard Room. There was twenty-four hour coverage, the night duties being from 7 p.m.–7 a.m. When women became involved too, the membership grew to around seven hundred by 1943. There were Fire Fighting

INCENDIARY BOMBS !

Dear Friend,

      Some of the inhabitants are much concerned regarding the safety of life and property in the event of INCENDIARY BOMBS being dropped in our area during the day or night, particularly since our wooden houses would very quickly be beyond saving.

      As you may be aware, constant watch is being kept every night in order - should the necessity arise - that PROMPT ACTION may be taken to assist you, but YOUR help and cordial co-operation is needed TO MAKE EFFECTIVE PROTECTION POSSIBLE.

      It will be clear that fire-fighting materials (water,sand etc.) cannot be transported from one part of the Colony to another quickly enough to be of any use. This means that it is necessary for these materials to be kept handy at each house in a known and easily accessible place, so that any available apparatus (such as Stirrup Pumps) can be brought to the fire and put into action at once.

      With this end in view,it is suggested that all householders should keep handy (under cover outside the house) AT LEAST one bucket (or other suitable receptacle)of DRY sand, fine soil or sifted bonfire ashes, also AT LEAST one bucket of water, and some damp sacking, rugs or old coats, for use in beating out, or smothering the fire. A spade, or shovel, should also be kept in the same place. (A Warden will call upon you in a few days to note where you keep these things, in case the unexpected happens in your absence).

      These few simple precautions would materially assist the Wardens and be to the advantage of all concerned in the perfectly possible event of Incendiary Bombs falling on **Whiteway**.

                 Yours fraternally,

                   F.H.SHOTBOLT.(+)

(+)	(	P.ELLIOTT.
	(	W.B.GIBSON.
	(	G.H.HOLMES.
On behalf, and with	(	A.MAXFIELD.
the approval, of the	(	H.MERRETT.
f o l l o w i n g	((Mrs)	R.MITCHELL.
Acting-Wardens.	(	G.PARKER.
	(	G.PHELPS.
	(	J.PORTLOCK.
	(	B.ROBERTS.
	((Mrs)	B.ROBERTS.

28th September 1940.

Whiteway Colony Incendiary Bomb Leaflet.

Strachans Fire Guards and Members of the Civil Defence Services in October 1944. In Civilian clothes The Mill Fire Guard. In Uniform standing L–R: C Young (Decontamination Service), H Webb (First Aid). Seated: F Urch (Special Constable), J Blair (First Aid Service), WR Achlam (Observer Corps), J Allison (CD Incident Officer), Mr Stewart (Major, Home Guard), KW Green (CD Incident Officer), G Watkins (Head Warden Randwick), J Apperley (Senior Warden Selsley), L Birt (Decontamination Service). Front: C Spalding (Warden), K Gazard (CD Control), V Smith (Warden), R Bashford (Decontamination Service). Courtesy of Milliken.

Demonstrations, which were performed by teams from Stroud and Stonehouse who toured the district, and a team competition when Stonehouse won The George Pearce Cup.

The Battle of The Fields took off as German submarine action claimed our food imports. Britain's farmers, now paramount in food production, assumed unaccustomed importance, with guidance and advice from the government. Questions awaited them in the papers. Was their machinery neglected? Were they wasting tractor fuel? Was their seed dressed with an 'organo' to reduce seed-borne diseases? Had they thatched their stacks in good time, and were their potatoes clamped correctly?

More wheat and barley production was advised for making bread, as were potatoes, because of their iron content. Advertising campaigns urged everyone to 'Utilize every crust', or to 'Eat more potatoes to save on the wheat'. Subsidies and fixed prices were offered for potato production. Posters shouted 'Your part in the Potato Plan', 'Potatoes help to win the War', and people convinced 'A pound of potatoes eaten daily will produce a healthy body', refused all other foods to 'Eat More Potatoes Instead!' Potatoes replaced fat in 'pastry' when mashed with flour and rolled out in the normal way. Betty Morgan used this mixture for meat pies which were, 'Quite nice this way'.

However when the war was finally over, the potato, which had sustained us so well, itself fell victim to the rationing scourge. Even the stalwart Bedford Street Restaurant was unable to obtain their one-and-a-half hundredweight daily supply.

Therefore 'Dig for Victory' became 'Dig for Victory over Want', with all producers continuing hoeing and growing as before. Some energetic gardeners, for whom producing a productive plant was an enjoyable pastime anyway, found satisfaction in growing large quantities of produce knowing it was so urgently needed. They willingly used all available daylight hours to convert untamed land into productive acres for the good of the local community.

The aptly named Violet Gardener, a woman of no large stature, did that very thing in an orchard a mile from her home, which resulted in an abundance of produce which she trundled in her wheelbarrow ready for sale. At the end of wartime shortages, when the paddock reverted once more to grassland, she transferred her energies to her own flourishing garden, which she was always pleased to share with her visitors. None left empty-handed. Their admiration of a plant swiftly led to a rooted offering in damp newspaper, or a few blooms for a vase. Her plants were for sharing and enjoyment, and many people must have a clump or two in their garden which began their lives with Violet.

Wheelbarrows had countless uses apart from gardening. When Ada Webb needed somewhere to put her eldest daughter Margaret to sleep, now that her cot was being used by the new baby, Mary, Ada's mother's ottoman, in her home near Salmon Springs, seemed the perfect answer. One evening, Leslie and Ada, and their wheelbarrow, visited Mother on the Painswick Road, the iron barrow wheel creating a dreadful din as it trundled along the hard road. On the return trip, fully laden, and now with dusk approaching, two men in conversation at Wallbridge came over to investigate. The noise drew attention to the box, which could have contained anything (even ammunition or a body!) but their torch revealed nothing but a good laugh. Anxious to get home before it got dark, Ada and Leslie proceeded up the Bath Road at a good pace, until when they were passing a three storied house at the road's edge, they heard a masculine voice, 'Just listen to that, here they come again!'. Obviously, the noisy barrow had been mistaken for a fleet of bomber aircraft, similar to those heard the night before.

Allotment card.

Although farmers were the main growers, anyone with available ground, however modest, was cajoled into cultivating something. Prized flower borders succumbed to the spade. Root crops, vegetables, and cabbages replaced grass, and Dig for Victory committees sprang up. These were a positive, enthusiastic approach towards encouraging the flagging gardener. The Council gave some land, but some was not used. The Bowling Green at Stratford Park was left intact, but potatoes were planted on its neighbouring acre.

Many people were surprised at the sudden shortage of food, not realising how desperate the situation had become. Consequently, information on future food shortages was published in the newspapers, along with offers of seeds to interested people. Once the French spring salads dwindled, these enthusiasts, equipped with their allocation of seeds, dug, manured, and sowed to be ultimately delighted with the fruits of their harvest.

Not all years were productive though, and the new gardeners suffered some disappointments. Ray Hay, in his *Stroud News* gardening column, blamed the weather and pests for the disastrous bean crop of 1941. It was too dry for the runner, and too blighted for the broad. The aphids and caterpillars infested the cabbages, and the late May frosts ruined the tomatoes. It was the prolific pea crop which saved the day and encouraged growers to, 'Dig on, and keep on top of the work'.

Glasshouse owners, unless living in an agricultural area with special permission from the Regional Controller, were prohibited from using fuel for heat, although growers of salad crops, tomatoes or seedlings did receive some favour. Flower growing became a thing of the past, for commercial flower growing without a permit was prohibited.

The keeping of poultry increased dramatically during wartime; the visions of roast chicken and limitless eggs well worth all the labour. The Domestic Keepers Council concentrated on egg production for family use and discouraged selling for profit, gauging their coupon foodstuff allocation in proportion to the number of birds kept. It was more economical to purchase 14lb of Balancer Meal, which allowed proportionally more for each bird per quarter, than the hundredweight allowed for 120 birds.

However, Stroud district, because of its rural situation, did allow some small poultry keepers to supply a few customers legitimately with their egg quota. The information a new poultry keeper needed to choose his chicks, with advice on rearing and feeding, and 'How to Construct a Movable Bird Coop', which was essential to a small garden, was supplied by *Feathered World* and *Poultry Keeper* magazines.

I frequently helped father feed our chickens before setting off for school. Their squawks as daylight approached were enough to wake the dead. We ladled their combined mashed potato and meal breakfasts into their tin bowls, and opened their little trap door so they could all come tumbling down the ramp. The small boiled potatoes cooked the night before were delicious dipped in salt, which meant that on some mornings the birds' rations were slightly short.

Rabbit keeping ensured a ready supply of meat for those who could cope with eating their 'pet bunny'. We could not face rabbit meat, although at one stage we kept two black and white Dutch rabbits as pets called Bubble and Squeak. Bubble soon had to leave as he made Squeak squeak too much. The magazine *Rabbit Keeping* advised on rabbit-keeping for food, where it seemed a rabbit's future hung in the balance at four months old. Then, bucks destined for the table, it said, ideally weighed three-and-a-half pounds, and owners of does had to decide if they were there for food or breeding.

There was at this time a large demand for rabbit skin goods, which if they were sleek, shiny, and devoid of white patches fetched 7s 6d. Some owners even added cod liver oil to feeds to boost the glossy coats. Little wanted were the poor old rabbits with baggy skins and bony backs: they were even no good stewed!

Although domestic rabbits received stroking and pet status, even if reared for food, their wild cousins foraging freely on the nation's crops were detested and hounded. There was a constant human battle against wild rabbits and, if they were not shot, gassing was the chosen weapon. The gassing powder, Cymag, was sold in 7lb tins costing 18s. One teaspoonful was adequate for each treatment. Contact with the damp earth was essential to activate the poisonous gas, and the insertion of the powder into a narrow burrow hole was difficult and tedious. This was achieved by using a small shallow tin which was attached to a stick and slid in flat before tipping over, then sealing all the outlet holes with turf and dirt.

Osborne Ayers caught rabbits with ferrets and Jim Dickinson could get 2s 6d for each one he shot, if he took it to Charlie Holford of Snows Farm, who sold it on in the village. 'In war, people would eat anything that moved', said Jim. The Americans particularly loved grey squirrels.

Jim Dickinson was twelve years old when he was first allowed to use a gun. The clappers that he had once used to scare off the birds were left at home. One day at his post, he shot a pheasant down by mistake. Wondering what to do about his problem, he pushed it inside his coat, hoping he could get it home without anyone seeing it. As he neared home, Mr Wigmore, an old country character, called out, 'I heard the shot, lad, did you get anything?'. Jim answered 'No' before he realized the tail of the pheasant was hanging out below his coat!

Rats were the subject of another battle. Their invasion during 1941 was so great that a 'Rats Order' was enforced, requiring a fence to be erected around stacks before threshing began. The rats which ran from the rick were meant to be killed before they could escape into the fields to multiply. Many farmers did not bother, even when threatened with fines of £170. They simply carried on as before, their only personal precaution being the tried and tested string tied below the knees!

CHAPTER SEVEN

SALVAGE, SAVING AND ENTERTAINMENTS

Nearly everything was saved during wartime. The increasing inability to obtain normal everyday items prompted many schemes for recycling. It seemed as though only pests could be destroyed!

Therefore, from June 1940 salvage schemes introduced by the Ministry of Supply organized collections of a range of items hitherto discarded without a second thought. Paper, bones, rags, rubber, metals, and pig food could all be useful. Government appeals were accompanied by charts depicting equivalent shell fuse components, or boxes for cartridges per ton of scrap, resulting in large collections.

Paper shortage, caused through transport curtailment from the paper producing countries of Scandinavia, had already become intolerable, and the requirement of one hundred thousand tons boosted up the price to £6 7s 6d a ton. As a result of the appeal, bundles of newspapers and dog-eared magazines appeared from attics and recesses, and a National Waste Paper Competition scheme emerged, whereby districts and wartime charities shared the profits.

Scouts throughout Stroud district conducted waste paper collections; their Scout Headquarters became paper dumping grounds, before the precious waste was delivered to a paper collection point such as the builders' merchants, Selby Bros at Lightpill.

In April 1940, paper wastage figures approaching fifteen thousand tons came to light; a Paper Rationing Order was introduced, and paper collecting tightened up. Paper usage was reduced by 30 per cent from what was used twelve months before, and people became liable to summons if paper was destroyed, or mixed in with other things. Goods did not receive wrapping any more; all luxury paper goods such as serviettes, paper tablecloths, cups, plates, and even confetti, disappeared from shelves. People took their own bags to the shops with which to wrap their purchases.

Stroud held a 'book drive' in 1943. The John Street Council Chamber became

Selby's building business began with Fred Selby in the 1930s with three lorries, but in 1950 a Selby lorry assumes an Hawaiian theme. The dancers decorated the lorry at Ruscombe and made their own costumes which they donned at Margaret Steel's house. Fresh flowers were worn in their hair.
Back L–R: Elsie Kirby, Margaret Steele (now Hazell), Joyce Mills, Maureen Whitaker, Jon Harper, Jill Steele, Betty Kirby, Muriel Steele. Front: Eddie Bolton, Margaret Harper, Marian Keene, Bert King (driver), Tony West, Dave Stiff.

their distribution point. An enthusiastic response provided hitherto unwanted books and magazines for schools, libraries, the Forces, and pulp. Careful examination by the Scrutiny and Sorting Committee (a body composed of the National Book Counci, the WVS, the Waste Paper Recovery Association and Stroud Council), discriminated between informative, rare, technical, and academic books, and those too decrepit for anything but scrap. Paper collecting continued for many years after the war, people's meticulous saving habits slackened along with the end of the black-out.

Rags, rope, sacking, carpets, mops, and rubber (scarce due to Japanese control of rubber producing countries) all became part of the compulsory saving scheme. Anyone throwing away these items was liable to be prosecuted. People thought twice before renewing their vehicle tyres, which caused another problem in itself, as it was an offence to use tyres until they were bald, and the fabric within could be seen. Therefore, a new brand of tyre was introduced, incorporating a bold wavy strip of colour into the tread, which showed up clearly when the unsafe limit was reached. With replacement difficulties, it was just as well wartime travelling was restricted.

Rubber shortage only bothered families who were directly affected, when wellingtons leaked, or babies' dummies became chewed. When my dummy became badly gnawed, and mother was desperate, Aunty Kate, who lived in the small village of Brean in the Forest of Dean, secured not one, but two from their village shop. My parents made the trip there to collect them.

Soon brass, once vital to Victorian kitchens, but old-fashioned and out of favour with women in the 1930s, joined the Salvaging Scheme. Its value escalated to £45 a cwt, along with copper, aluminium, and iron. All manner of iron objects, bedsteads, cycle frames, and vast amounts of ornate wrought ironwork, was accumulated from homes, gardens, and streets. The highly unpopular 'Requisition of Unnecessary Iron Railings' became operational on 26 January 1942, and invited people to make a free gift of their railings to the nation, with compensation if they required it. Posts, gates, bollards, chains, and stiles, along with many miles of railings, were affected. Hospitals, schools, military institutions, and historical artefacts were the only positive excuses for exclusion. However, some could remain if it was felt life was endangered by their absence. One Stroud vicar applied for a reprieve for his churchyard railings on that count, but his hopes were dashed.

Wilf Merrett, remembers the men and their lorry arriving with their acetylene equipment to collect the railings in Bell View Road. 'One man cut them off, while another picked them up'. Only the bit near the ground remained to show that railings once stood proudly there, 'with their nice little spear on the top!'. Even the garden gate was taken. 'We had to have a wooden one after that!', sighed Wilf. Landmarks did not escape either. Two cannons, trophies from Sebastopol, went from their railing-enclosed positions in the front entrance of the Subscription Rooms; and a 12lb Cannonade which Lieutenant-Colonel Edmund Gilling Hallewell, Assistant Quarter Master General of the Army of the East had presented to Stroud in 1855, from its mantelshelf inside.

It is hoped that the German gun which was housed at The Armoury at Merrywalks, a relic of the First World War taken to protect us in the Second World War was not destroyed. The heavy machine gun from Victory Park, which like the rest was hurriedly bundled off, may also have survived as much iron taken was never used. The haunted gates of Nether Lypiatt Manor stayed in place (would life have been in danger had they gone?), and in later years the still intact Cannonade was rescued from Mr Cousin's scrap-yard at Lower Mill Thrupp by Mr Dauncey, a director at Daniel's. Following renovation, and mounted on a brand new oak carriage, it was placed in front of Daniel's building.

Other items also had to be saved. These included bottles, razor blades (two thousand were requested), toothbrushes, glue, destructor tin scrap (which was baled into twenty ton lots at Merrywalks) and aluminium metal toothpaste tubes (collected at chemists).

The humble bone, usually unnoticed unless encased in plaster or roasted in a joint, assumed enormous potential in wartime, when its versatility promoted it to inconceivable heights. People discovered that 75 per cent of bone was usable. The glue extracted from it was vital for aeroplane manufacture, shell cases, camouflage paints, ARP gummed strips, paper and matchmaking, as well as in bone breeze, feeding matter, and fertilizers. Housewives were requested to 'save every bone, large or small (two ounces from each person weekly if possible). From chop bone to gnawed dog bone'.

Throwing anything away became offensive. One can therefore imagine the outcry when a large quantity of rationed food was discovered on a refuse tip. The 'waste' included many pounds of jam, large hams, bacon and beef joints, loaves of bread, and over a hundred cooked sausages. Investigation revealed the culprits were the Forces!

Few people knew what happened to their salvage after it went into the bags and bins. None, apart from the pig food, was of much value to the ordinary man or beast. For enlightenment, War Weapons from Every Home issued a 6d booklet, The Amazing Story of Weapons made from Waste which, through its text and diagrams, described how modern science, through skilled craftsmen, transformed people's scrap into brand new equipment and deadly arms. Metal became guns and helmets, perished rubber produced waterproofs, gas masks and knee pads, and paper became wads for cartridges and explosives.

National Savings Certificates also contributed largely in the War Saving plan. An untaxable investment to benefit both people and the nation had been introduced in 1916 and its flexibility encouraged saving by everyone, whatever their age or income. An investment of 6d or half-crown in savings stamps could be accumulated to buy certificates which could be cashed in later.

Kingscourt Primary School pupils took their sixpences, or occasional half-crowns, for savings stamps to school each Monday, where the teachers issued them following the dinner money ritual. The stamps were large and colourful, but we as children were not bothered about their monetary value. Our chief objective was to fill our book quickly, although we were pleased to realize their worth when we cashed them in later.

Fund Raising Weeks began in 1941. A different service benefited each year after that. War Weapons' Week was in July 1941, Warships' Week in March 1942, Wings for Victory in June 1943, and Salute the Soldier in July 1944. In the first year, £562,730 was raised, a submarine was funded in the second year, twenty Bisley Bombers and forty-eight Typhoons in the third, and a Gloucestershire Regiment maintained in the fourth. In total, £1,958,957 was raised over four years.

Strachans Carnival Band in Stroud in 1938. Their trainer was HW Green, Drum Major, Doreen Horton. In 1936 the Committee of Stroud Show instituted contests for bands formed by workers at local mills and factories. They were awarded points accordingly for appearance, deportment, marching, music etc. There were bands at Holloway Bros Ltd, Hill Paul & Co, Strachan & Co Ltd, Wm Playne & Co Ltd, Newman Hender & Co Ltd. In 1938 Strachan's won 1st Prize at the Three Counties Show Gloucester, 2nd Prize at Stonehouse Show, 3rd Prize at Stroud Show, 1st Prize at Newman Henders Sports and 3rd Prize at Trowbridge Carnival. That year also they contributed £15 12s towards the Spitfire Appeal.

All the 'Weeks' were large, well organized affairs. They provided a programme of events which everyone could participate in and enjoy. The Week was always opened with a grand parade, which terminated at Fromehall Park. War Weapons' Week was officially opened by Mr W.J. Jordon, the High Commissioner of New Zealand, and there was a boxing tournament, a bathing costume parade, open air dancing, and a 'wartime slogans' competition running throughout the afternoon.

Many villages contributed to the competition. Bussage thought 'Thrift Will Help The Nation To Win The War'. Cainscross advised, 'Put Every Penny You Can Into Defence Bonds', while Chalford thought 'War Weapons' Week, a Winner'. Eastington claimed 'No Safer Security In The World – Britain', which won them 60s in National Savings.

The target set, £250,000, was reached within the first four days, and was double that by the end. It would seem Chalford's slogan should have won first prize!

Warships' Week was unable to reach their set target of £425,000, although a commendable £391,890 was raised to contribute towards the submarine HMS *Usurpeter*. Keith Browne, who at nine years old attended a fund raising event at the Church Institute, remembers an enormous submarine on the backdrop at the back of the stage. A year later there was a need for another collection when the news arrived of the loss of the submarine and its crew.

National Savings played a large part in Wings for Victory Week, which furthered war-plane building. As encouragement, so all contributors might see where their money would go, a list of components and their prices was compiled. Sixpence would buy one rivet and was at the bottom of the list, a sparking plug for 8s came about the middle, while £1,500 for an undercarriage, and £2,500 for an engine were at the top.

The grand parade on this occasion was comprised of troops and service members, and the Home Guard, which was marshalled by Captain White. Chasmen Charlie, riding an assortment of contrived bicycles, entertained at Fromehall helping to amass £494,017 by the Week's close. The total raised was over £9,000 more than was originally anticipated.

Stroud was no novice at fund-raising for war planes, having in 1942 contributed towards a speedy, Rolls Royce-engined Spitfire fighter, *Stroud*. The final 'Salute the Soldier' Week in 1944 sucessfully raised £511,320 to sustain a Gloucester Regiment for a year.

Smaller money-raisers were continually in operation. There was the Red Cross 'Penny a Week' Scheme, where a penny from the weekly pay packet bought provisions and medical equipment for friends fighting abroad. The slogan was 'Make Your Penny Save Your Pal!' If six workers donated for a year they could buy a sterilizer drum, forty workers could manage an operating table, while eighteen thousand could buy a complete X-ray apparatus.

Villages everywhere ran collection schemes. Stonehouse placed a defused

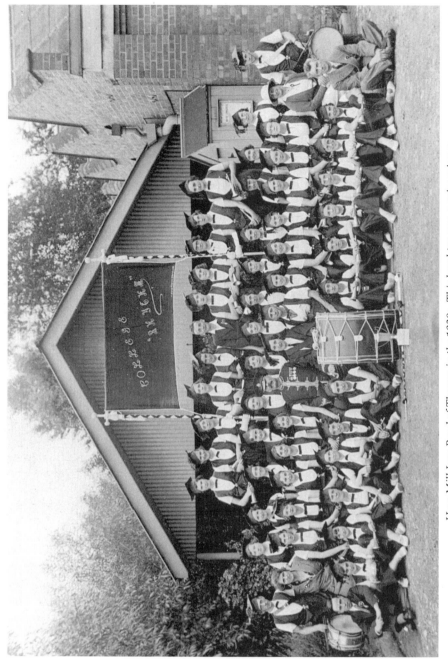

Ham Mill Jazz Band of Thrupp in the 1930s. This band too was a prize winner.

Chalford Silver Band in 1939 at Chalford Primary School Playground. Back, L–R: Les Stratford, Hector Stratford, Frank David, Ernie Fletcher, Jack Latham, Sonny Ward, Bramwell ? Middle: Alec Cook (Secretary), Lionel Riks, Bill Hayward, George Wear, Harry Buckingham, Harold Gardiner, Wilf Young, Bob Niblett, Mr Freeman (School Caretaker). Front: Harold Taysum, Joe Roseblade, Ernie Workman, Ken Gardiner, Percy Stratford, Walter Philip Gardiner, Albert Hayward, Archie Hawkes, Len Smith. Drummers: Jack Warren, Walter Parsons.

This was the last photograph taken before the Second World War. The Chalford Hill Brass Band was founded in 1885 under the conductorship of Mr J Garey, bandmaster. Early rehearsals were at The Duke of York Inn, either side of a long deal table in the glow of oil lamps. A variety of engagements followed: a bazaar at Chalford in August 1886 in the presence of Sir John and Lady Dorrington; the annual Sunday School Whitsuntide treats (the largest of which led a parade of 1,100 Sunday School children on Queen Victoria's Jubilee); the Ascension Day Blessing of the Wells at Bisley; charabanc trips to Birdlip where the George Hotel provided tea following their performance; the Cranham Feast weekend parade from the Royal William; the annual day out to Bourton-on-the-Water, Stow-on-the-Wold and Moreton-in-Marsh; the Stratton Flower Show; an occasional trip Severn Beach, and the inevitable carols at Christmastime. The Band changed to 'Silver' in 1935 when they purchased the instruments, drum kit and uniforms from the disbanded Ham Mill Band for £90, and used them (possibly for the first time) at King George V's Silver Jubilee. Following the war the Band reformed, and formed a Junior Band in 1972 whose success prompted a visit from John Craven of BBC television. Success followed when both adult and Youth Bands entered the world of Brass Band contests to win contests and acclaim throughout the country.

77

bomb outside The Ship Inn, on to which 6d National Savings stamps were stuck. Bisley had their 'Bisley Bomb' which was painted in blue and red, which was what the artist reckoned to be German colours, and transformed into an effigy of Hitler's face. It was placed by her garden gate, which was to the left of the New Inn (now the Stirrup Cup), and passers-by were invited to throw their coins into the vacated fuse hole which formed Hitler's mouth. Underneath, the inscription 'Choke the Bugger' or something similar was printed, which was designed to add impetus towards aim and contribution.

At intervals the 'Bisley Bomb' required emptying, and this hefty task was performed by Harold Gardiner, a man whose height and strength enabled him to achieve such a mammoth task. The story of the arrival of the Bomb is more fascinating than those aiming their coins at Hitler probably knew. Miss Gompertz, the Head Warden for Bisley, transported all five hundred pounds of its finless bulk to the village in the boot of her Morris Eight, but mistakenly began her journey home with an active, undefused bomb. She had travelled some way up the road before realization dawned. A cautious return procured her the safer one!

Mrs Edith Gardiner, a mother of six, was crippled, but her disability, although impairing her movements, by no means prevented her raising money for Red Cross comfort parcels. Apart from contributing through 'knitting parties', when groups of ladies knitted sea-boot stockings, socks, mittens, pullovers, and anything else required for warmth, she concocted another method, her dolls' house.

Mrs Gardiner's dolls' house was a wooden black box, with a slot in the top, wallpapered walls, and a glass front. Inside, clearly visible through its windowed front, dolls conducted their own replica knitting parties, just as their human counterparts did outside. When she was seated on the wall of her home in Bisley High Street, with her 'house' on display, admirers showed their appreciation by dropping a coin through the slot, the accumulating total resulting in a bit more to send to the troops.

Parcels of food were regularly sent abroad to Prisoners of War, through the Red Cross, and St Johns Brigade. These parcels contained tinned food, jam, soap, games, and musical instruments. In 1942 Stroud district had fifty-one POWs abroad. There were seventy thousand countrywide.

Despite the anticipation of war, but possibly spurred on by the 1938 Holidays with Pay Act, some people planned for holidays away, quickly realizing when confronted by wire netting and sandbagged buildings that any normal holiday would be out of the question. Instead they became resigned to remaining in their own district, and in 1941 a Holidays at Home scheme resulted. A holiday on your own doorstep became the pattern.

Several towns became involved, but not always at the same time, which allowed interaction. Stroud's Holidays at Home were organized by Stroud Urban Council. The principal events occupied about a month, usually from

Ethel and Ernest Gardiner.

Red Riding Hood *in 1946 at the Church Institute Stroud. The first of three pantomimes performed by The Stroud Red Cross Youth. Back, L–R: Valerie Watts, Iris Latham, Kate Bateman, ?, John Lardner, ?, Pat Jarvis, Alec Brakespeare, Barbara Cleveland, Eileen Latham, Bert Waldron, Audrey Phillips, ?, Joan Pride, ?, Gordon Ford. 3rd Row: Lexa Watts, Ken Davis, Ann Waller, Monica White, Len Hemming (Wolf), Zena Wager (Fairy), Mary Bird (Witch), Mary Tuft, Iris Emberson, Les Cook. 2nd Row: Bill Watts, Geoff Miller, Valerie Blakesley (Red Riding Hood), Meriel Arthur (Principal Boy). Front: ?, ?, Pat Chell, Sheila Bidmead, ?, Evonne Lampard, Jean Trotman, ?, ?, ?, Pam Wood, ?.*

mid-July until the second week in August. These were the traditional factory closing weeks in Stroud district, around the Bank Holiday. Holidays at Home events were in addition to the usual comprehensive programme of organized events which ran from Easter onwards, throughout the summer months, winding down at the end of August.

Easter Bank Holiday was usually the beginning of the season. A grand fête at Daniel's Sports Ground was held on Easter Saturday, sporty pastimes such as tennis tournaments, skittles, and darts on Easter Sunday, and a horse show, gymkhana and fun fair at Fromehall Park normally occupied Bank Holiday Monday. Prize money became a large attraction of the holiday enterprise, by drawing in crowds of people to 'spot Mr X' or the chance to win hundreds of pounds offered through War Savings Holdings as prizes.

The summer events brought picnics in parks, bandstand concerts, fairs, and visits to beauty spots. In addition, there were sports meetings, swimming galas, bathing beauty contests, junior athletic meetings, garden shows, and wrestling at Fromehall Park. There was a mass return to the great outdoors, and Stroud's citizens made the most of what was on offer. A leisurely feel in general abounded, as so many were on holiday together. Sports obviously suffered

The Opening Ceremony of the re-levelled ground and the new Headquarters of Stroud Rugby Club at Fromehall Park by Sir Wavell Wakefield MP on Thursday September 27th 1951, followed by Stroud v JV Smith's International XV Match. On Wavell Wakefield's left is Stroud Skipper BW Smith, and holding the ball is JA Endacott the Stroud President. This photograph marked a turning point in the Club which was founded in 1873. Their building became two-storeyed and was extended in length.

STONEHOUSE A.F.C.

SUPPORTERS' CLUB

Official Programme   1949-50   *Price Three Pence*

Listen for announcement or watch the board for to-days Lucky Number, the holder of which will receive a voucher to the value of 7/6 to be spent with any of the advertisers in this programme. Voucher to be collected from the Supporters' Club Hut during the interval.

Souvenir Programme, Thursday, Aug. 25th, 1949

WELCOME

WHILE we naturally anticipate the appearance of many sporting personalities, it is feasible to assume that none will be more famous than our guest tonight, and we of the Stonehouse Football Club, fully appreciate the honour that Billy Wright has conferred on us as we begin our great adventure into the realms of professionalism.

Less than three weeks ago, Billy Wright's performance at Edinburgh set the whole football world talking, and both the English and Scottish Press compared him with the world's greatest half-back ever. That is, in itself, a really great tribute to his abilities—here was an English Captain at his brilliant best.

While no words of ours will adequately express our thoughts, we can at least say, "Thank you, Billy, for your presence here tonight." We must also record our thanks and appreciation to Manager Stan Cullis for making his appearance possible, and we know that the footballing fraternity throughout this district will join us in wishing both these sportsmen, the very best that the great game has to offer.

Football leaflet.

with so many away from home; any organized County team matches were impossible, but cricket and football games, and other team games, were achieved locally between clubs.

According to Colin Timbrell, historian to the Gloucestershire Football Association, the outbreak of the Second World War brought a halt to football almost everywhere, but the Stroud and District League did form a wartime section in 1939. It met with limited success due to severe weather, and also players leaving to join the Forces, and had to close in 1940. The League was revived with two divisions, fourteen clubs and twenty-one teams, in 1945 and by 1961 numbers had risen to three divisions, thirty-seven clubs and forty-five teams. Ten of the clubs playing in 1945 were still members sixteen years later. These were Forest Green Rovers, Brimscombe, King's Stanley, Chalford, Rodborough Old Boys, Minchinhampton, Avening, Dursley Town, Uley, and Hoffman Athletic.

The Stroud Hospital Cup, which had been started in 1922, continued during the war and became the Stroud Charity Cup in 1948 with the advent of the National Health Service. There was also a Stroud Wartime League run by the late Harry Greening, a legendary figure in Stroud football. The clubs competed for a wooden 'cup'.

In the immediate post-war years local football attracted large numbers of spectators but, by the late 1950s, television and the motor car had eroded this support. There was no shortage of players, however, and the Stroud and District Youth League, formed in 1947, expanded steadily.

In the refereeing world, the Stroud area can be proud of its own outstanding 'man in black': David Smith of Stonehouse, who started his refereeing career in the Stroud League. He went on to referee the Centenary FA Cup Final at Wembley in 1972.

People also started having weekend trips out and Stroud's abundant common land became a haven for visitors. Haresfield and Painswick Beacon, Rodborough, Selsley and Minchinhampton Commons encompassed endless acres of land, and many varied walks. Weekends, of course, were the main times. Tom Long's Post on Minchinhampton Common, and Stratford Park Pool, reckoned to be the 'Most up to date in the West' (165 feet long, 60 feet wide, and 10 feet deep) became crowded with visitors. People wishing for a quieter time used their bicycles to cycle through the lanes, mainly locally, although some cycled further.

Ada and Leslie Webb thought nothing of cycling to Weston, setting off at 5 a.m. and arriving back at midnight. Six hours of sun on the beach was their reward. Once they cycled to Blackpool, which effort entailed an overnight stay. Ada remembers that all the exercise kept her slim. 'I was so thin my father said I would break off in the middle', she laughed.

Cinemas played a major part in wartime entertainment, claiming themselves to be the most popular leisure activity. Ardent fans visited several times every week as there were two or three cinemas and a choice of films. Pre-war Stroud had been disappointingly limited in cinemas, The Palace Theatre being the only one. In 1935, following refurbishment and with a brand new heating system, it was re-opened as the Gaumont Cinema. Hylda Griffin remembers, 'busloads

Stonehouse Community Centre

BELONGS TO **YOU!**

ENSURE ITS SUCCESS BY BECOMING A MEMBER.

MEMBERSHIP 6/- PER ANNUM — PAYABLE QUARTERLY.

YOUR TEAM FOR TO-DAY.

STONEHOUSE. (1) 2.

Goal
STOPFORD

Right Back (2)　　　　　　　　　　Left Back (3)
FARLEY　　　　　　　　　　　　　STOLES

Right Half (4)　　Centre Half (5)　　Left Half (6)
BROWN　　　　　　TAYLOR　　　　　　GARFIELD

Outside Right (7) Inside Right (8) Centre Frwd. (9) Inside Left (10) Outside Left (11)
PHILLIPS　　CARTER 1　　A. GILES　　E. GILES　　BENNETT 1

Referee: Mr. L. H. Hook.

Kick-off 6.45 p.m.

DEAN 2.

Outside Left (11) Inside Left (10) Centre Frwd. (9) Inside Right (8) Outside Right (7)
FITZ　　CROWE　　MOSCROP　　BUCKLAND　　BOND

Left Half (6)　　Centre Half (5)　　Right Half (4) BUCKLAND.
HORDER　　　　　WHITNEY　　　　　TOVEY TITCOMBE.

Left Back (3)　　　　　　　　　Right Back (2)
HARMER　　　　　　　　　　　HILCOCK TITCOMBE.

Goal
COLTMAN

OUR VISITORS FOR TO-DAY. (1) 2.

CHELTENHAM TOWN. (1) 2.

NEXT MATCH: DOUGLAS AT STONEHOUSE.

REGAL CINEMA, STONEHOUSE

Showing To-night: KIERON MOORE and DULCIE GRAY in MINE OWN EXECUTIONER

MONDAY, AUG. 29th, TUES., WED.　　　　　MONDAY, SEPT. 5th, TUES., WED.
NELSON EDDY　::　ILONA MASEY　　　　　DAVID FARRAR　::　GRETA GYNT
END OF THE RAINBOW　　　　　　　　MR. PERRIN AND MR. TRAILL
Also WEB OF DANGER　　　　　　　Also: PENNY AND THE POWNALL CASE

THURSDAY, SEPT. 1, FRI., SAT.　　　　　THURSDAY, SEPT. 8th, FRI., SAT.
JOHN WAYNE　::　HENRY FONDA　　　　　ROY ROGERS　::　DALE EVANS
FORT APPACHE　　　　　　　　　　HOME IN OKLAHOMA
Also FULL PROGRAMME.　　　　　　　Also NOTHING VENTURE.

Saturday Continuous from 5.45 p.m.　　　Monday to Friday Continuous from 6.15.

Stonehouse Community Centre.

OUR VISITORS

Cheltenham Town Football Club has been in existence since 1892.

Were prominent locally for a number of years and decided to adopt professionalism. Made club history in 1933, when they reached the 2nd Round of the English Cup Competition only to be beaten by Blackpool after having visited and defeated Carlisle in the previous round.

Have been members of the Southern League since 1935.

Joined the Western League Division II in 1947, and nearly gained promotion in their first year, when they finished third to Salisbury and Weymouth. Achieved their objective last season, when they were runners up to Chippenham United and only dropped 13 points. Tim Ward of Derby County and England, and Peter Goring, who is being spoken of as Arsenal's leader for this season, are among many players transferred to football's higher spheres.

Mr. Cyril Dean who played for Aston Villa and Reading is their present Manager, and they are looking forward to a successful season.

"GOOD LUCK"

On behalf of the Football Association, I send to the Chairman, Officials, Players and spectators of the Stonehouse (Glos) Association Football Club best wishes for a successful season. I have noticed with interest the development which has taken place in the Club and I much hope that the enterprise will have satisfactory results.

SIR STANLEY F. ROUS. C.B.E.

I wish you the very best of luck in your new venture. I am sure that under the leadership of Mr. Frank Twiselton, the team will reach a high standard of play, for Mr. Twiselton has done a great deal of work as an F.A. coach in Gloucestershire.

W. WINTERBOTHAM.
Director of Coaching.
F.A. England Team Manager.

SUPPORTERS' CLUB GOSSIP

TONIGHT, we start a new chapter in the Fifty-one years' history of Stonehouse A.F.C. this is the evening that so many "Magpie" supporters have waited for, to them and all our visitors we extend a cordial welcome. We trust the football played here will be in keeping with the best traditions of our great national game, and that it will provide endless pleasure for players and spectators alike. While we realise our ambitions and expectations are high, we are convinced that the achievement of such is not beyond us, and remembering the great effort already made here, we face the future with an inspired determination to do everything possible to further the interests of our parent club. The Supporters' Club proudly record a present membership of 2,000, and will gladly welcome others.

We record our grateful appreciation of the services rendered by a loyal band of voluntary workers, who have since April changed this onetime ploughfield into the ground you see to-day. Without any intention to differentiate, we feel special tribute must be paid to Messrs. F. Baldwin Senior and Junior, who thanks to their experience, have been towers of strength throughout.

We hope that Manager Twiselton, Gib Ainge, Jock McInroy, Denny Rogers and the players will have a successful season, that will in turn add lustre to the club's good name.

May I, on this grand occasion, send my very best wishes to you all, for a very successful season and may Dame Fortune be kind. Stonehouse F.C. I am sure, will prove themselves in their first season of higher grade football. May the supporters rally around, and ensure success to the club, a good crowd is always a big help.

RAY WARREN.
Captain Bristol Rovers F.C.

First let me apologise for being unable to get to Stonehouse as I had hoped to do, but it was impossible on this date. I send my very best wishes to the Club and to Manager Frank Twiselton.

"Twissy" and I played in the same team in Scotland for two seasons during the war, and he is an old friend. I can assure you that everyone at Blackpool welcomes your Club into professional circles, and on their behalf, I wish you all the very best of luck.

There goes the whistle!
All the very best,

STAN MORTENSON.
Blackpool and England

83

Stroud Swimming Pool in 1939. John Clements from Bulls Cross was the first man to jump from the top diving board. Photo by courtesy of Peckhams Stroud.

flocking to see *Evergreen* with Sonny and Hale and Jessie Matthews, who looked beautiful'.

The expanding Gaumont British Picture Corporation offered a full and varied programme, their performances beginning at 6.30 p.m., and continuing non-stop until 10.30 p.m. at night. Mother often missed the end of her film, having to rush to catch her bus, and so she was pleased when 'rotation screening' began later. However, it sometimes meant seeing the end of the main film first. She sat in the stalls, while 'the elite sat in the balcony'.

The Pathe News was avidly watched during the war, it being one of the few opportunities people had of viewing the action 'live'. Even though it must have been slightly out-of-date, all attention was focused on it, any chattering reserved for refreshment time.

The Saturday Morning Pictures during the 1950s was a great success and always played to packed houses. Snowy White from Uplands played the piano. The films, which were usually some kind of adventure story, always ended in a cliff-hanger so that everyone would go along the next week to see what happened next.

Winstone's pitch at Tom Long's Post required a £5 licence, but you would not have seen their van there during the war years. Instead the business which Albert Winstone had begun by selling sweets following his redundancy from Woodchester Piano Works in 1925, but had since become an ice cream concern selling from two motor bikes and side cars, completely closed down. Albert went to work at Newman Henders for the war effort, while his wife Doris went down to

Ham Mill. On re-opening in 1945 a specially built Austin 10 from Gloucester, followed by a converted left hand drive American Ambulance which did 12 m.p. gallon, but 'went like a bomb', and a French Talbot van exploded their increasingly popular business, into which Frank became a partner at twenty, and with which sisters Mavis and Jill assisted. L–R Lewis Cook, Frank Winstone, cousin Wendy and sister Jill.

Today people still flock as they did when I was a child to their shop for one of their delicious ice creams, or buy from one of twelve retail vans, four kiosks, or five wholesale delivery vans covering a hundred mile radius. This is Albert Winstone at his shop on Rodborough Common in 1983.

Two Programmes

We make no apology for recalling here in full detail the Programme of our first effort at Sunday Concerts. We look back on this occasion with many pleasant memories and are happy in the knowledge that a number of our patrons at that Concert are still supporting us as ardently at the last.

SUNDAY, NOV. 12th, 1939

Compere .... P. COOMBS JERRARD
Official Accompanist ... ALEXANDER N. COURT

1. JACK PARKER .... Piano Accordion
2. TOM SADLER .... Entertainer
3. SALISBURY BAKER .... Baritone
4. JUNE CHALIER .... Child Impressionist
5. "DEVANO" .... Electric Guitar
6. CHICK FOWLER ("Glo'stershire George") ... Entertainer
7. WENALLT THOMAS .... Tenor
8. MERCIA STOTESBURY .... Violin
9. MUSIC BY ORCHESTRA .... (Leader, Harold Lusher)
10. CHICK FOWLER .... Entertainer
11. STROUD'S WARTIME DISCOVERIES
    GNR. E. C. LAWLER .... Saxophonist
    GNR. J. C. BARR ..... Non-Smiling Comedian
    GNR. C. J. DYER .... Bass
    GNR. K. W. LEWIS .... Impersonator
    (Accompanist: GNR. WHATLEY)
12. COMMUNITY SINGING

Programme under the direction of STAN CRATCHLEY.

SUNDAY, DEC. 30th, 1945

Compere .... FRANK E. WEST
Official Accompanist ... G. R. COOMBS

1. We open with LES LESLIE—A Fool and a Fiddle.
2. Some Clever Dancing by TONY AND PAUL—The Dynamic Dancers from West Indies—assisted by Barbara.
3. Comedy by FRANK E. WEST—5ft. 2in. of Mirth.
4. We present JOSEPHINE ANN PHILLIPS, The Great Little Star.
5. DYNAMIC GLADYS (WILL) HAY AND ALBERT, Comedy Harmonists, will liven the proceedings.
6. TERRY WATERS, Stroud's Queen of Song, in Tunes You'll Love.
7. CLIVE WHITTOCK, The Wonder Boy on the Drums and Xylophone.
8. JEAN WATTS shows her Steps.
9. HARRY HEMSLEY, The King of Child Impersonators, complete with Horace and Winnie.
10. BILL FARTHING and His Uke.
11. STAN CRATCHLEY in a Joke and a Monologue.
12. WE PRESENT THE COMMITTEE.
13. BERTI. BERESFORD AND LESLIE HINTON, with Laughs by the Score.
14. TONY AND PAUL in another Spot of Dynamic Dancing, assisted by Barbara.
15. CLIVE WHITTOCK AND JOSEPHINE ANN appear jointly for the first time in any Programme.
16. LES LESLIE will wind up.
17. AULD LANG SYNE.

THE KING.

Ritz Commemorative Programme showing opening and closing programme. The weekly Stroud Popular Concert Programme was 2d, and there were about nine turns. WJ Barber was the Director of Programmes in the early 40s, and the Stage Manager was Ralph Meadows.

Ritz interior.

Sometimes there were competitions. In 1937, when Billy Butlin opened one of his first holiday camps at Clacton-on-Sea, a competition was run at The Gaumont to list films in a specific order, the winner receiving a holiday at Butlins with everything (even the train fare) thrown in. Billy Butlin, whose grandfather had been vicar in Leonard Stanley, became useful to the government because of his speedy building technique. He was asked to erect camps for the Forces, which later provided non-stop entertainment for war-weary holiday makers.

After the Gaumont re-opened following refurbishment in 1935, *Ruggles in Red* with Charles Laughton and *Two heads on a pillow* with Neil Hamilton were shown on the opening night. However, on 26 August 1939 the exclusiveness of the Gaumont Palace was threatened. Competition arrived with the glitzy, newly-built Ritz Cinema in Kings Street, built by Mr Walters, and managed by his sons and his wife. It took about nine months to build, and was modern, plush and spacious, boasting seating capacity for 1,250, and the latest in projector and sound equipment. Lighting was composed of three hundred feet of luminous tubing in pastel green, and there were four sets of double doors in black and ivory. The foyer décor was in peach, blue, and flame, and from there the stalls were reached via a wide staircase.

Above was The Cadena Café, an increasingly popular trend in 1940s' cinemas. The Café was reached either by stairs from the cinema itself or from outside, and was thus available for refreshments independently of the cinema.

Underneath, was a large car park, providing parking facilities for a hundred cars. Admission prices for the cinema, compared with today, were minute. A circle seat cost 2s or 1s 6d, and the stalls 1s or 6d.

From the day it opened the Ritz was an overwhelming success. Hylda Griffin says the first film she saw there was *Sweetheart* with Nelson Eddy and Janette McDonald, but the longest ever was *Gone with the Wind*, which lasted four hours. Queues for this stretched right into Stroud.

Stroud's second cinema had arrived at exactly the right time, because within a month the district's population had swelled by hundreds as our evacuees arrived, many of whom were accustomed to a fuller social life. Now, with two cinema houses in operation, Saturday Morning clubs, and Sunday performances, there was more choice.

At the outbreak of war all cinemas throughout the country automatically closed. In this respect our evacuees did Stroud a favour, as their presence allowed us, as a reception area, to re-open our cinemas within five days. War did not hinder people flocking to 'the pictures', where they could lose themselves in the extravagances of Hollywood, where nothing was rationed and people lived in mansions. There was no trouble filling seats. Obtaining the films was the difficulty.

On Sunday 12 November, with an increasing demand for entertainment, Sunday Entertainments made their apppearance. The Ritz Cinema and The Gaumont alternated throughout the season. Hylda says they were run by ENSA, and the tickets were sold on Monday mornings from 8.30 – 9a.m., and cost 1s 6d and 2s 6d. The shows began at about 8 p.m. and ended at around 10 p.m.

Hylda managed to get tickets for most of the shows and went whenever she could. She recalls the first film star who came was Ronald Franco who sang 'The man who broke the Bank of Monty Carlo'. Also seen were Florrie Ford, Tessie O'Shay, Beryl Orde, Will Fyfe on the bagpipes, and Flotsam and Jetsam on the piano. She continues, 'I remember all the gorgeous bands: Henry Hall and his Dance Band, The Squadronaires of the Air Force, King's RAF Band who were stationed at Aston Down, the KOYLI Army Band stationed at Woodchester, REME who were at Standish Court, and the Royal Engineers at Paul Camp at Edge.'

Those early days also brought the well known violinist, Miss Mercia Stotesbury, and radio celebrities such as Ann Shelton, Harry Hensley the vocal impersonator and ventriloquist, Tommy (ITMA) Handley, the famous radio comedian, and Jack Train, the impersonator, who struggled through snow, ice, and then an electrical breakdown to perform.

The programmes were always crammed with different acts, many local performers taking part when the popular Stroud's 'Wartime Discoveries' began. Following the adult talent competition success, a juvenile talent search opened on 25 February 1940 entitled 'Youth Takes a Bow'. The age limit was sixteen, and a variety of singers, elocutionists, and instrumentalists appeared following an audition at Audrey Butts' studio in Church Street. Mr Walters' own talented daughter Terry, then about ten years old, appeared.

Most of Stroud's population attended Sunday Concerts at some time, those requiring a seat always advised to book in advance, or risk being turned away. The tradition of 'the show going on if performers were willing to take the stage' built a reputation far and wide. Only a short break during the summer months offered a well-earned rest, before everyone returned in the autumn.

Sunday entertainments did not please everyone. The Church felt Sunday shows and films affected the quality of Sunday life, disturbing the peace associated with the Lord's Day, and forcing people to choose between the entertainments and church services which sometimes overlapped.

A unanimous resolution by the Church Council protested against 'The growing menace to our church ideals which Sunday evening variety shows (and cinemas) have become in Stroud'. Their conclusion stated, 'We think this (wartime) is the very last time when people can afford to neglect the proper observances of the Sabbath Day'.

The entertainment supporters, putting their side of the argument, described the benefits of light-hearted entertainment to dispel the grimness of war. It kept bored soldiers off the streets during the dark wintery Sunday nights, they insisted, reducing the crowds which inevitable arose on a day when they were free. All this prompted one Stroud resident to suggest that Sunday concerts should continue all summer.

The move to prevent Sunday cinema opening grumbled on for several years, culminating in a three-and-a-half hour debate in July 1942 of both Houses of Parliament who approved Sunday cinema screening. Both the Stroud cinemas were issued with licences for a two month trial, but the hours were fixed from 4 to 9 p.m.

The end of the war, and the troops returning home finally settled the situation. Sunday concerts closed on 29 December 1946, with six years of successful variety shows, and £15,000 for charity behind them.

Dancing was another very popular pastime during the war. Hylda Griffin recalls that dances were mostly held on Saturdays at the Subscription Rooms, lasting from 8 to 12p.m. She went with her friends, and remembers there were about three hundred on the floor. The admission fee paid at the door was 1s 6d and 2s 6d, and that provided a whole night of enjoyment. There were many servicemen, including Canadians and Americans. Some of her friends later married them, and went to live in Canada or America. If it was too crowded at the Subscription Rooms, Hylda and her friends went to Tucks instead, which cost them 1s 6d.

She also suggests that before the war there were other marvellous dances.

A dance at Tuck's Premier Hall during the 40s.

Among them the Red and White, and Western National, which ran fancy dress evenings, and always had two bands, one at each end. Entrance was by ticket only (they were 2s 6d and were limited). There were also balls, including the Police Ball at the Premier Hall, The Rugby Ball, Stroud District Council Chamber of Trade Ball, and The Valentine's and Old Year's Night Balls.

Alison Hock remembers the dances too especially the Church Institute on Thursdays, the Subscription Rooms on Wednesdays and Saturdays, the Co-op Hall at Cainscross, and Brimscombe Poly, from which one had to walk home.'You took it for granted you walked home. Goodness only knows what time the young man who walked you home got home himself'.

Nancy Hawkes enjoyed the dances too, despite the loss of her evacuee 'kindred spirit', Joan Barber. On dance nights, she regularly rushed home from work to eat and change on the run, before cycling from The Riflemans to Mrs Poulton's along the Slad Road, where she left her bike before catching the bus to Aston Down, or wherever the dance was that night.

She rarely arrived back home until the early hours, often having had a long walk home. One night a loose carthorse loomed up ahead of her along the dark

A cricket match in period costume at Stroud Brewery Cricket Field at Colonel Godsell's Stratford Court during the 50s. Jack Hillier, then manager of Stroud Wines and Spirits Dept is batting. His son Russell later became manager of Stroud Rugby Club.

Slad Road, initiating a leap over the fence in her panic to get away. She wakened Mr Kemp nearby who, despite the early hours, walked her all the way to The Vatch before finally saying, 'I think you can walk the rest on your own'.

Despite the war, Nancy always wore lovely clothes to her dances. 'Beautiful high-necked, low-waisted dresses, which Barbara Ingram's mother made up from material sent by the Americans and Canadians, along with high heels and stockings'.

Nancy enjoyed life, diving off the top board at the newly-opened Stroud Swimming Pool at Stratford Park, and coming third or fourth in a bathing beauty contest which was held when it opened. 'It was always packed solid,' she says. She spent D-Day at Bournmouth, 'where the atmosphere was electric and people burnt deck chairs and jeeps', and later VE day in London, 'where I had a wonderful time'.

A more serious campaign, originally tackled in 1916, but mentioned very little was VD. No one talked of it openly, and when it was broached it was with hushed tones. Stroud's information centre was a cinema van, which toured factories and canteens, youth centres and organizations, clinics and libraries, and public lavatories, where posters were exhibited. The campaign attempted to remove VD's shameful image, and to persuade people to seek treatment. There was information about the 278 treatment centres where cures were available, in the hope of sparing men, who had already survived the war's brutality, from further misery when they did re-unite with their loved ones during peacetime.

CHAPTER EIGHT

THE LURE OF FOOD

The year 1942 drew to its close with the ringing of church bells, which had been banned under wartime restrictions, and not heard in England since 1940. On Sunday 15 November their clear triumphant tones rang out, broadcasting the victory of the Eighth Army in Egypt, whose successes were such a tonic to British moral.

Just a few weeks later, on Christmas Day, their peels echoed again, uniting families in seasonal festivities. Some were fortunate to have their loved ones with them at home, others were resigned to the fact that they were needed elsewhere.

Bedford Street Canteen, which had operated without a break since its opening in September 1939, when evacuees, midday meals were their predominant aim, began its day at 7 a.m. serving breakfast to fifty postal workers, plus many hungry extras. The room, decorated for Christmas by volunteers under the wing of organizer Mrs Pane, was prepared for lunch immediately breakfast was finished, in readiness for the 130 visitors arriving for Christmas dinner at 12 noon. They were not disappointed with their fare. They feasted on roast pork and apple sauce, roast beef and Yorkshire pudding, along with Christmas pudding and fruit jelly: a meal equally as fine as the one served during their first Christmas in 1939, which had had the addition of turkey. On Boxing Day 240 troops were fed.

This year, 1942, when everyone was adequately fed, the afternoon offered the conjuror Ward Waterman, before the King's Speech whetted appetites for more food. A Christmas cake, cooked by Mrs Bendall, along with mince pies and chocolate biscuits was enjoyed for tea. The £2 5s collection for Prisoners of War seemed adequate proof of everyone's appreciation.

Although no one knew it then, this was the last time Bedford Street would serve Christmas lunch under its 'Canteen' label. Three months later, on 1 April, it was to change management and format and join the British Restaurant group, becoming one among hundreds of nationwide feeding centres. These had operated since 1940 under the guidance of Lord Woolton, the Minister of Food, providing a cheap nourishing meal, without a coupon in sight, for ordinary working people.

The Bedford Street Canteen had had a good record, managed during three and a half years as a canteen by a band of volunteers, who worked daily from 8a.m. to 10p.m., seven days a week, serving a daily average of seven hundred meals. In total, nine hundred thousand meals had been provided.

The change of title heralded a change of image, achieved through extra finance. British Restaurants were backed by the government and run by the Council, which thus ensured well-designed and well-equipped kitchens. The interior fittings, décor, and furnishings of the restaurant were designed to make the surroundings as attractive as the building allowed. Meals were plain but adequate, usually including soup, a roast joint, and pudding, costing about 2s, but never more than 5s.

Stroud's Bedford Street Restaurant refurbishment necessitated closure for three weeks, from 13 March until the beginning of April. When fitted out as described, and decorated in chocolate, stone, and green, it re-opened on 1 April. Its new Council status was clearly recognized on re-opening by the presence of Admiral Sir Arthur Strickland, the Chief Divisional Food Office, and an assortment of urban council hierarchy.

The first change obvious to patrons was the opening hours. The services were not available all day, as they had been before when voluntarily controlled, but fixed at specified hours. Lunchtime was 11.45 a.m. – 2 p.m., tea 3 – 6 p.m., and supper, 6 – 8.30 p.m. A fraction over a shilling purchased a two course main meal.

There were other Restaurants in Stroud district too, at the Ritz Café, Dudbridge (opposite Redlers), Stonehouse, Thrupp, Painswick (at the Institute), and Nailsworth (in the old Co-op). The latter's opening on 5 April 1943 providing two sittings of eighty, just for lunches. Soup was 3d, lamb, vegetables and Yorkshire pudding 8d, steamed jam pudding 4d, and coffee and tea for 3d and a 1d.

During the early part of 1944, the Thrupp Restaurant closed, followed by Stonehouse in June the following year, and Painswick on 28 September 1945 (which had served 150,000 meals during five and a half years under the care of Miss Bulley). Their good work as food providers continued when the Restaurant became a canteen for Painswick school instead with Mrs Gerrish in charge. The children walked through the churchyard from their school, where Painswick Library is today, to partake of their daily meal at the Institute. This left Bedford Street, the Ritz, and Dudbridge, as the only Restaurants remaining to carry on a while longer.

Although Bedford Street remained self-catering, Dudbridge and the Ritz, managed by Miss Payne, relied for their 1,400 meals on the Dudbridge food depot. This was one of several food depots countrywide which from 1941 appeared on town outskirts to supply emergency meals. Stroud's Dudbridge depot, which consisted of two huts erected in 1942, also supplied school lunches, the premises being purchased for £2,000 by Gloucester Education Committee in 1950 for that sole purpose. Previously, some seventy children with no canteen facilities had availed themselves of the Bedford Street facilities. The Dudbridge depot achieved its substantial output with only a head cook, a male cook assistant, five women helpers, and a stoker (the Ministry ruling that all depots should use solid fuel and steam, and have independent water supplies in case the mains were damaged).

The Bedford Street Restaurant carried on until 30 April 1949 when, now under civic restaurant status, and ten years since opening, it put down its shutters for the last time, despite a protest to keep it open by three hundred and eighty protesters. The Ritz Café changed its name also, upgrading to trendy Cadena status. Some eating places remained in private hands. Some readers may remember Hancock's restaurant in Gloucester Street, which the Citizen Office occupies today. In 1945, a plate of faggots and peas could be bought for 1s 11d here.

In November 1940, the Ministry of Labour made it compulsory for munitions factories employing a workforce of 250 to provide canteens, where food allowances were gauged in accord with manual output. Shortly afterwards, other factories, not necessarily involved with government work, also became included in these rules. A spate of canteen facilities, many with accompanying music to give a happy work-along feel, sprang up in the Stroud valleys, providing subsidized meals for around 9d a head.

Lunch-hour concerts began to be held throughout the country, the BBC's *Workers' Playtime* broadcasting live midday variety shows from factory premises. Many shows involved well-known entertainers from stage and radio. In 1949, Hoffmans, the ball and roller bearings company, broadcast one show from their factory during their fiftieth anniversary year. Their premises were now considerably larger than ten years before, when their canteen began, and they grew vegetables on the site to help supply it.

Workers employed in outlying districts, far distant from works' canteen or restaurants facilities, could sometimes receive food through local mobile canteens, manned by voluntary organizations, such as the YMCA, and the Salvation Army. Stroud's contributions through fund-raising enabled their first mobile canteen, which cost about £200 and was manned by one lady worker, to become operational in March 1941.

Eventually, finances allowed the purchase of four more, each manned by a growing number of lady supporters who serviced and drove the vans themselves, over a two hundred mile radius. During each visit, mainly to RAF establishments, teas, cakes, cigarettes, and toiletries were provided, and each evening on their return the vans were washed, loaded , checked, and put ready for emergency call-outs.

The Canteen at Strachans.

The voluntary services also provided for American servicemen. Gwen Phillimore, from Horsley, remembers a Black American Only Club, in the Old Co-op in Nailsworth, which was used by the soldiers based on Minchinhampton Common, and George Webb recalls the fascination of seeing a black face in Frampton-on-Severn.

The Americans' arrival had a tremendous impact on most English people. 'Fabulous, god-like creations to the young ladies, and generous and kind' to childen, but 'resented' by the British men who could offer no comparison to 'peach jam and nylon stockings'.

As a child Jo Bessant, living in Vicarage Street in Painswick, certainly remembers their outgoing generosity. The Blacks camped in the Plantation, and the Whites in the grounds of Painswick House, she said. 'They gave us small tins of Nescafe, with pull-off tops, chewing gum and sweets'. George Webb compared their presence at Frampton Green as 'almost on par with the hard-as-lead 3*d* blocks of ice cream, which came in following war and tasted of nectar.'

Three thousand American servicemen, complete with tents, ambulances, medical men, and trucks, in fact a whole town, descended upon Frampton-on-Severn. It was a wonderful time for the children there, who compared them with the film idols whom they had seen regularly in Frampton's cinema. The servicemen apparently 'adopted' boys, and generally spoiled them. George's adopted American was Jack Johnson, a religious, very kind man, who gave the nine-year-old George tinned peaches and sweets.

Jim Dickenson from Slad also benefited from the Americans. Once an American on sentry duty supplied Jim with money and a load of empty bottles with instructions to purchase him and his mates some drink from The Plough at Sheepscombe. The American was genuinely surprised, said Jim, when the drink actually appeared. This earned Jim some tins of fruit and Spam.

For most children, it was the first time they had seen a coloured American, and they might not have seen one then, had not two black Americans ventured from their own unit, which was an all black American camp by Saul Junction, on bicycles into Frampton. They were immediately surrounded by children, who pursued them all the way back to the Junction.

The Americans stayed at Frampton for about six months, their presence completely overwhelming the five hundred inhabitants in the village. Then one day, they left as suddenly as they had arrived, and life to George and his pals seemed very dead.

Their sudden quick dispersal was typical of many American or Canadian units. Jonathon Tidy remembers it happening at Whiteway Colony when a Canadian convoy moved into a field nearby known as Clay Piece. They lined their lorries and Brengun carriers up against the hedge and in the same way as at Frampton, became targeted by children, of whom they made a fuss, and gave rides on trucks around the field. One serviceman, who had formerly worked as a cowboy, discovered Juliet Parker's pony, and was soon riding it up and down the verges. Suddenly, after about a week they moved out in convoy without warning, leaving behind just memories for those youngsters.

In the Gloucester Street area of Stroud there was a similar occurrence. Apparently, the Americans were occupying much of the living accommodation above the shops. One Saturday night they were all there, drinking the milk of which they were so fond; the following Sunday morning by 9.30 a.m. they had gone.

Bryan Durn, with his friends Titch Neale and Gordon Ponting from Summer Street, used to frequent Lypiatt Park and The Old Stroud Workhouse where the Americans, along with their vehicles for invasion, were billeted 'in thousands'. At Lypiatt there were some sectional wooden huts for the officers, but the majority of the troops slept in tents. There was a supply of water, which the Americans had installed themselves, together with a filtration plant, a pumping station down in the old quarry at Bisley Road to boost the water up the hill, and a large water container on stilts.

Titch's mother worked at Walter's Cakeshop, and sometimes brought cakes home for the family. When one of the Americans from the Lypiatt Park camp asked 'Can you get us any cookies?' and Titch said he could, he was told to, 'Bring us up some, sonny', and arrangements were made through Titch's mother. Several large sponge cakes were bought, for which Titch's mother received her money after the delivery had been made.

After a while, greed took over. The boys evolved an idea whereby, by inflating the price slightly, Titch and his mates could eat one of the cakes themselves, yet still take the correct money home. This they did for some time, ripping one cake apart on their way there, and sharing it out. One day, through a spot of trouble inside the camp, the guard was doubled on the gate, and the boys were unable to deliver the cakes. When they returned minus one cake, with no money, their secret was out. This earned Titch 'a bloody good hiding'.

Following a stay of about six months the Americans suddenly left. Bryan thought something was strange when the cookhouse bugle, which sounded from the camp, and got him out of bed every morning at eight to go to school, did not sound. 'The gang' rushed up to Lypiatt, which by then was deserted. 'There wasn't an American on the place.' After jumping over a wall, they looked in one of the sectional huts, which was used by the officers. There was a pot of still warm coffee, and several sacks of provisions which had been left behind.

As soon as the news broke, people were over at the workhouse, and up at Lypiatt Park, acquiring pots, cutlery, chairs, tables, and bedside cabinets. 'They didn't live like dogs', said Bryan. Bryan took some cups, coat hangers and tins of pineapple, which had not been seen in England since the thirties, while other 'gleaners' availed themselves of coffee and sugar, which remained by the hundredweight. Sackfuls disappeared, the tell-tale trails of coffee through Summer Street Woods leading to the culprits' homes. The following Saturday morning, about a week later, Scotts' removal lorry, accompanied by 'Copper Mills' and Detective Buck, whom everyone feared, called at each house, asking if they had taken anything from 'The Camp'. Bryan's mother admitted what Bryan had taken, but only the large items were wanted back.

Mike Hawkes also remembers when the Americans left. A few still remained, clearing up, when he made his last visit to Lypiatt Camp. One asked him, 'Would you like a plane, lad?', and Mike was given a demonstration Mustang Recognition model aeroplane to take home.

Once a Canadian serviceman stayed, during his week or so of leave, with the Hawkes family, and Mrs Corday who ran the Riflemans Arms pub next door. Both households contributed towards his fare. Sometimes local people took servicemen into their homes to give them a break from camp life. This

Stew.

particular Canadian's name was Stew and, as he had no civilian clothes, the family fixed him up with an assortment of theirs. He immediately fitted into family life, and was great fun, not even minding when the Hawkes children put holly in his bed as a joke.

Stroud missed their flamboyant visitors when they had gone, even though the Blacks and Whites frequently fought when the pubs closed and they met up in the street. The pubs were used in the same segregated manner as the camps. For example, The White Americans used The Post Office Inn in Stroud, while The Blacks frequented The Foresters just a few yards down the road. It was also the custom for the Americans to send their washing out locally. A jeep delivered the dirty washing, and women in the neighbourhood competed to do the job.

Following the factory canteen influx Sports and Social Clubs were started, which offered a wider range of leisure activity to workers. Hoffmans Club began in the basement, where their wartime air raid shelter was situated while Erinoids received their smart new acquisition in 1948 when it was opened by their Managing Director, John Harvey.

Erinoid's Annual Show was a family day for its employees and was introduced after the war. The first show had forty-six horticultural items, but the number had risen to 620 by 1953. There was a carnival and a carnival queen, and a large exhibition tent, which could be clearly seen from our garden high on Rodborough Common. My friend Eileen, whose father worked at Erinoid's, was able to attend, but I felt left out as I viewed all the activity below me from my vantage point on 'the tumpt'. Father enjoyed the County matches played there, which he viewed through a pair of binoculars without even attending. Unfortunately, Erinoid's field was prone to flooding, and during these times often resembled more of a lake than a pitch when viewed from the common.

The authority plan for school dinners, augmented by the need for a cooked midday meal while mothers worked during the war, eventually resulted in even the smallest Primary school providing a fresh hot daily meal for its children from its own kitchen. Children from low income families received theirs free.

Victorian school buildings were converted to make dining facilities or a room was added. Church Street Boys' School, whose pupils had formerly marched to Bedford Street for dinner, converted their indoor sports area to a canteen, which was manned by five ladies under the control of Miss Manley. However, this deprived the boys of their room for indoor recreation. With no field on which to play near the school, the boys had to march in crocodile to their playing field at the top of Stratford Park. They usually lost a few boys in town in the process.

The County Council operated their canteens within a framework of administration and costing. They employed cooks and assistants, and insisted on fresh ingredients. Until the fifties, some foods were still rationed, and six pounds of meat or fish for fifty children was deemed adequate. But vegetables were plentiful, some of which were supplied locally, as at Painswick School's canteen in the Institute, who received fresh vegetables from Mr Perrin's allotment.

School cooks required little qualification, except the ability to produce edible fare, and balance the books. At Kingscourt School, mother stood in for our usual cook when she was ill, sometimes for several months at a stretch. On receiving a hastily written note via a panting messenger (me), she abandoned her weekly washing (as it was usually a Monday), while dashing to and fro, amid moans of 'I wish I'd known earlier'.

Kingscourt School canteen was a converted classroom, divided from the head teacher's classroom by only a door. As morning progressed, delicious aromas wafted through the cracks, causing stomachs to gurgle in impatient anticipation. At midday, following grace, and lined up to collect our meal, every child received a little of everything, even when they said they did not like it.

Kingscourt School about 1951 when there was only one class. Miss Wilkinson (later to become Mrs FE Wake) retired in 1953, when she was presented with an enormous bouquet of flowers. Back L–R: Miss Wilkinson (Head Teacher), Derrick Hogg, Michael Lewis, Peter Fletcher, Mrs Taylor. 3rd Row: Marlene Young, Margaret Webb, Christine Buckingham, Barbara Herbert, Janet Turner, Gillian Oldmeadow, Cynthia Hammond. 2nd Row: Mary Webb, Deanna Mitchell, Joy Furley, Anne Boulton, Pricilla Herbert, Angela Stephens, Johnny Oldmeadow (kneeling). Front: Timothy Chambers (kneeling), Keith Thacker, Graham Hill, Bobby Oldmeadow, David Boult.

I remember how fussy we were. If meat harboured the slightest gristle, we would cut it off, and line it round the plate. One girl could hold her unwanted food in her cheek, even through the pudding course, spitting it over the wall when we went out to play! The puddings were lovely, leading to queues for 'seconds'. When mother cooked for the school, regulations ruled that no leftovers could be used the next day, so she often brought some unwanted food home, and we ate it for supper.

She says she tried her best to remove any fat from the meat. Once, on one of the 'hasty summons' mornings, beef stew was on the menu. With only fifteen minutes to go, she mistook the bicarbonate of soda tin for salt, and its addition caused instant frothing and bubbling. Thinking calmly amid rising panic, she and Mrs Buckingham, her assistant, tipped the lot into a strainer, ran the remaining meat under the tap, and added a tin of stewed beef.

Kingscourt catering and teaching Staff. L–R: Nora Furley (mother), Mrs Buckingham, Mrs Metcalfe, Miss Roberts (top class teacher), Miss Wilkinson (head).

The children's meal went smoothly, and no one commented. Mother's ordeal continued, when the teachers took their turn. As the pudding plates were cleared, and coffee took their place, Miss Wilkinson, the Headteacher, looked up saying, 'Thank you again, Mrs Furley. That was an exceptionally tasty stew today, most enjoyable!'

CHAPTER NINE

KEEPING THE HOME FIRES BURNING

In 1947 the coal shortage was at its worst. Other commodities could, to some degree, be substituted as they became scarce, or even dispensed with altogether with little physical harm to those deprived of them. Coal, however, because of its nationwide domestic and industrial usage, and being the basic fuel for electricity and gas, was difficult to replace.

During the thirties and forties the majority of industry was dependent on coal for its production, but when coal output fell by over fifty million tons, compared with 1939, cause for concern escalated.

In pre-war days, the export of coal was an important part of national finance but now, with none to spare for any export market, alongside the subsequent exchange of imports, production at home suffered. For example, lack of imported building materials slowed up house building plans.

Pit modernization could have provided an answer, but the pits were owned by many separate small firms, who during these hazardous years were unable to finance such an expensive enterprise. Even if they had, there would not have been guaranteed materials and manpower to see the project through. Men who, through wartime duties, had seen a bit of the world outside Britain, gained experience in other fields, or embarked on new lines of employment through the Forces voluntary training schemes, did not always relish returning to their previous dirty, and dangerous, underground work, especially when an abundance of clean employment, along with improved payment attractions, were plentiful above ground. Most men viewed a return to mining as a retrograde step.

During 1944, following an overall review by the Conservative Government, a coal governing body was recommended, under whose wing a reduced number of companies would operate. However, when in 1945 the Labour Government under Mr Attlee came to power, nationalization and The National Coal Board became the way forward. This was a popular move in the eyes of many miners,

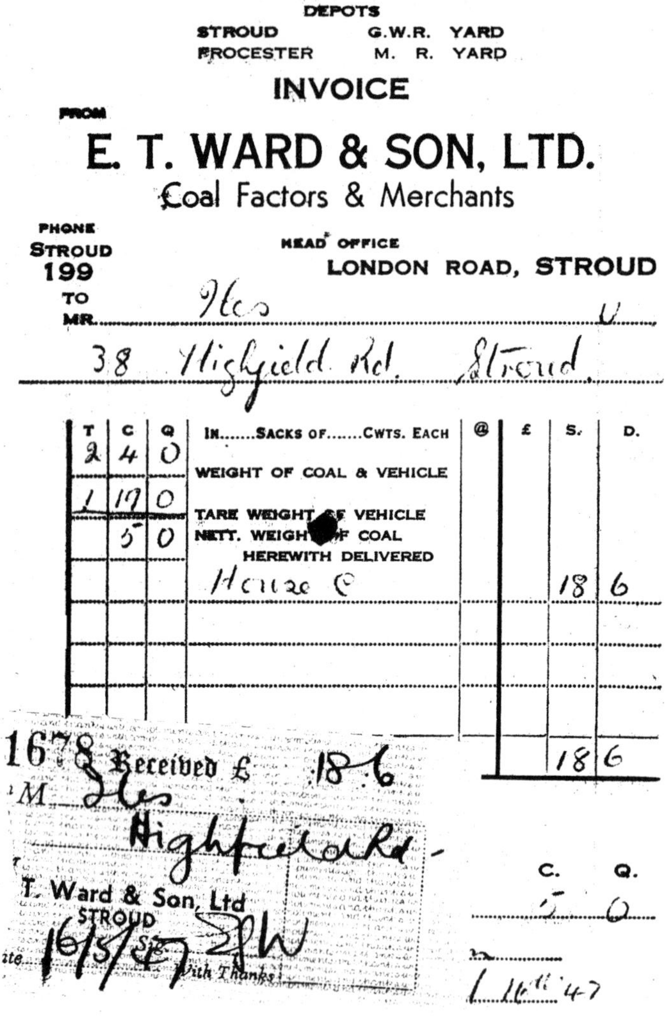

INVOICE

FROM

E. T. WARD & SON, LTD.

Coal Factors & Merchants

PHONE	HEAD OFFICE
STROUD	LONDON ROAD, **STROUD**
199	

TO MR. _Iles_   U

38   Highfield Rd.   Stroud

T	C	Q		@	£	S.	D.
2	4	0	IN......SACKS OF......CWTS. EACH				
			WEIGHT OF COAL & VEHICLE				
1	17	0	TARE WEIGHT OF VEHICLE				
	5	0	NETT. WEIGHT OF COAL				
			HEREWITH DELIVERED				
			House C			18	6
						18	6

1678   Received £   18.6

M   Iles

Highfield Rd

T. Ward & Son, Ltd
STROUD
16/5/47   SW
With Thanks

C.   Q.
                            16th 47

PARAGON (REGD.) LAMSON PARAGON, LONDON. E.16

Wards Coal invoice 1947.

104

who had hankered after such a move from First World War days. Thus it was that from 1 January 1947, 800 companies and 1500 pits entered the new state of nationalization.

Almost immediately, a lengthy, hard winter and transport difficulties, combined with increased fuel usage for industry as the country resumed post-war trade, affected the newly formed Coal Board. The coal stocks became so depleted that every business connected with coal, including power stations, and electricity for industrial and private users, was affected. Realizing that without drastic measures the whole country would seize up, Polish men were recruited for labour, new machinery was installed, and a five day week was introduced as an incentive. The result was a strike in forty Yorkshire pits, whose miners wanted Saturday overtime working.

To highlight the desperate coal situation, a fuel economy drive was launched entitled, 'We must save fuel For Britain'. This replaced the previous slogan, 'We must save fuel for Battle'.

Posters and shop window displays urged the general public, particularly women, who it was assumed had more dealings with this valuable commodity for cooking and heating, to find ways towards sensible coal usage. Teachers educated their pupils, and 'Mr Therm' of the Stroud Gas Light and Coke Company demonstrated how one single therm of gas would heat enough water for ten baths, cook four dinners for a family of six, warm a room 12 x 12 x 10ft for over six hours, as well as operating a small refrigerator for more than a week!

The local fuel overseer controlled coal distribution within his area, ensuring that no one exceeded the fixed 15 cwt of kitchen or house coal, or coalite. Special certificates of exemption from the Regional Coal Offices allowed hospitals and schools more supplies.

As time progressed, the situation worsened. Supplies of coke and anthracite became limited, and existing stocks became depleted. Only lesser quality coals, such as unscreened coke breeze, anthracite grains, duff and washery slurry, bituminous fines, and Welsh dry steam, were available. To ease the situation, government dumps, put by as emergency stock, were opened up and weekly withdrawals were made to supplement the reduced supplies arriving by rail. Stroud helped slightly with some stock from the Forest of Dean, and the Gas Works supplied the coke.

Regardless of the lack, ordering was still encouraged, although customers were asked not to harass their merchant. He was the one whose coal was rationed, and he could only give them what he had. Mother, who was the wife of a coal merchant, put it this way, 'There were changes in the coal wagon delivery. So much coal was allowed to him to sort out for each person'. Consumers were warned their deliveries might differ from their usual orders: the types and sizes of coal might vary, and the order might not arrive exactly when they thought. Soon everyone, whether the lord in his manor, or a family in run-down accommodation, knew what Nutty Slack was.

Over the following months the rules became more rigid. No customer with more than 5 cwt of fuel in their possession was allowed a delivery, until their existing stock had dropped to the authorized set limit, nor were they allowed an amount exceeding 10 cwt a month, or 15 cwt over three months. Only customers with no facilities for stocking large quantities of coal received priority delivery, which enabled a constant trickle to keep them going.

In January 1945, The Black Diamonds Exhibition opened at Cheltenham, where numerous uses of coal in wartime, along with labour-saving devices and daily fuel economy hints, were demonstrated daily. The wireless, now owned by most families, broadcast hints and people were asked to shorten their coal fire's burning time. One suggestion was to confine all living activities to the kitchen during daytime, and use the sitting room only in the evenings. Another advocated sitting rooms to be abandoned entirely, and wanted everyone to spend the whole winter in the kitchen. Yet another suggestion was for the entire Nation to go to bed early where no heat would be needed at all!

A variety of inventive methods for procuring heat for warmth and cooking were adopted. Logging, firebricks, coal dust, or slack (which was recommended as good for baking), hay-boxes and one-pot cooking were all favoured. There were also thermos flasks, which were impossible to replace when broken. The basic overall message was, 'Light fires less and never in Summer!'.

For all coal merchants, these years were fraught with difficulties. Each merchant, like father, allotted the appropriate measure to his customers according to the set number of wagons allocated to him. Accurate weighing assumed enormous importance, a tremendous difficulty when an item is stored outside. Labels and tabs ensured that each customer received the due weight of coal, but this did not satisfy everyone. Some who felt they deserved more went to extraordinary lengths to prove they were short-changed. One customer, father told us, dried all his coal quota bit by bit in the oven to prove his point, while another report stated a woman chopped up her clothes line to gain fuel for warmth.

One of father's customers told me that following their modest delivery of coal they just stood and gazed at it for a while, as it stood shiny, black, and complete in the pile before filling their bucket and benefiting from the warmth.

As the coal allocation dwindled, more wood was sold to supplement customer supplies. Wood had not been dealt with much while coal was plentiful. Another difficulty for father was finding workers. Young men were not often available, and those who were around disliked the heavy dirty work and being seen with dirty faces. A delivery of coal required manhandling about four times before coming to rest in a coal-house. Jack Russell (Uncle Jack to me)

It was about 1915 that my father (Alfred Finley) started up in business, by buying for £9 a small piebald pony, and a small cart, which my brother (Francis) drove, he was then about (16), delivering wood-blocks, and coal, in 5 cwt lots.

Later as the business increased. the pony was sold and a larger one purchased. which was strong enough to pull 10 cwts, about this time another one was bought an ex Army horse, as this was during the 1914-1918 war, and most of the horses were used by the army.

This second horse and another cart was driven by a young man after leaving school, which we employed.

Then as the business still increased my father left the work he was doing, and joined my brother + employee, making 3 horses + carts. it was about this time 1916. that the started hauling coal for the Stroud Coop. Soc. to gether with their own Coal customers, as time passed other horses + carts were bought and more men employed, to cope.

It was in 1924 that I (Edward) left school, working for my father, driving a the trace horse, which was placed in front of the horse + cart. for pulling the heavy loads up the hills.

As I became older I then had my own Horse + Cart delivering coal and general haulage, where was plenty to do.

In 1930 the first 30c Motor Lorry was purchased and which I leared to drive was bought, driven by an employee which I leaned to 12 months later another one this reduced the horse + carts to 3. My father continued to drive his Horse + Cart. still doing a load of coal, to the places unfit for Motor Lorry's until he was 75.

My brother. retired 13 years ago, it was then left to me to carry on, his place was taken by my nephew Mr. C. M Maule who is still with me and, will be. taking over in the new year. in the business

$$\frac{78}{\frac{65}{13}}$$

A history of the Furley Coal business written by Father for the Stroud News and Journal on his retirement at the age of 70. Although this is a rough draft using a ball point pen instead of his usual finely chiselled wedge pencil or broad knibbed fountain pen, Father's writing is still a pleasure to behold. All his business accounts were written this way, and took an hour or two each night except Friday. Although Thursday was his busiest evening he always took time to produce a good result.

Francis and Edward Furley beside the old MST Bedford 2–3 ton Short Wheel Base End Tipper lorry, which was being taken away following a lengthy spell parked by the drive.

was a shining light among a succession of irregular workers. He worked for my grandfather for thirty years, beginning with the horses, with which he was marvellous, and when the lorries came along he went with father as his mate, as he never drove himself. He was kind and honest, and called me 'missy.' On the days when work was slack, he walked from Brimscombe across the common, or sometimes he went to the Wharf at Wallbridge in Stroud. He helped to mend coal baskets, cleared up the yard, assisted with haymaking, and later he visited us every Christmas morning for a glass of 'something strong' until he was too old.

Occasionally, when I was quite small, I spent the morning with father and Uncle Jack in the lorry, sitting on a board placed over the gear stick, which was wedged between the driver and passenger seat. Father's office was at the LMS yard and was owned by the Co-op. Inside it had a tortoise type stove, which was lit first thing before anything else was done, and the kettle put on it for tea.

Uncle Alf, a 'proper' uncle, worked for grandfather too during the early days. He also began with the horses, but progressed to become the driver of the second lorry. When he left, Uncle Francis, who could not drive at all, took his lorry over. Uncle Francis did not want to drive, but coaxed by father, and following a few lessons, he eventually went on his own and continued that way until his retirement. Sometimes he would appear just in time to save me the long climb up Rodborough Hill following a detention after school (usually a result of three reports for not wearing my beret, difficult with a pony tail hairstyle). At other times, if I had done an errand, he would say, 'I'll give you an orange at Christmas', which I realize now after wartime restrictions meant a treat.

Coal was registered until the early fifties, Spiers, Baddesay Spiers and Arley Spiers, being the best coal Merchants in the Stroud district received their supplies from Littleton, Coventry, Mansfield and Stafford, and the Midlands and South Wales, from where Dry Steam and Anthracite was obtained. Coal merchants were allocated one or two trucks a month, from which coal was delivered, straight from the truck and weighed accordingly, or loaded into stock piles, as a surcharge was paid if the truck stayed over two days.

Wards' coal yard, which began at the turn of the century, was on the GRW yard (where Stroud's multi-storey car park is now) and their coal office was across the London Road on the corner opposite the Union Inn. A unique feature of their shop was the enormous block of coal that stood outside which, according to Mr Alec Alder, who ran the company from 1947 and eventually owned it, came from the Aberpergym Colliery in an ordinary truck of coal. I asked him if people ever tried to chip bits off it, and he said, 'Yes, the American soliders had taken off lots'. But most people of Stroud, such as Jenny Bailey, were content to stroke its polished surface as they walked by.

When Ward's Coal closed down in 1970, the Stroud Ladies Circle held a competition to guess the weight of the lump, the proceeds of which purchased a bed for Stroud Hospital. Afterwards, the coal lump went to Stroud Museum to sit amongst the tradesmens' signs.

After the war, Mr Alder recalls, when coal was still registered, a quarter of coal or half a cwt of coke was permitted to anyone, and people came to Ward's yard to collect it. One particularly bad period for all businesses was during the rail strike of 1948, when no trains were running to bring in supplies. Ward's overcame this disaster by collecting their own allocations from the Midlands while the strike lasted.

Cordwell's Garage · Ltd.

AREA DEALERS	**AUTOMOBILE ENGINEERS**	AGENTS FOR
VAUXHALL CARS		STANDARD CARS
BEDFORD TRUCKS	**EBLEY, STROUD, GLOS.**	TRIUMPH CARS

BRANCH SERVICE STATION: CAINSCROSS, STROUD
TELEPHONE: STROUD 264

Messrs Alfred Furley & Sons.   Dec 12th 1950.

	£	s	d
To one new Bedford 2/3 Ton Short Wheelbase Tipping Truck, complete as per makers specification and terms of sale.	488	0	0
Purchase Tax.	106	2	4
Delivery ex works.	5	0	0
Number Plates fitted.	2	0	0
Tax for year.	27	10	0
£	628	12	4

2076

Received of . . . .

the sum of. . . . .*Pounds,*

. . . .*Shillings and*. . . . .*pence.*
Per Pro. CORDWELLS GARAGE

. . . .

Date. . . . .

CUSTOMERS' CARS STORED AND DRIVEN AT OWNERS' RISK

Cordwells invoice for the new lorry in December 1950.

110

Cordwells was formed in 1926 on the premises of G & R Fasteners Cainscross by Mr Cordwell of Cordwell's Brewery. In 1940 as a limited company it moved to its present premises at Ebley, where it worked for the Ministry of Transport throughout the war years. In the mid-1960s it amalgamated with Haines and Strange, Vauxhall dealers of Cheltenham.

Mike Samson with the restored lorry. Although the old lorry was bought by Geoff Mayo, it was Michael Samson who swapped his older TK Bedford for Father's lorry and restored it to its former glory. It took him seven long years, during which time he rebuilt the engine, and sought spare parts wherever he could. Father managed some from his accumulation of old lorry parts, but it was Norman Aish at Poole of Bygone Bedford Bits who supplied the new evasive parts. Finally Bryan Durn, now emerged from youthful antics into respectable signwriting replaced the Furley name on the doors (which Father painted himself), to the Samson one. Michael was used to working with coal, having done so from ten years when he had emptied Wards railway coal trucks and delivered for them as he grew. Finally he started on his own, and was running three lorries until he retired from hauling in 1991.

Over fifteen tons of coal were loaded by hand on each trip, over a period of eight weeks, before any deliveries at home could be thought about. Moreover, the enterprise proved so successful that larger lorries were employed regularly to transport some of their supplies from Mansfield and Pleasley, which was about 133 miles away. Normally the trains were exceedingly prompt. Mr Alder says. 'If a colliery said they would send it for 7 a.m. or 11 a.m., you could be sure it would always arrive on the dot'.

One notable event which Alec Alder remembers happened during the atrocious winter of 1947, when Arthur Russell (he could be related to 'Uncle Jack' but there is no way of knowing) went off in his lorry with a delivery for

The old family yard at Little London. When newly built the buildings to the right were stables, cart sheds, a tack room, a workshop and a hayshed. The other sheds appeared with the lorries. When I was young this yard was alive with activity, and a haven in which to play. My friends and I made dens in the large piles of reject coffin boards which awaited the saw, or baked potatoes on the stove in the tack room, bathed Shep the dog, or chalked crinoline ladies on a slate which leaned against the wall. Later it saw a revival of horse-power when cousin Claire and I groomed our ponies until they shone. Sunday mornings were especially noisy when the saw, powered by a pop-popping station engine, screamed across the valley to compete with Woodchester Church Bells. However Sunday evening was quiet. The yard was deserted and people walked to Rodborough Chapel, as I rode my fat-wheeled bike back and forth along the road, or attempted a horse carving in the workshop with a blunt old chisel. Those days are gone now, the yard is decaying. For me it died with Dad in September 1989.

Miserden. It started to snow on the way there, but on the way home the weather deteriorated so badly that Arthur had to abandon his lorry by The Fostons Ash public house. There it remained, completely enveloped and securely immovable, for the best part of three weeks. Only the Ward's Coal sign on the top advertised that a vehicle was there at all. Moreover, when it was eventually retrieved, the bag of coal which had been buried along with it was still intact.

Another source of power, electricity, was at the mercy of the coal supply. Coal-fed power stations endured regular power cuts, and their workers suffered losses in wages accordingly. During peak periods, stringent measures were introduced to preserve power. These were between 8 and 10 a.m. in the morning and from 4 to 6 p.m. at night. There were warnings of further cuts if the load rose above manageable proportions .

Increasing factory consumption caused by newly-installed electrical machinery and domestic consumer goods made the situation worse. Fearing local industry might be forced to close down due to curtailed coal deliveries, thus affecting the nation's recovery, the local paper conducted a fuel check on a cross-section of Stroud's main employers.

Newman and Henders in Woodchester, who used coal for smelting (anthracite being their main heating fuel), remained optimistic and predicted their stocks could last a further month. Stonehouse Brick and Tile Company, who weekly consumed 120 tons and Daniels, the Engineering and Fibre Board manufacturers of Lightpill, said 'they were alright for the present'. Chamberlains, the Leather Board Company at Nailsworth, were justifiably worried about obtaining their enormous requirement of 170 tons weekly.

As confidence in coal supplies diminished, alternative methods of heating and fuelling industry were sought. Many factories turned to oil to keep up their production now that Britain's goods were once more in demand. Strachans of West of England Cloth fame, situated in Lodgemore and Fromehall Mills, became frustrated with the uncertainty of their coal supply. They converted their Lancashire boilers to oil, and installed storage tanks which were capable of holding twelve thousand gallons of oil. Hill Pauls, the large tailoring company at Rowcroft, followed suit. The Great Western Railway converted forty locomotives, and installed new overhead filling tender tanks at Swindon, which were capable of holding thirty-six gallons of fuel.

No one could have foreseen the substantial rise in oil prices before the year was out!

CHAPTER TEN

CAN WE SEE THE LIGHT AT THE END OF THE TUNNEL?

The Stroud News summed up the feeling in Britain perfectly when it wrote, 'We enter the year of 1945 with mixed feelings'. Planning ahead was all very well, but ultimately everything depended on winning the war. With victory postponed, and an end to war the previous summer dashed, the British questioned, 'Did we underrate the remaining strength of the Germans?'

Since May 1940 when, under the leadership of Winston Churchill, a coalition government was formed it had been apparent that expansive social reforms should be planned for those future peacetime days which everyone hoped were not too far away. Britain's people were entitled to a worthwhile life in the land they had fought to protect.

With this in mind, 'The Beveridge Report' was published in December 1942. It was an overall social plan which encompassed a wide range of issues: poverty, health, education, employment, and housing. Each was dealt with by the war cabinet's Reconstruction Committee, through a series of White Papers.

Much happened during 1944. There was the Education Act which planned for overall secondary education; a National Health Service Scheme to provide comprehensive medical care; an Employment Policy to deal with post-war employment; and National Insurance, which introduced compulsory contributory benefits. Then in March 1945, a Housing Policy endeavoured to provide a home for everyone.

Anticipation of the war's end in Stroud became more of a reality in February, when the Fire Guard, which had been suspended since the previous September, began to wind down. Helmets, eye-shields, and stirrup pumps (which could be purchased for 7s 6d by gardeners), were mostly collected up and handed in. Quantities of protective apparel appeared from hidden corners, but some, like the pile of helmets neatly stacked and unused in our old tack room, were not returned at all.

In March, a 'thank you' stand-down dinner was held at the Stratford Hotel

The Committee formed to organise Street Parties etc at Castle Street. Back L–R: Eddie ?, ? Mr Jones (Min Brownes father), ?, ?, Mr Tuck, Mr Payne. Front: Mr May, Mrs Payne, Mrs Tuck, Mrs West, Mr West.

for Stroud's Auxiliary Firemen, many of whom had helped during the city blitz, and the Marling School football ground was used for their farewell parade on 24 June. In the future, any fire assistance had to be obtained by dialling 0 or 01 (war having prompted a massive increase in subscribers and public telephones), when The National Fire Service, or the Warden on duty, would deal with the blaze. However, this latter instruction changed when the wartime civil defence was dismantled too.

The long-awaited news of the end of war finally arrived on 7 May, when the surrender of the German army, and the disintegration of Nazism was announced. At last the struggle in Europe was over. Tuesday 8 May was chosen as VE day (Victory in Europe) and Wednesday as a public holiday. The following Sunday became a 'Day of Thanksgiving and Prayer'.

Bryan Durn, living now at 1 Vale View, Old Bisley Road, on hearing the bells ringing, and knowing there was no invasion, announced to his friends, 'The bells are ringing. The war's over'. The boys at Wycliffe College, still in Wales, kicked the tops off the Belisha beacons down the street to demonstrate their happiness.

The people of Stroud was already well advanced with peacetime

116

Margaret Webb.

preparations. The Gas Board had been hard at work replacing the dim emergency 'star lighting' (from 1943) with for new powerful overhead lights. Loudspeakers, in readiness for Churchill's speech to the nation, were appearing in the town. The inevitable queues had formed at fishmongers and bakers, in readiness for the holiday ahead. Festive food was prepared for street parties, and bunting and flags decorated streets and buildings. Bonfires grew like mushrooms throughout the district, village parades were organized, and fancy dress costumes sorted out.

VE day was wet, but not enough to dampen the enthusiasm of those celebrating, and throughout the morning people headed for the town. Stroud Parish Church, which was packed to the door during its special midday Service, opened proceedings with 'The National Anthem' and ended with 'Land of Hope and Glory'.

Due to the half-day bus service, the town had filled up by the afternoon. A crowd outside the Holloway Institute thickened as 3 o'clock approached. Churchill's speech was due to be broadcast over the BBC Forces News Network.

Ada and Leslie Webb walked in from Kingscourt. Ada had the pram and five-month-old baby Mary, and Leslie brought Margaret in the pushchair.

'There were people and police everywhere', recalls Ada. The Webb family took up an elevated position at the head of Gloucester Street, from where the victory grand procession could be clearly seen coming up the hill. Behind them in the crowd were two 'Yanks'. One, spotted Margaret, her dark eyes alight with wonder and excitement, and bent over her saying, 'Gee, honey, where did you get those eyes?' This comment sums VE day up completely for Ada. 'Everyone happy together', she said. 'It seems like yesterday.'

Following Churchill's victory announcement there was dancing. Clearings were made in the crowd, and people danced to the ATC Band, and the jazz band from the top of the town called Our Gang.

Public houses, which reverted to their 6 p.m. opening having survived indiscriminate opening times, soon ran out of beer, as their patrons filled and refilled their glasses and carried them outside to escape the inside crush.

All the villages celebrated in their own way, organizing parades and processions, by dancing, and burning bonfires. The effigy of Hitler was a popular addition to any bonfire. Painswick's effort was just one of many.

Stroud Hospital had a bonfire (where the maternity hospital stands today), and Stonehouse Boys' Brigade led a parade to theirs. Woodchester built and burned two. The one at Bisley Old Road was 15 feet high, topped by their version of Hitler, who wore a white boiler suit and was stuffed with hay, but still needed a can of creosote to set him alight at 10 p.m.

Harry Hill, of Frampton-on-Severn, built their enormous offering on the Green, while Fred Hazell, who had carefully hoarded fireworks throughout the war especially for such an occasion, ceremoniously let them off in a dazzling display.

Some celebrations were noisier than others. The ten-minute whistle blasts from Brimscombe's Great Western Banker engines ensured that everyone remained awake!

There were processions by torchlight, and dancing until well into the early hours. Nailsworth and Minchinhampton danced until around four in the morning in Cossack Square, The Cross, and Minchinhampton Market House.

Numerous villages held sports and street parties and blocked off the roads. Trestle tables were set up, and people produced feasts. Sometimes surprise luxuries appeared. *The Stroud News* reported that a large bottle of sweets, bought in 1939, was handed round at Rodborough Avenue.

Painswick's Vicarage street party, according to Jo Bessant, had 'two pianos, and tables and bunting from the top to bottom'. There was a free fish supper from Mr and Mrs Hyatt who ran the fish and chip shop, and The White Horse Pub, which was kept by Mr and Mrs Larner and known locally as 'The Pony', was handy for drinks.

Bryan Durn's street party was outside the Spread Eagle Inn, and the one at Kingscourt, according to Ada, 'was on the flat stretch of road by Lewis' sweet shop'. Trestle tables and benches were set up, and everyone supplied food.

A Street Party in The Street, Leonard Stanley. Typical of hundreds held throughout Stroud district to celebrate VE Day.

Betty Morgan at Sudgrove stayed at home to garden, because Les her husband, who had caught measles from their son Tony, was very ill in bed.

Wednesday was a day of brilliant sunshine, and an afternoon bus service was in operation to enable people to get into town. People congregated around Sim's Clock; and the Ritz and Gaumont cinemas, no longer slaves to the black-out, switched on all their lights. There was an illuminated 'V' sign on the flag displayed outside the Ritz, and a huge picture of the Allied leaders at The Gaumont.

Thursday, although theoretically a working day, still maintained a holiday feel as the Gas Board, spurred on by further light, plodded steadily on installing yet more lamps.

Throughout the week, church services played a major part. Worshippers from all the services, civil defence, youth and voluntary organizations, joined with family gatherings to fill the churches, the village church bells freely resounding throughout valley and hills.

T

8th June, 1946

I send this personal message to you and all other boys and girls at school. For you have shared in the hardships and dangers of a total war and you have shared no less in the triumph of the Allied Nations.

I know you will always feel proud to belong to a country which was capable of such supreme effort; proud, too, of parents and elder brothers and sisters who by their courage, endurance and enterprise brought victory. May these qualities be yours as you grow up and join in the common effort to establish among the nations of the world unity and peace.

George R.I

A commemorative Victory Message issued by Stroud High School for Girls.

To celebrate the war's end, The Gas Company introduced a new cooker, The Victory Coronet. The speed, economy, efficiency, and durability attributed to it were all qualities which Britain would need during the difficult times ahead.

Soon local Prisoners of War began to return home, including servicemen from Downfield, Horsley, Paganhill, Ebley, Nailsworth, Middle Street, Minchinhampton, Bisley, and Thrupp. One had attempted to escape eight times, another had escaped but had been recaptured, and one father saw his four-year-old daughter for the first time.

Demobilization did not happen immediately, as it was thought the rehabilitation of four million service men and women was best achieved in easy stages. To keep up their morale, people at home were asked to keep sending parcels. There was a bulk cigarette collection system in the Gaumont foyer, where patrons were asked to donate into a box, or 'A Link 'Twixt Him and Home', at Fred Wright's shop in Stroud High Street, provided duty-free bulk packets of Players at 5s 6d, or packs of two hundred Woodbines for 4s.

Overcrowding on the buses got worse as the war ended, prompting the question, 'Is your journey really necessary?' Many travellers decided it was, and continued to cram into buses amid increasing resentment by understaffed conductresses. Although normally cheerful, the clippies threatened strike action unless laid-off staff were replaced. Two strikes hit The Red and White Service in 1945. Passengers continued to omplain about queuing for buses which did not come, and asked for termini, waiting facilities, and bus shelters. 'It's worse than during the war', said one frustrated traveller. A Red and White Bus Service holiday advertisement at the time united the feelings of both bus crew and passengers when it stated, 'There was a time when Bus and Coach solved the holiday problem. War has put a stop to that form of relaxation!'

Travellers on the trains fared better. Their restaurant cars were restored.

Shopping restrictions disappeared with the end of the black-out, and shops reverted to pre-war opening times, although some shopkeepers felt it a waste of time to open longer while goods and shop assistants were scarce.

On 23 May, two weeks after VE day, a 'caretaker' administration replaced the coalition government. There was a lull in which to choose a new government.

All the main parties were united in their support of the Beveridge plan for rebuilding Britain, the Labour Party favouring industry nationalization in addition. Stroud's candidates were Flight Lieut. Ben Parkin, a Stonehouse man, and member of Wycliffe College staff, who proclaimed 'Labour Fights for Human Freedom'; Peter Egbert Cadbury, the Liberal representative, formerly Fleet Air Arm, and test pilot with the Gloucester Aircraft Company; and National Conservative Flight Lieut. Robert Perkins who 'backed Churchill's team'. There was also an Independent candidate, Mrs Victor Bruce, who withdrew in June to give free rein to the three main parties.

All the party promises were practically identical: five shillings family

Detailing bus staff for overtime in the Old National Garage Yard at London Road during staff and conductor shortages in the early 50s. L–R: Fred Cooke, Frank Washbourne, Percy Clarke, Larry Harding, Mervyn Bennett, John Nottingham, Inspector J Hall, Ken Shelly, Martin Hyde, Dave Cruikshank, Reg Mansfield, Eric Bridges, Doris Phillips, Nat Hammond, John Shipton, Vick Watkins, Inspector Ireland, Roy Anns.

allowance, free school meals, sickness and unemployment benefits, and maternity grants, widows' pensions, the early release of skilled men from the Forces for urgent reconstruction work, training for the disabled, homes for servicemen, and a return to jobs.

'We're not going to have them selling matches on street corners', said the Nationals.

'Every method, public or private, for homes permanent or temporary, will be employed, and all obstructions, from whatever quarter they come, will be dealt with by the whole power of parliament and the Nation', promised Mr Churchill.

'A possible two-and-a-half million homes if all united and co operated', thought Mr Perkins.

The next few weeks witnessed hectic campaigning, averaging eighty speeches per candidate. Finally, following a week of last minute pre-election speeches held consecutively at Stroud Subscription Rooms, Stroud's citizens voted Labour's Ben Parkin in on 5 July as their Member of Parliament. His 22,495 votes gave him a majority of 949 over the Conservatives.

A nail-biting wait of three weeks followed, during which time ballot boxes remained sealed while British citizens abroad placed their vote, whereupon the announcement on 25 July proclaimed a Labour Government. Labour's triumph prompted a rapid change in prime ministers, Clement Richard Attlee claiming within the hour Churchill's place as leader. The future plans for Britain were announced in the King's Speech on 16 August.

VJ day (Victory in Japan) arrived on 14 August. An unconditional surrender by the Japanese Government had followed the August bombings of Hiroshima and Nagasaki.

The news was welcomed quietly in Stroud, partly because the announcement came at midnight when many were asleep. The Americans, however, reacted differently, roaring through the town in their jeeps and trailing tins and blasting horns.

The next day, more celebrations followed, which were relatively quiet compared with those of exuberance on VE Day. Bunting and loudspeakers went up again, and there was dancing on the Ritz forecourt, and fireworks at night outside the Subscription Rooms. But no buses ran, and the shops and workplaces remained closed. Some, not having heard the news, arrived for work but were unable to get in. Those who have remembered VJ day have done so because of other reasons. Peggy Perrins did because her son was born that day, but most people felt, 'It was more like a Sunday!'.

With the prospect of troops returning home, 'Welcome Home Funds' appeared. Each village, because of the 1940 War Charities Act, had to apply for permission to the Council. Committees were formed as a result to arrange the events.

Stroud town itself did all manner of things. There was a celebration dance at The Premier Hall, a grand whist drive at the Church Institute, a flag day, a mammoth jumble sale at The Liberal Hall, a garden party at The Acacias in Bowbridge Lane, and a competition in the *Stroud News* awarding the ever-popular National Savings Certificates as prizes. £396 15s 11d was raised, its exact distribution causing serious deliberation.

Each village was independent in raising funds: those raising the money deciding on its dispersal. Some, like Uplands, considered cash gifts were best and shared their £250 between the returning troops. Some other uses were for help for widows, or a community venture which benefited everyone.

Stroud's 'Welcome Home' committee, unable to make their decision, sent their service people (through relatives), a questionnaire asking what they would like the money used for. Some requested nothing, only a return to home and family. The majority appreciated an event which would make returning home special.

Fêtes formed the basis of most 'Welcome Home' presentations. Their venue was usually the grounds of a large local house. Selsley held theirs in Stanley Park, Woodchester was at Benwell House, while Painswick used The Court House, and Chalford had a Melody van and carnival.

War, which regulated most things, could not ration pleasure. To most people, tomorrow was another day, the present one was here to enjoy. For women, remaining smart was part of it. Madame Pompadores, the King Street hairdressers, catered for this therapy by offering a 'New Cold Permanent Wave, No Machines, No Heat!' A boon to women like Mother, who had previously endured ceiling stringing, along with hot roller torture. The envy of a curly-headed friend was the source of her agony. Mother's hot perm used to take four hours, from which she emerged with first degree burns, tight curling, and dreadful frizzing on washing. However, her real pain usually came as Father exclaimed, 'Oh Nora, you've ruined your hair', and she believed him when she could not get her comb through it later!

CHAPTER ELEVEN

HOMING IN

The housing problem had been tackled before the war but hindered because of it. It now progressed from a headache into a migraine, triggered off by an influx of marriages, births, and made worse by the loss of buildings through war. Of all the issues highlighted by the Beveridge Report, a home to return to was the dream of most servicemen.

In 1939 there had been twelve million houses in Britain, of which seven thousand were destroyed or damaged throughout the six years of conflict. There was little hope for the four million promised homes which every party manifesto offered, and it was totally unrealistic when viewed against post-war monetary, manpower and material shortages. The shortage of bricks (only a third being manufactured compared with pre-war quantities), combined with the scarcity of steel and timber, which normally came from Canada, Germany, or Sweden, made the problem worse. Housing development was to prove a slow frustrating procedure.

Fifteen thousand homes were initially required in the South Western Region, but following an inspection of five-and-a-half thousand existing properties, thirty-three per cent were declared uninhabitable. This situation was disregarded by desperate homeless people who took them on, paid too much, and incurred debts.

From 1930 the Labour controlled council, under The Greenwood Act, embarked on a slum clearance and rehousing plan, with new and general need subsidies. New council housing appeared at Foxmoor Lane, Highfield Road, Paganhill, Summer Street, Summer Cresent, and Bowbridge, but further developments came to an abrupt halt when the National Government took over in 1933.

Under their control, funding was geared towards the Five Year Clearance Plan, until desperate overcrowding proved the need for further homes. Painswick, Cranham, Stonehouse, Leonard Stanley, Woodchester, Minchinhampton, Whiteshill, Chalford, and Thrupp gained their council homes as a result.

Whiteshill Carnival by St Pauls Church in the 1940s. The School's Headmasters house, then occupied by Mr Billit, is in the background.

Wartime conditions reduced building to a minimum, although a scattering of housing, which had already been started, appeared at The Tynings in Nailsworth, Doverow Avenue in Stonehouse, Dallaway at Thrupp, and Cutler Road, Folly Lane and Thompson Road at the Uplands. The return of the servicemen soon made it obvious that Stroud's housing would not be adequate, and empty housing was requisitioned by the council to house the needy. Reports of squatting added fuel to an already inflamed situation as forty thousand people in desperate need of homes began to occupy the many disused Forces camps throughout the country, relieved to find somewhere to settle, however temporary and primitive.

Half-hearted attempts were made by the authorities to discourage them, but in reality the squatters' newly adopted life-style removed a few homeless families from off the council's backs and the housing list, and gave a bit more breathing space to those trying to solve an unsolvable problem. In Stroud district, five of the huts left by the Americans at Lypiatt Park in 1944, now knee-deep in undergrowth, were taken over by squatters and converted into homes. Each hut was adapted to incorporate a living-room, bedroom, and scullery. Some Nissen huts at Stanley Lane, which had formerly housed a potato, grass seed, and fertilizer store, received the same treatment, as did an RAF hut at Avening Court.

Eventually, as time passed and Stroud District Council felt that enough was enough, some of the Lypiatt huts had their roofs removed to deter future home-seekers, while the others were demolished. But at the same time the Leonard Stanley huts were reprieved and, following repairs, were deemed fit to last for several more years.

The housing dilemma called for immediate measures, forcing Aneurin Bevan, as Minister of Health, to embark on a plan of emergency housing throughout the country. The old, neglected. war-ravaged properties were patched up, and local authorities took over vacant buildings. The temporary prefabricated houses, erected hastily to provide shelter for bomb victims during the war, were succeeded by a number of better quality, more substantial, prefabricated homes. These provided a reasonable substitute for permanent brick-built housing, although theoretically temporary, were surprisingly popular, their new occupiers delighted with their new, damp-, and damage-free homes. Throughout the country, large numbers of 'prefabs' arose like mushrooms, a life saver to the homeless and councils alike.

Ron Smith's family, who lived at The Leazes, were given a newly-erected prefab at Cashes Green when the council removed them from their home for slum clearance. Ron remembers that the first ones there were at Springfield and Etheldene Road, and were asbestos with tin roofs. His parents were delighted with the modern house, so different from the cottage they had just left which had no gas or electricity, and where the toilet 'seemed miles away and there were rats'. It was perhaps a bit too hot in summer, and cold in the winter-time, but generally his family were pleased with their home and all its facilities. It even had a gas fridge. Ron recalls later housing at Cashes Green, at Mosley Road, Mosley Court, and Hyatt Road, 'which was where the posh council house people lived'.

Obviously, all councils would have preferred to accommodate their tenants in a traditional sturdy home, but prefabricated housing was realistically the quickest way to handle the shortage. A hundred Airey-type houses were requisitioned by Stroud District Council to help their immediate need, accompanied by appeals for local builders to erect them. The builders had been enduring a tough time, being very much restricted in their choice of post-war building. Only one private house was allowed to be built for every four in the public sector. Even the simplest building job demanded licences and permits, a cause of frustration for builders small and large alike. The eleven months from August 1947 to June 1948 proved particularly irksome, when all private building was completely suspended, to enable the local authorities to have a free rein on labour and materials in hand.

The Airey house prefab, of metal girder construction, came with the shell already made, being erected in no time, once their foundations had been laid. Their interiors incorporated storage units throughout, which was a boon at a time when obtaining furniture was difficult. Haste, however, can have its drawbacks, and within the year some prefab inhabitants complained of squeaky floors. It turned out to be a hidden hazard of metal floor joists.

In January 1947, the coldest winter for years, thirty Hawksley aluminium-framed prefabs arrived in Stroud after a hazardous journey. The final half mile up Stroud's narrow, steep, and slippery High Street, en route to Jim Knees' field at Bisley Old Road, was decidedly the worst part. However, once on site all problems, except the snow which had cut Bisley off from the rest of society, melted away.

The proven teamwork of the construction companies could apparently override any building problem. A gang of twenty men, including a cook and welfare officer, lived and worked on site throughout the building duration, and could erect a basic house in under an hour. It was just double that when fully fitted out with water and electricity. As, on this timetable, at least four homes were habitable after the first day, the team were able to live in those while continuing the building of the rest. It is reported that several houses were already erected by Thursday that week.

Doreen Ireland remembers Jim Knees' field before the prefabs came, when it was the venue for the celebration VE day party, and a carnival was held for the little children. Bryan Durn recalls Jim bringing his horses up after a hard day's work, and letting them loose to canter up the road into the field, which was then practically open countryside all the way up to Bisley. 'The road was so narrow scarcely two vehicles could pass'.

Hill Street in the snow.

Jack Milton owned the farm on the other side of the road until the council estate around Mason Road was built in 1956. One foggy Saturday morning, the area experienced the arrival of a very low and spluttering aircraft, which turned out to be a Model plane with an RAF pilot. On landing he was immediately surrounded by most of the young ladies who lived nearby, but eventually ended up in Joan Rockett's house. For about a week, his aircraft stood in the field, continually overlooked by Copper Mills and his associates, until it was eventually manoeuvred into a corner, whence it shot off in the direction of Bull's Cross, as everyone watched it over the wall.

The weather also caused delays on other sites. Forty prefabs planned for Cashes Green, Ebley, and Bisley Road could not be completed because the installation of their plumbing was hindered. One was finally ready for inspection in March, and as the weather warmed, several more by the end of April.

Throughout the atrocious weather, the rural districts of Painswick, Waterlane, Stancombe, and Camp accommodated limited numbers of Swedish homes, and other more permanent council housing at Painswick, Stonehouse, Minchinhampton, Whiteshill, and along the Cirencester Road. Swedish house

129

designs were completely different from conventional prefabrication, as they were constructed of wood and supposed to last fifteen years. 'We were told they would be replaced with dwellings of a more traditional nature', said Ivor Gardener, surveying those still sturdily evident across the lane from his cottage in Camp. All post-war council homes had two things in common: they had good-sized gardens and reasonably spacious rooms.

In an attempt to shorten the waiting list further, the Conservative authority increased housing subsidies, and Woolaway and Utility housing made an appearance. Both were of sectional design, but more spacious than the others. Utility homes occupied thirty-three square feet of ground area, had a larger landing, three bedrooms, numerous fitted cupboards, a porch, a store shed, and undercover W.C. But their colour made Stroud residents unhappy, being red when Stroud wanted buff, like those recently erected in Bath. The colour did not influence the rent, which was eighteen shillings a week, four shillings more than any other type of council housing.

Stroud's new 'Water Plan', a scheme whereby ten villages received piped water, was implemented in 1948, together with a 'Joint Sewerage Plan', designed to provide comprehensive drainage for Stroud and Nailsworth districts. The sewerage work commenced in the Spring of 1948, following many years of referral, from its initial idea in 1929, through its shelving in 1931 as the grant diminished, another ten years when the war came, until eventually coming to fruition.

The water scheme, in contrast, although expensive at an estimated £15,000, appeared to the onlooker to be swift and smooth, as it reconstructed the Chalford Pumping Station, installing electrical pumps to replace the two steam ones, and provided a service reservoir at Thrupp. This enabled a constant lift of water to Minchinhampton's reservoir 600 feet above sea level. By January the scheme was well advanced. Cashes Green was one of the first on tap. Areas further out waited longer and paid more. Simply laying the pipes between Bisley and Camp, just fourteen houses and one farm, cost in the region of £1,000.

Farms in particular noticed the benefits. Cynthia Shaw, who milked cows at Bisley's Rectory Farm in 1941, clearly recalls all the water-fetching from the wells each day before any milking could begin. Similarly Ada, struggling with countless trips to the spring in The Street, Kingscourt, on washing day, recalls the hardship of it all, but still maintains nothing could ever compare with the spring water's soft taste. 'Leslie always fetched two buckets each morning before going off to work. If I needed more, I had to fetch them myself'.

Once the weather was so bad she was unable to reach the spring at all, and Leslie had to dig a passage through the narrow, steep path leading to the spring when he came home from work. But for many living in the country, water carrying was a way of life. 'Even a simple visit to the lavatory down the garden required a pint or two of water to throw down afterwards'.

Mr Peters was in charge of the water scheme, and was surely rewarded by the consumption of 35,000 gallons a day. This was approximately 3 gallons a person, just a small portion of the vast supplies of water which the Water Board subsequently struggled to sustain in following years.

Despite the installation of water and sewerage facilities, an incredible number of Stroud's existing homes were still desperately in need of attention, and were labelled as unfit for human habitation. A survey throughout sixteen parishes revealed that many homes failed to comply with the Ministry of Health's light, water, and sanitation service requirements. Chalford alone had 139 condemned out of 723 homes inspected.

To encourage householders to mend and improve their homes, a £10 allowance spanning a period of six months was offered, with an additional £2 a month to cover the labour. Subsequently, as there was nowhere else to go, occupants remained where they were, relying on village meetings and rehousing plans for their future, and welcoming any council plans towards home improvements, while continuing to resent the word 'slum', which they felt portrayed visions of squalor, filth, and destitution.

Eventually there was a pleasing outcome as a hundred private homes were given reprieves and modernization, receiving bathrooms, hot water systems, sanitation, kitchens, and larders, which furthered their life by another fifteen years. Grants were available for half the improvement expense if the cost exceeded a hundred pounds. There was a pamphlet, 'Inprovement Grants for Old Homes', which strongly advised obtaining official approval before commencing work. Otherwise, recompense might not be forthcoming if applications were tendered after the job was done.

For other properties, though, slum clearance continued to sweep 'dangerous and inconvenient' old properties away for ever. In the top of the town area, Ron Smith remembers, 'hundreds went. Acre Street, Parliament Street and Hill Street. It was a rough area, very much like living in Victorian times really'.

Jottings by Jonathon felt the demolishing of their premises, to make way for progress in the area, would result in more cars or the modern biscuit boxes going up all around. 'Properly cared for these old homes make friendly and comfortable homes . . . how precious they are and how foolish is this generation to discard them so lightly . . . it makes one sad to see them go.'

The allocation of council houses was fraught with problems when it came to deciding who needed a home most urgently. Obviously, when faced with a waiting list of such length and need, some system was urgently required. The higher powers of government offered no hard and fast rules, so each locality was left free to decide their own scheme.

Stroud adopted the points system, in which all applicants received points according to circumstances to determine their accommodation. Children each received two points, there were five for the dwelling which was inhabited at the present time, with an additional three points each for pregnant women, ex-

Leonard Stanley showing the orchard in front of St Swithins church. A Village Hall was to have occupied the corner of this field.

servicemen and TB sufferers. Enormous trouble was taken to achieve fairness, but sometimes a word from the doctor could ease the waiting.

Ada and Leslie were over-snug in their tiny one-bedroomed cottage containing their family of four, having patiently awaited developments from the council for nine long years. Every three months, as was required, Ada religiously renewed her application, replying each time to enquiries of, 'Has anything changed?' with, 'No, they haven't, the children are still getting bigger!'.

The growing pressure on space eventually prompted Leslie to sleep on the landing, where his single bed nudged the chest of drawers accommodating the family clothes, and restricted the doorway. One day Margaret was sick in bed, and Doctor Mould came. As he negotiated the landing he lost his jacket button, and the Webb dilemma came to light. His recommendation ensured swift transferral from the ordinary council house list to one of priority, and soon a new council house at Leonard Stanley was theirs.

Ada will never forget the day the letter arrived confirming their allocation. 'It stated the house was practically finished and there would be a short wait. It

Ruscombe in the mid 50s.

was like a mansion after that tiny cottage. It had a lovely large sitting and dining room, two bedrooms and a lovely large garden, all for 11s a week. You'd have to pay a lot more than that today!'

Stroud's urban population was about sixteen thousand at the close of 1948. Two years of post-war building had provided 213 new houses, of which 116 were permanent, 37 aluminium, 40 temporary and 20 private. Rural areas had acquired 166, which for farmers requiring homes for their agricultural employees 'was not enough'. They were unable to use many of their tied cottages, which were traditionally part of the farm worker's employment deal, a large number having deteriorated considerably through lack of maintenance. Mindful of the farmers' point the authorities took note and placed agricultural workers' housing, along with that of miners, at the top of their list.

Despite housing shortages, council house rents rose. A two-bedroomed house suffered an increase of 1s 6d weekly becoming 9s 6d, while those in three-bedroomed accommodation paid 2s 9d more, becoming 11s 6d. The prefabs at Bisley Old Road cost 12s per week.

Rates rose too. During the ten years from 1940 to 50 they rose in urban areas to 23s 4d, an increase of 6s 4d, while residents in rural districts paid an increase of 6s 3d, making a total of 21s.

133

A series of changes in living accommodation habits permeated the fifties and sixties. It seemed that no sooner had increased council housing solved the housing problem of twenty-odd years than private home ownership became an object of desire. An increasing number of newly married couples looked towards buying their own home, and regarded council housing as a thing of the past.

When Pat Hawker married in 1941, one of the two million brides tying the knot in wartime Britain, her accumulated allocation of coupons bought her a wedding dress from Bon Marche in Gloucester. She obtained extra rations, 'which were hardly noticeable really', for the wedding reception, and there was a good deal of scrounging for extra butter, tea, and sugar. All her neighbours contributed something, resulting in a fine, sit-down meal of cold meats and vegetables for her seventy-five guests at the British Legion Hall in Horsley. Two women did all the catering and serving, and three blind brothers entertained them with a melodeon.

The newly-weds had no honeymoon, nor even a home to live in. Instead, as in countless other wartime unions, their first two years of married life were spent with parents. In 1943, the chance of a home came their way, one of a row of three cottages at Bowbridge, owned by Orchard and Peer. It had no kitchen, just a gas cooker at the top of the steps leading to the cellar. 'I suppose all smells went down there!', said Pat. However, there was gas lighting downstairs, but they had to use candles upstairs. The communal wash-house and a flushing outside toilet was shared by all three households.

Pat put her name down on the council list, but had two children by the time a letter arrived to say she had a house. Even then it was not her desired dream, but a prefab at Kilminster Road, in completely the opposite direction to the one she had asked for. Although disappointed, she collected the keys and went to look. 'It didn't look much from outside, but when I stepped inside it was like a palace. Everything was built in, cupboards, a cooker, a fridge. How many had fridges in those days? There were two bedrooms and a lovely bathroom. It was just great!'

In 1956 the Kilminster Road tenants were obliged to move from their prefabricated homes to brand new houses on the newly-built Bisley Road Estate, across the road on Jack Milton's land. Pat said, 'Kilminster Road tenants had first choice. We chose one which had been used by the builders for their 'cuppas' and so ours was reasonably aired. When we moved, we simply carried all our furniture across the sports field, except for the piano which had to go the long way round by road on a trailer.'

Later Kilminster Road was pulled down.

When Nancy got married in 1947 (the same year as Princess Elizabeth) at Slad Chapel, she borrowed her wedding dress 'which was a marvellous creation' from a friend. A slight problem arose because her younger brother,

134

Mike with Slad cricket team at Daglingsworth. L–R, Back: J Rickets, L Mynett, J Cook (Capt), E Allard, H Cook, J Ward. Front: ?, Mike Hawkes, J Wynn, Jackie Wynn, E Bartlett (Rev). During the season of 1950 Slad Cricket Club First XI played Redlers, Frampton, Stonehouse, Kings Stanley, Frocester, Hoffmans, Stroud Brewery, Chalford, Amberley, Sheepscombe, and the Second XI British Railways, Mr Birts XI, Avening, Cranham, Box, MA Hawkesley, Bathurst Estate, Thrupp and Minchinhampton. Their President was Mr T John, Chairman Mr E Allard, Secretary-Treasurer Mr A Ward. The Captain of 1st XI was Mr J Cook, and Captain of Second XI Mr L Gardiner.

Mike, who had turned up in scruffy clothes in readiness for a cricket match (choosing to miss her reception in order to pursue his passion) appeared on her wedding photograph, sitting on the nearby wall. She was so infuriated by his messy appearance that she wanted the photographer to cut him out of the picture, but his smudged form is still in it. Nancy continued to live at home following her marriage as her husband was in the Forces. As soon as Slade Cottage at the end of Summer Street became vacant, she was off to seize the opportunity, and moved in with the rats and mice.

Forty years later in 1980, council house tenants, who in years past had waited and wished for their name to come forward for house allocation, were able to purchase their council house at a reasonable cost under the government's Right to Buy policy, becoming house owners in their own right.

Large scale council house building was abandoned, and replaced by estates in the private sector, DIY home improvements and mortgages.

The private housing boom raced freely ahead now that builders and materials were once more in abundance. Numerous private estates grew up around Stroud, and people dug in their pockets to purchase one of the many properties for sale throughout the district. A new house on a mortgage could be bought for between £2,500 and £3,000, while a four-bedroomed house with a garage in Painswick was £3,000, or a three bedroomed one at Oakridge, £2,850. These factors influenced the rise from twelve per cent of homes in owner-occupation at the start of the fifties to fifty-six per cent by the end of the decade.

CHAPTER TWELVE

EDUCATION

The war brought an expansion to the organization of education in England. The government, realizing that a wider range of subjects and opportunity was essential for Britain's future economy, looked towards reducing the existing all-inclusive elementary schools, where often a child's complete schooling was conducted under one roof. Instead they wanted to create a more varied education system for pupils from 5 to 18 years, conducted in well-equipped separate buildings.

Until now, only the cleverest working-class child could progress from their state or voluntary elementary school to one of the twenty-five per cent of places available to them in grammar schools. Their wealthier middle-class contemporaries had more such opportunities, where money rather than ability, appeared to open the door to a better life. Clearly, although grammar school entrance was an unfair process, it was vital towards gaining a foothold away from working-class employment, and the only route towards the possession of the school certificate, which was essential for university entrance.

Before the war, ninety per cent of all children from the age of five, until leaving at fourteen, attended elementaries. Many school buildings resembled the churches from which their education originated, with high Gothic windows to obliterate all outside interest, presumably to avoid loss of concentration. Two systems operated: the church or voluntary school, which was compulsory, and maintained, controlled and dominated by the church, and the state elementaries which were funded by the authorities through the rates, while the church provided and maintained the building.

The 1926 Hadow Report envisaged separate senior schools for every child, regardless of scholarship results, along with new schools to house them, and an increase in the leaving age to 15 years. But economic conditions and then the war, halted progress until R.A. Butler, the President of the Board of Education, and the Beveridge Report took the matter of widespread educational reorganization in hand.

The 1943 Norwood Report suggested three types of secondary school: the

Children in fancy dress on Sheepscombe House Lawn about 1948. L–R: Colin Liptrot, Pat Morey, Maureen Beard, Jennifer Liptrot, Dorothy Hearne, Freda Scott, Ruth Scott. The little girl in the front is Alice Scott. The boy is Ronnie Beard.

'Grammar' for intellectual minds; 'Technical' for engineering, craft and future apprenticeships; and the 'Modern', which was for a large proportion of Britain's future labour force. In theory, each establishment was realistically geared towards pupils' aptitudes and their subsequent type of employment.

Stroud already had grammar and technical schools, so only required the new secondary moderns. But many towns only achieved a modern and a grammar, because their technical training system did not get off the ground.

Stroud's Marling School had begun in 1887 on seven-and-a-half acres of land in Cainscross Road, and was supported by prominent local businessmen, of which the Marling family played a leading role. Established predominantly for middle and lower class education, the funding for poorer scholarship entrants was provided by charities and the intake of fee-paying day boys and boarders. Even then, gaining a place did not always mean the boy or girl who had qualified could attend. Jack Ireland and his future wife, Doreen, both gained places at grammar schools but neither was able to go. Jack should

Cainscross Voluntary C of E School when John Webb (Ada's son), the last but one in the front row attended there in the early 60s. Ada said they walked each day to St Matthews Church 'come rain or shine'. When Gerald Arthur attended in 1939 the intake was from 4–14, there were two playgrounds, one each for senior and junior pupils, and outside toilets. Victory Park was their playing field, the car park was the school garden where the pupils learned gardening skills, and woodwork lessons were on the site of Ebley Supplies. There was a school photo each year, and Cosham Tea, which was charity-orientated and exists no more. Norman Smith took class 4, Miss King class 3, and Mr Giles, the Headmaster took the senior classes 11–14. Miss Ratcliffe took class 5, which was prior to the scholarship which took Gerald to Marling School. At Marling he joined the Army Cadets and Youth Volunteers, and potato picked at Kings at Forest Green for a shilling an hour.

have gone to Marling, but the expense of the uniform, and the books which parents were required to supply, prevented it. Likewise Doreen, having passed for Eastdene Grammar School at Cinderford, had to surrender her place to another girl whose parents could pay, while she went into service instead.

A secondary grammar school for girls was started in 1904, firstly at the School of Art building in Lansdown, and after 1911 at their newly-built premises in Beards Lane, Cainscross which are still in use today. Junior departments and a kindergarten at Stroud Girls High were maintained until 1944 when the fee system was abolished.

Marjory Hook attended The Stroud High School for Girls in 1937, having been one of two chosen from Ebley Elementary (the other was John Smith). She had started school at four years old with Miss Beard, being tutored in the top class before sitting the entrance scholarship. She read aloud to the headmistress, Miss Brew, at her oral, and used the school's front door for the only time during her school life. When she was there the rules on dress were very strict. If a blazer was worn, the students had to wear socks, but with the long coat it was black stockings. While she was awaiting her school certificate results in 1942, Miss Dancer asked her where her interest lay for future work. When she said 'figures', she was chosen by Lloyds Bank to work for them, but she found it disappointing as she was 'in the basement and on machines'.

The Craft School was started in Stroud within four years of the grammars. The lessons were held at the Lansdown Hall until the move into their new County Council funded premises in Beards Lane in 1910. The school provided training in woodwork, metalwork, technical drawing and textiles, alongside the general subjects. A test and an interview determined entrance.

In 1926 the existing schools were joined by the Central School for Girls opposite the Boys Craft School, which was renamed the Stroud and District Central School for Boys in 1921.

The Girls Craft School, which also changed its name, to The Girls Technical School, following the war, was an amalgamation of pupils from Badbrook, the School of Art juniors, and several district elementaries. It was unique of its kind, the tuition based on self-motivation, pride, and creativeness, and the students learned general subjects in combination with domestic science and art. Book-keeping and secretarial tuition, in which pupils specialized in the fourth year, were all much in demand in and after the war.

Pat Robinson, then Mavis Berry, remembers: the school May Day revels, when the second year group customarily Maypole danced 'in summer uniform come hail or shine'; the November 'beating the bounds' ritual, when the entire school walked round the perimeter fence chanting, 'that's mine, that's mine' as they touched it with sticks; potato planting in wartime at Slimbridge, where 'the field stretched out to infinity and we were told to keep well away from the Italian prisoners of war'; and the coach trip to Wills Tobacco Factory for a sports meeting, where 'We shrieked as the air balloons swarmed overhead (we had never seen so many before) and our teacher said, "Girls, girls, we are not on a common factory outing"'. There was also 'plantain digging', a quaint punishment exclusive to the Girls Central School, in which the whole school indulged when necessary .

The move towards 'modern schools' brought schools to Brimscombe, Nailsworth, Stonehouse, and Rodborough. The immediate Stroud area chose

Rodborough School 1941. Keith Browne is second from the right at the back.

Rodborough Primary School site for their school 'because it seemed a good place to have one!' Their first intake of pupils moved in during the summer of 1951 following a spate of alterations, several additional prefab classrooms for woodwork, arts and crafts, and a science laboratory 'just inside the gate'. There was a delay when it was discovered that the installation of lavatories had been overlooked. Clive Maton recalls separate playgrounds, one for girls just behind the science lab, and one for the boys behind the woodwork building, with an area between where anyone could go. During the early days the boys played football on Daniels ground. Hockey was up on Rodborough Common by the lonely tree, 'We ran up and the teachers drove', recalls a pupil, and netball in the school yard.

Although initially adequate for its intake of 160 boys and girls, when numbers rose to 360 accommodation had to be sought elsewhere. Domestic science was taught at Badbrook, art-related subjects were taught at the Art School in Lansdown, and there were several classes held at the Old Boys Club in Church Street. Needlework took place at the public bath premises in Bath Street, from where complaints came of 'keyhole peeping'.

Mr Loosley was the headmaster during those years as a secondary modern, and Mrs Shepherd was senior mistress, and games and P.E teacher. In 1951 Fred Clark was the music teacher, and Mr James and Mrs Drew also taught there.

The Blackboy School displaying their Christmas decorations in 1958. Margaret Hawkes (née Iles) is half hidden to the end of the 3rd row, and her twin sister Sue is 4th from the right in the back row. Others include Christine Bickle, Pat Weaving, Margaret Young, Molly Wheatley, Ann Price and Mary Tipple.

When faced with a school whose pupils were destined to follow a less academic career, they and the rest of the staff at Rodborough were determined their students should flourish in other ways. Miss Shepherd, despite poorly equipped practice sites, produced county champions at netball, players whose skills cast fear and dread into the hearts of every opposing school, and who were regarded with awe. But despite this achievement, some pupils still felt they were merely seen as ' factory fodder'. Clive Maton nevertheless enjoyed the factory visits which were laid on by local businesses to provide an insight into their world. 'At Arthurs' Press and Redlers we were given cream cakes for tea, and the Bon Marche trip was a pretty good day out too!'

For some pupils, there were courses at Stroud's new Technical College, which many progressed to after on leaving at fifteen.

Margaret Hawkes arrived in 1959, only a year before the move into comprehensive status at the newly built Archway. She also remembers the wide spread of the premises used for lessons. 'We spent a lot of time walking', she said, 'In fact we walked the whole of the first day I was there, visiting one classroom after another, back to school for lunch, and then off walking again, until we walked home!'

In 1959 almost all her lessons took place at Church Street in two rather gloomy classrooms, only English or games necessitated a trip to Rodborough.

During April 1960, Rodborough Secondary Modern moved lock, stock, and barrel to Archway, the younger pupils having a few days off, while the older ones helped to move the equipment. Gradually, the staff and pupils adjusted to their new name and increased space. Margaret clearly remembers Mr Loosley, in his new role as a comprehensive head, addressing them all on opening day in their spacious new hall. 'He stood on the platform and said how pleased he was to have this new school, but he feared it would never be big enough!', she said. How right he was, for the expansion did not match the future number of students, and within eighteen months terrapins began to appear, to cope with the extra pupils.

During the twenties, although grammar school education was far beyond the reach of average children with modest means, the technical schools provided an insight into an unexplored world. In 1920, my father, from a working-class family of six children, was one of the two accepted that year from Kingscourt elementary.

Mr Hall was the headmaster, and the skills which father gained within the school's walls enriched his life beyond measure. Violin tuition, taught by Mr Perry, would definitely have been beyond his grasp had he not attended Stroud Craft School. The extravagance for the family in fees was insignificant in comparison with the pleasure he gained thereafter. When I was a child, Christmas Day was when the violin usually had an airing. A rendering of 'Silent Night' on the piano sparked off a careful tuning ritual and an inevitable

Father at The Stroud Craft School. He is 2nd from the right in the third row.

snapped E-string. Today father's violin is no more; age and woodworm have hastened its demise, although a lovely fretwork medicine cabinet remains, as does a beaten copper plate, both relics of opportunities received by a lucky few during the first half of the century.

In 1945, in line with the technical school influence, the school changed names again to become Stroud Technical School for Boys. In 1944 Mike Hawkes from The Vatch started there, his third school, having previously attended Slad and Uplands which he left at eight years old. He recalls there were forty-four boys in his class, and 'no art lessons at all during wartime'. However, being artistically talented, he was able to attend the Art School part-time for two terms on Friday afternoons, frustratingly missing sports in the process, which was the real passion of his life.

His memory of changes during that time include the introduction of the school's first fifth form in 1948, which thereby initiated a five-year course, and a two-stream entry. Perusal of his ageing report book reveals that there were twenty-two in his class. One also notices a good technical drawing mark, 'for a quiet boy who could do better in time'.

144

Slad School in about 1939. Back Row L–R: Alan Green, Margaret Hearne, Barbara Thomas, Pat Ballenger, Roa Porter. Middle Row: Norman Holford, Claude Hearne, twins Pat and Jean Brooks, Dorothy Puttick, Maureen Edwards, Edgar Avery, Guy Gearson, ?, John Phillips. Front, seated: Mike Hawkes, Jean Phillips, Derrick West, Dougie Hearne, Norman Hooper, Raymond Holford, Jane Webb.

Slad School just before closure on September 5th 1966 after a long fight. The authorities felt the bank behind the school was unsafe, but it is still there today. L–R: Christopher Warner, Jefrey Close, Robert Smith, Grand Lewis, Clive McGovern, Hilary Gardiner, Delia Gardiner, Pauline Close, ? Gardiner, Andrew Broderick. The teacher is Miss Hicks and the Dinner Lady Mrs B Ballinger.

Keith, my husband, who was a pupil from 1954 chose to go to the 'Boys' Tech', 'because my friends wanted to go there.' He stayed until eighteen and emerged well-equipped in academic and practical work, with a determination to do everything properly. Keith's outstanding memory was of the canteen, which was by the railway, where the dinner was served in two sittings. Each table seated six boys with a senior boy at the head to dish out the food. On one occasion some salt hurled itself into Keith's custard, instilling an instant dislike of the stuff, which was never eaten again.

During Keith's schooldays, Mr Elliott (Chappie) was headmaster, and 'Ghandi' Levitt took English. 'Taffy' Evans was the history master, and Harry Cooke was the PE and RE master. 'Ganger' Neale was the metalwork master, and Marchant Stanley and Stan White taught woodwork. No external exams were taken until after the war. In 1961, when Keith took his exams, he had to walk over to the modern Stroud Technical College at Stratford Road every day.

At the outbreak of war the schools were crowded, and it became apparent that there were not enough teachers for the job. Any teacher who did well at college was automatically offered a degree course, as women were desperately needed in the classroom. One teacher remembers having fifty-six pupils in her class, and seats for only forty. 'I just prayed for a few to be ill', she said. As the war progressed, teaching materials became terribly short. 'You should see the scraps of paper we used. We tried to manage without too much writing.'

In 1944, to prepare for the new education system and the influx of teachers required to sustain it, an Emergency Training Scheme was introduced, which was a one-year intensive course in teaching. Training establishments, based in an assortment of unlikely buildings, provided classrooms for an estimated twenty thousand applicants from the Forces, civil defence, and industry, who over a five year period, in over fifty emergency colleges, boosted teacher numbers up to somewhere near the seventy thousand mark.

Stroud's schools were fortunate during wartime to retain an adequate compliment of staff, although they could have done with considerably more when the Handsworth Grammar School Boys and Edgbaston High School Girls arrived in September 1939. Margory Hook remembers then that High School evacuees only stayed a short while, so her classes were not disrupted too much. But the boys at the Marling were around much longer. The two schools had to split the day between them, one occupying the morning while the other took the afternoon. This, according to Wilf Merrett, led to overcrowding, the need to remove all his belongings from his desk, weekend classes, extended school hours, shorter holidays, and more homework. There were many extra pupils and some strange buses, which he descibes as a dirty maroon colour with Oldham Corporation Buses written on the side. One 'foreign' bus was a double-decker with an open stairway, and every schoolchild wanted to ride on it.

At Stroud High School for Girls and at Marling School, deep trenches occupied the school field. They were zig-zag, not straight, to prevent any bomb impact from carrying through, and were roofed with corrugated iron and covered with soil. They were equipped inside with benches on which pupils sat for practice sessions. Sirens were at Hill Paul's, and repeated by bells at school. When these sounded for practices every pupil went scurrying to the shelters, to claim their seat on the bench.

Both grammar schools played an important role in arranging billets and accommodating those with nowhere to go. During the black-out, most after school activities, social events, and games were abandoned, but pupils over sixteen were able to fire-watch, an activity which most enjoyed as they were paid, and it was treated as fun. At the Girls High School, the fire-watch room

Edward Godsell, who today farms at Church Farm, Leonard Stanley, with Jim Dickenson at Lampeter, Wales.

containing a couple of beds was 'in a little room off the back corridor', but the whole school was at their disposal. When Marjory Hook fire-watched with Joan Barnes, they went down Beards Lane for a walk in the middle of the night, which was terribly exciting as it was not the sort of thing they normally did.

Wilf left Marling in 1940, when Nick Carter was headmaster. 'Only the academic type went into the sixth form', he said. So he went to Erinoids, earning four and three farthings an hour, later raised to sixpence. Here he worked in the colour shop, mixing and matching the colours, before proper manufacturing in the main plant took over. Wilf, however, did not reach his increase in pay, for sensing that the cellulose acetate involved in plastic production was unhealthy, he left for the planning office at Newman Henders, valve production, and twenty-five shillings a week. Eventually he went to Aston Down, and then Horsa Gliders in 1942.

In 1934 Jim Dickenson first attended Slad School, moving to Marling and Form 1 at nine, and remaining until the age of twelve. The fee was £5 a year, and the headmaster was Nick Carter, but a master known as 'Tramp' was the teacher all the pupils feared. The prevailing silence in class as his footsteps echoed down the corridor was the reason for his nickname. The next move was

The Parrott Family leaving Peterwell in Lampeter by horse for their trek home to Stonehouse after the war. Mr PJ Parrott was a master at Wycliffe college which was evacuated to St David's College Lampeter from 1939–1945.

Wycliffe College, where he spent three years, and then Lampeter in Wales after the Air Ministry commandeered the Wycliffe buildings.

Jim says the schools encouraged their pupils to join some organization to assist the war effort. For many it was the Sea Cadets, the Air Training Corps, or perhaps the Home Guard. Jim joined the ATC and experienced a complete 'turnover' manoeuvre on his first flight in a Tiger Moth, with a Czech instructor, who was on a rest period from his squadron. Three weeks later, everyone was shocked to hear that the Czech had been killed in combat.

Although Technical schools received financial assistance from the Council for their buildings, and moral support from educational authorities who supported their progressive schemes, the grammar schools had to survive mainly on donations from benefactors, charities, boarding and tuition fees, and means tested grants from the Council. The passing of years, and increase in pupil numbers had led to a shortage of space, and although the girls' school acquired their new hall and other additions in 1939, Marling's accommodation was very cramped. With financial control now firmly in the hands of Gloucestershire

County Council following the Education Act, hopes for improvements to Downfield's delapidated buildings rose, only to be dashed time and time again, when other essentials claimed the County's money. Moreover, when presented with the end of the war and an ensuing buoyant economy they did not finance the grammar schools, but launched into their building plan (which was implemented in the Act), which was not for Moderns as anticipated but for the new Comprehensive system, with designs on equality for all. Therefore Stroud's Grammar and Technical Schools were again left behind to wait for desperately needed improvements.

Educational reform enabled everyone, regardless of means, to have a chance of education. This was increased further in 1947 when the leaving age was raised to fifteen, with plans to increase it to sixteen. Subsidized school meals were provided, with dining rooms, free milk, dental and medical services, and (in secondary schools), gyms, assembly halls, libraries, art and projector rooms, and playing fields for all.

Stroud High School suddenly had a shower room. This was a positive nightmare for new pupils, such as myself, aged just eleven. Naked as the day we were born, we walked self-consciously around its strategically aimed water nozzles, one hand protecting our attributes, while the other held the towel around our head. Afterwards, the towels were put to dry in a heated towel room which, as first year nerves evaporated and confidence grew, served (albeit somewhat smelly), as a perfect haven in which to hide during cold winter break times.

A favourite mistress was Miss Parsons, who taught English and wore a flamboyant black and purple cloak. Friday afternoon English lessons could sometimes result in stories of the London blitz, and mysterious tales of nights when she and her sister shared a double bed in an old house where ghosts dripped blood (only a tap actually) in the dark crevices of the room. At other times we learned great chunks of poetry from The Golden Treasury, 'Water, water everywhere, nor any drop to drink,' from the Ancient Mariner, or a page or two from the Lady of Shalott. Miss Parsons promised us a version of this favourite volume if we sent her a piece of wedding cake on our marriage. I did not, but a couple of the girls did and were surprisingly rewarded with a lovely leather Golden Treasury by which to remember her.

Having school playing fields again changed the school day. When Kingscourt Primary School pupils were let loose in the school field, a small paddock across the lane, freedom entered our lives. The hedges became dens, we ran, and played rounders, or rocked and day-dreamed on the old uprooted tree stump in the corner. Sometimes we sat on the grassy slope during long dinner hours, singing 'Coming Round the Mountain', 'Ten Green Bottles', or 'Old Macdonald's Farm' with our playground supervisor, before the bell summoned us back into class.

Miss Roberts helped us to cultivate gardens by scratching out the turf and drilling in the seeds. Flowers bloomed and a few vegetables grew. It was all so much better than broad beans in a jar. Our field was never smooth and manicured, but wild and interesting, and no inter-school matches were ever played on it. It is built over now. It ceased to be needed when the school closed, but whoever had the idea of school fields was a genius.

Education did not exclude the Forces men and women who needed to adjust back into civilian life. The authorities realized that the current circumstances could prove difficult for those whose lifestyle had changed so dramatically and allotted a few hours compulsory education for them on all manner of subjects. This was to prepare them for demobilization and future employment at home.

CHAPTER THIRTEEN

GETTING TO WORK

The year of 1947 had begun with one of the severest winters on record, the coldest of the century. There was a wet autumn in 1946, and an appallingly bitter, snowy, and lengthy winter, and the resulting cool spring, and disastrous flooding warded off any warmth until the end of May. May Day itself was a mere forty degrees, and most trees and vegetation remained in extended dormancy, which heralded reduced crops, financial losses approaching £1,000 and subsidy grants of £15 an acre for potatoes, £10 for sugar beet, and £5 for oats.

There had been hints around the previous Easter-time, but the euphoria of peace combined with Easter weddings had masked the problem. The people queuing for oranges and bananas in holiday mood were blissfully oblivious of such things.

In July 1946, bread had to be rationed, and housewives took to using oatmeal, and purchased the 'National Loaf' while complaining of its wholemeal content. Mother says a National loaf never entered our house as, 'Mr Cooper always produced a white one for us from somewhere in his van!' but I fear she was misled, as all bakers were forced to use the same standardized flour. For Stroud's bakers, the rationing of flour was, 'An utter disaster.'

Hardings Bakery, which had been purchased from Percy Goddard in 1933, was originally at Whitehall and then, from 1938, at Cowle Road. During the war, they produced the 'National Loaf' and only managed to make pastry products about twice a week. Their allocation of flour was calculated on what they had used the previous year, which made life difficult when they needed more through expansion of the business. Sometimes they were able to buy flour from another baker who needed to cut down, perhaps through war, and who had an excess.

To keep the price of bread down, there was a bread subsidy of about 1*d* or 2*d* a loaf which meant a large loaf was 4$\frac{1}{2}$*d* and a small one 2$\frac{1}{2}$*d*. Bakers were regarded as having top priority for fuel, and Hardings used coke, only

The Harding Bakery Ford van, reg. DG7575 on Weston sands in 1935. L–R: Eileen Harding, Granny Beale, Florence Harding (née Taylor), Elizabeth Harding (née Beale). Colin Harding is in the driving seat.

Colin Harding seeing the first lot of flour down from a bulk white flour tank and a new Redler conveyor (possibly the first in Gloucestershire) following installation in 1965.

*Leonard Stanley's Bakery last day of baking
and delivery before Mr Wother's retirement.*

converting to gas in about 1950, when new equipment was installed. The baking began at 4.30 a.m. in those days. They often went on to deliver as well, and could sometimes be delivering up until 6 p.m. around Uplands, Tower Hill, or Bisley Road. Mr Harding remembers people ate a lot of bread then. 'You could load a van and sell the lot to Summer Street alone'.

The floods came in March when the snow melted on the hills. Titch Neale was the Sunday paper delivery boy for Henry Marriott, around the Bisley district, which had been cut off from civilization by the blizzards for several weeks. As at least two weeks' supplies of papers had arrived by train and were awaiting delivery, Titch, assisted by Gordon Ponting and Bryan Durn, and egged on by Henry, loaded up a sledge, and set off towards Bisley, by way of fields and over walls, despite the concern of the boys' parents. The drifting snow had made the roads inpassable. Towards Stancombe Corner, where the snow was telegraph-pole high, Titch disappeared from view as he fell through the roof of a Riley car, hidden beneath a massive mound of snow. Further along, they encountered a double-decker bus with an open staircase, whose upper deck was at least a foot deep in snow.

The horsedrawn Co-op bread cart at Leonard Stanley.

Bryan Durn, and school mates at Parliament Street School in the snow of 1947. The photograph was taken by the headmaster Mr William Smith. Back L–R: Bryan Durn, Douglas Harding, June Jordon. Bottom: Constance Gobey, Valerie Wheeler, Jean Hodges, Gordon Ponting.

Car in the snow at Stancombe.

On approaching Bisley, they encountered twenty or thirty men digging themselves out. Seeing the boys with their stock of newspapers they said, 'Go on down to the village'. So Titch and Gordon dumped the papers, in return for the hot drinks and bread and jam given them by grateful Sunday paper readers, before making their way home through walls of snow 12 to 15 feet high.

Another time during this icy spell, the local milkman, Frank Boulton, was unable to deliver as he could not reach the farm to fetch his supplies. Though fierce winds drove the snow back again as soon as they had dug it out, a gang of kids from the top of the town dug out a channel as far as Farmer Hiram's farm, just wide enough to get out two churns and enable Frank to carry out his deliveries. Frank, a bachelor, was quite a character. He always wore leggings and a pork-pie hat, and delivered the milk using a hand trolley.

Tuesday 4 March sticks out in Jack Ireland's mind as a day to remember, as it was the day his bus got stuck in the snow for three days on the Bisley Road, with snow up to the windows. (It was most probably the one encountered by our paper delivery boys). Throughout the lengthy winter, snow had alternated with freezing conditions. On this particular day, the Western National sent

This Western National Bus was trapped in the snow between Stancombe and Bisley from March 4th 1947, until it was dug out by those pictured on March 7th. L–R: A Ryland, H Morris, W Hill, C Larner, V Watkins.

word to the relevant factories, such as Hill Pauls and Holloways, to warn them the last bus to Oakridge would leave at 3.30 p.m. Near Myers Lane, a car was stuck in the road, and the bus was unable to pass. Within only a short time the snow had drifted and travellers had to begin their walk home. Only one passenger remained on the bus, because her mobility was inhibited by an iron calliper. With Jack's assistance, and kindly accommodation at the Pike House, she too left the bus, and Jack was fetched down by a breakdown lorry.

The floods which resulted when the snow thawed caused the old tried and tested wartime emergency services to leap into action as before. The Red Cross, together with the St Johns Ambulance and their mobile canteen, were readily on hand to distribute tea, soup, hot pies, and sandwiches to stranded victims around the St Mary's Square area in Gloucester. A precariously-balanced plank between two doorsteps was often their sole access to those flooded. Where the water was too deep, Gloucester Rowing Club assisted with their boats. They were manned by Rangers and Sea Cadets distributing food, blankets, and clothing, which had been hastily transported from London overnight.

Roderick (Roddy) Smith's van in the snow at Bisley in 1963.

Doris Nipper with her grandson Robert Smith, in the Slad lane leading to Down Court in 1963, following several days of being cut off.

The spring remained cold even when the flooding has subsided, until quite suddenly, towards the end of May, summer arrived with a flourish. The August temperatures rose to remain well up in the seventies until the late autumn, until inevitably we had a drought!

By 1946 the German Prisoners of War, many of whom had worked on farms throughout the district, had returned home, and Britain's four-and-a half million servicemen and women were returning to a financially deflated and war-damaged country. Employment was plentiful, due to the Civil Employment job reinstatement plan which guaranteed work or training if none was forthcoming. Servicemen in no rush to join another organized body survived for a while on tiding-over sums or 'bounty', which was calculated according to rank and length of service. A woman's grant could be £146, but men had proportionally less because of their free suit.

John Powell, a gunner in the Navy for four-and-a-half years came home with £62 along with his free suit, a grey herring-bone overcoat and a trilby. When his family saw him dressed in this fashion, especially the hat, which he did not normally wear, they reacted with, 'Whatever do you look like!', and his coat and trilby duly formed the basis of a guy which they burned on the bonfire before the week was out.

Ted Hewer went to Exeter to be measured for his demob suit, where he picked out the style he liked, together with a shirt, tie, shoes and hat. Great coats, he said, could be kept for a couple of pounds, but all the other equipment had to be handed back. He and his wife Thelma, who was a nurse during the war, 'and a jolly good one', lived in the beginning with Ted's parents, while adding their name to the council housing list. However, following eighteen months running a grocery shop in Gloucester High Street, which did not do too well due to the limitation of goods, they moved to a cottage at The Heavens at Lypiatt, which had no electricity, required every drop of water to be fetched from the spring, and cost £1,200.

The gradual process of putting the country straight was already under way, a horrendous, lengthy task for the blitzed regions, but simpler for Stroud. Here, trenches across fields and commons were filled in by bulldozers, anti-invasion hazards and defence blocks were removed, and the old trough at Stroud's Sims Clock was broken up. Army huts disappeared from numerous camps throughout the district, and factories, at last released from government work, set about refurbishing their equipment, amid urges from the government, 'to revive their business and production lines, and get on with the exports'.

The woollen industry, with its numerous mills dotted through the Stroud valley, overlooked by the grand clothiers' houses from the hillsides above, had made Stroud wealthy. But due to many factors, including overseas competition, synthetic fibres, and a failure to update machinery and methods, a pre-war decline had set in. Mills had gradually closed down, or been converted to other types of manufacture, such as walking sticks, plastics, and engineering. In consequence, over three hundred thousand workers were lost from the textile industry's 1938 workforce of 1,126,000. The number of workers dropped dramatically to 687,000 in 1946. This was disastrous for an industry whose labour force once far outnumbered any other in England. Benefiting from this loss were the rapidly-escalating engineering businesses whose pre-war 862,000 work-force increased to 1,240,000 by 1946.

War produced an unnatural textile boom which lasted for several years, at first producing cloth and tailoring for the Forces' uniforms, followed by the expansive post-war production necessary to replace the shortages at home, and revitalize exports. To ensure full production, Poles and Irish immigrants were employed to bolster up the work-force, and the mills bustled with activity getting the orders out. Actually, however, realistically Stroud's textile heyday was over, and as the fifties and sixties approached, many industries closed down, their gradual fall into disuse setting in along with the obsolete canals beside them. A few old faithfuls remained: Howard and Powell's at Wallbridge, Marling and Evans at Stanley, Winterbotham, and Strachan and Playne at Lodgemore and Longfords. Each company continued producing cloth which was renowned and respected throughout the world.

An abundance of skills had developed because of the war. Steel, aircraft, and shipbuilding production improved. Electronics and radio, chemicals, plastics, and the motor industry also flourished along with an increasing consumer market. Full employment, an expanded education, and an expectation of better things to come, encouraged people to spend. A spate of new modern premises to suit the modern lightweight industries began to appear, the higher wages, and subsequent comfortable conditions, drawing in an enlightened and educated work-force to increase productivity and exports.

In 1946, the Labour Government launched a production drive through all aspects of industry, designed to instruct the British labour force in the importance of increased production. Their campaign, entitled, 'A Fair Day's Work for a Fair Day's Pay', was conducted in pamphlets, films, and factory pep talks, which explained ways of beating the increasing fuel shortage, and its influence over production.

Strachan's chairman, forecasting the struggle ahead, explained how if just one loom stopped work for only ten minutes, many yards of cloth would be lost. This would be a financial disaster when one yard was worth 20s. Needless to say, the forty-hour week, dreamed of by so many, was scorned by the businessmen who felt that, 'Machines should not stand idle, they should be kept running for double that time!' Their offered bonuses helped the workers to understand.

Marling and Evans, however, approached the problem in another way, by installing quicker, and quieter, twenty-four-hour Swiss automatic looms which were said to double production.

Long-established companies who had been commandeered for munitions work, such as Hoffmans, Daniels and Newman Henders had to rebuild their trade. Newman and Henders, in fact, who had produced a variety of munitions throughout both world wars while employing thousands of employees, had lost several outlets. However, public company status came in 1948, and, following the purchase of the Trowbridge firm of G.N. Haden and Sons in 1947, increased production of forged steel valves for the petroleum industry.

Endeavouring to increase nationwide post-war productivity, the government embarked on a drive to entice an estimated ninety-two thousand woman back into full or part-time work.

Women in the Stroud district were spoilt for choice when choosing a job. This was an area where so much of the industry traditionally suited female skills. The hundred-year-old Holloways clothing factory alone employed over two hundred women on their machines, with just a few men for cutting and pressing.

Ivy Lusty, 'at ninety five going with the year', began her working life at thirteen years of age at Holloways, where she earned three shillings a week. Her job had been arranged by her widowed mother, who worked there. On her first day she went off to work happily, but a problem arose when the School Board discovered Ivy was under age (fourteen was the school leaving age). So, very soon, Jimmy Morgan, the school attendance officer, was knocking at the door asking Ivy's granny where she was. It seems the family should have consulted the School Board, from whom they probably would have received a sympathetic hearing, if they had stated their case. For the moment, however, officialdom reigned and Ivy was sent back to school, but only a fortnight later she was allowed to return to Holloways, where she stayed for the next fifty years.

Ivy recalls that Holloway's suit and shirt production dropped when the war drew near. Men realized that new clothes would not be needed if they went off to fight, as the Forces provided all their clothes. So by the time war broke out and Holloway's male employees left the work-force, the gap was not too noticeable. The demand of work had already dropped and. as most employees were women machinists, there were enough remaining to produce the khaki Army uniform which the factory was assigned to manufacture throughout the war. The demand for suits did not even increase when the war ended. The Forces demob suits adequately covered several years of wear!

Some women did leave the factories along with the men when war came, but their departure was not for fighting, but to make more money in munitions' factories, such as Daniel's, making shells.

The shift and piece-work system was a godsend to women entering employment following the war. Shifts provided flexible working hours, which enabled adjustment to domestic routine, and piece-working gave an incentive

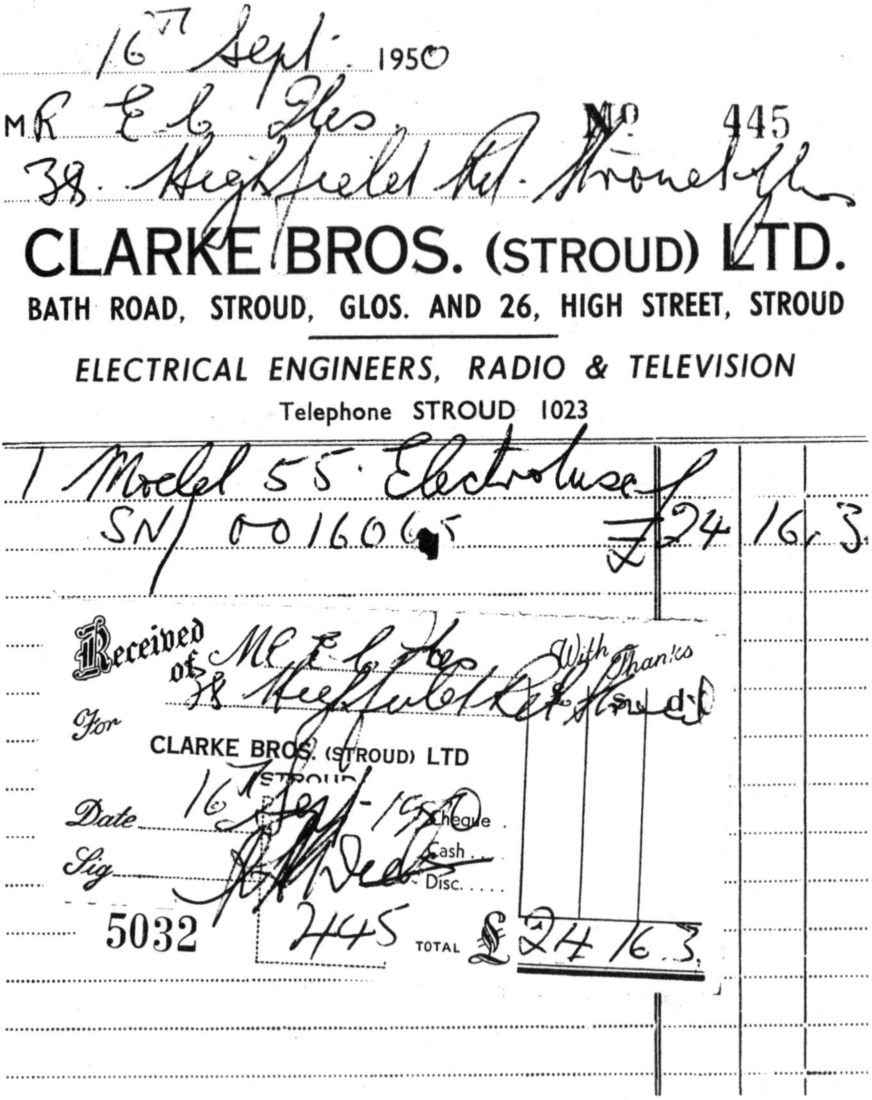

16ᵗʰ Sept. 1950

Mr E C Yes
No. 445
38. Highfield Rd. Stonehouse

CLARKE BROS. (STROUD) LTD.

BATH ROAD, STROUD, GLOS. AND 26, HIGH STREET, STROUD

ELECTRICAL ENGINEERS, RADIO & TELEVISION

Telephone STROUD 1023

1 Model 55 Electrolux

SN 0016065   £24 16 3

Received of Mr E C Yes   With Thanks

For 38 Highfield Rd Stroud

CLARKE BROS. (STROUD) LTD
STROUD

Date 16 Sep -1950

Sig

Cheque
Cash
Disc.

5032   445   TOTAL £ 24 16 3

Clarke Bros Electrolux receipt in 1950.

162

to work harder and earn more money. When working a five-day week system, women piece-workers (Class A) at Strachans earned 61s a week, 59s 3d if Class B. Even girls under eighteen could earn 47s 6d.

Therefore large numbers of women, once compulsory commandeered into wartime working, now changed their minds about staying at home, responded to the government's pleas, and re-entered the employment realm. The benefits of peacetime work were realized by the money in their pockets.

Wartime conscription proved that the traditional role of housewife no longer took all day; electricity and piped water had lessened the load. Now, their money opened the door to a huge variety of labour-saving aids arriving in the shops, providing they had the coupons.

Many women still preferred work traditionally associated with their sex, such as school cleaning, helping in the home and shop work. A cleaner earned £39 a year, a home help £3 10s a week, and a shop assistant at Clark's shoe shop could receive 62s for a forty-five hour week. In service employment, predominantly work for women for centuries, was decidedly on the decline, although the vacancies columns were still full of such jobs.

The increased school-leaving age, expanded education, and a general move towards middle-class living, determined other work choices. The long, restrictive, unsocial hours of living-in positions were shunned when other work was offered. Consequently, ladies who had previously been reliant on cook and parlour maids, resorted instead to their own labour-saving devices, such as wielding a vacuum cleaner (which could be purchased from Currys for £6 0s 3d).

Gradually, then, a change overtook a woman's day. The independence gained through work, and money in the pocket, brushed aside the leisurely pre-war afternoon tea habit. The factory tea break, works outings, and socials, replaced them. Domestic duties were performed at evenings and weekends, the family's tea was prepared following a day at work.

Ada, having left munitions' work at Hoffmans in the middle of the war, on production of a doctor's certificate, and a baby due, had little desire to return to work. The rush to Cainscross to catch the works' double-decker, the shortage of seats, her long fortnightly night shifts, all for £3 a week, were still fresh in her mind. She would happily remain at home for a little while longer!

CHAPTER FOURTEEN

THE FREEDOM FROM ILLNESS

National Health Insurance, in which employees, together with their employers and the State combined, was introduced by Lloyd George for the working classes in 1911. A compulsory contribution benefited men whose income was £250 p.a. or under, but excluded women (unless they worked for payment, which few did) and children. It entitled the family bread-winner to sickness benefit, and a doctor's services, but no optical or dental treatment. There was nothing at all for their wives or children, only a £2 grant when wives were pregnant. When their dependants needed any health services they had to pay.

Doctors charged for visits, or ran a sixpenny or shilling surgery, which often involved their wife and a maid, and was conducted from their own home. Their sitting-room doubled up as a waiting room, with a corner curtained off to provide for scales and measures. Tried and tested medicines such as Mist, Morph, Magnesium, Trisilicate (for stomachs) and Ipecacuanha (for coughs) were dispensed by the doctor. All the medicines were numbered, labelled, and corked in old-fashioned bottles. Anything more elaborate was provided on prescription by the chemist, working closely with the doctor. Every patient attending the surgery expected to be prescribed something.

The charge in 1942 was around 3s 6d when patients came to the surgery, and 5s when they were visited at home. If they genuinely could not afford to pay, the doctor did not ask for anything.

In 1942, the qualification required to become a doctor was five years training, after which application for medical registration could be made, and then the doctor went into practice. In wartime, a Resident House Officer employed by the Local Authority, had board and lodging provided with a clear £3 for personal use.

A substantial part of a doctor's practice was on the private side, maternity being a major portion. In addition there were branch surgeries in villages, usually in someone's house, and child welfare clinics, both of which continued well into the fifties. Doctors running such a practice between the wars could run a car, live in a comfortable home and employ a maid. In pre-war days, no

PHONE
STROUD 43.

AT HOME
MORNINGS 9—10.30 A.M.
EVENINGS 6—7.30 P.M.
FRIDAY EVENINGS EXCEPTED.

Waldringfield,

Stroud, Glos.

1·10·43.

Mr. Isles.

38. Highfields Avenue.

To Dr. W. G. B. Halliden.

For Professional Services, etc.

Sept.

£2 . 13 .

With Compliments.

Received with Thanks
W. G. Halliden M.D.

4/11/43

Receipt for payment from Dr Halliden in 1943.

165

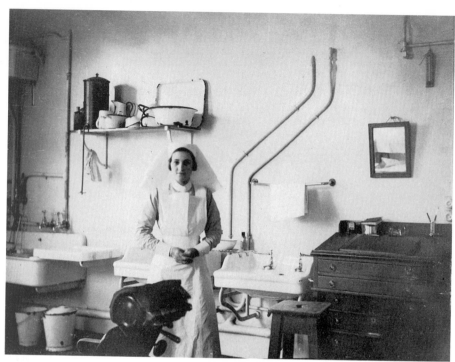

Nurse Price at Stroud General Hospital.

one called the doctor out unnecessarily, working-class expectations were not high, most people accepted without question what the doctor advised and did as they were told (but sometimes the affluent might demand a second opinion).

War highlighted the need for the reform of health and medical care. War service created a shortage of nurses at home, a total shortfall of three thousand nurses throughout the country. Persuading women to return to the nursing profession was difficult, as there were an abundance of other less demanding employment. Hospitals tried to reduce nurses' working hours to forty a week to tempt them back, and training schemes for older women and home helps, caring for patients at home, began. Still the immense pressure upon nurses' shoulders during wartime caused many to avoid following that road again when peace came. Doctors still retained their position of respect, and the District Nurse remained the main medical practitioner for the working-class sick. She provided her services twenty-four hours a day, seven days a week, with no relief system for her at all. Her services cost 1d per week (4s 4d per annum), or 1s for non-subscribers. Her workload had increased substantially

166

since 1939, alongside wartime marriages and births, which had risen by a third during the six years of war. For the nurse, there was little time to relax, for even following an all-night delivery, her daily visits still had to be done. Most of those in her care could not afford a visit from the doctor. Gloucestershire's charge for the doctor was 7s 6d a visit, far too expensive for a farm worker, whose pay averaged 30s a week. This situation resulted in many district nurses making two or three visits to a sick child or baby in a day, to save the family the doctor's bill.

The midwifery fee, including all antenatal visits, supervising the labour and delivery, with twice-daily visits for three days, and a daily one until the fourteenth day, was £1. But if a doctor was engaged for antenatal observance, delivery supervision, and postnatal care, his very presence increased the fee to £1 5s.

Hospital care was completely different, having until 1948 been organized in two separate parts; voluntary and Local Authority Hospitals, each operating and funded differently.

The 'voluntary' hospital was usually general in treatment, self-financing and therefore free from government intervention. Funds came through insurance schemes, charitable bodies, school contributions, and donations from wealthy industries in the district. Others, including some well-known ones in London, provided teaching and research work, and were therefore equipped with adequate facilities, unlike some of the smaller 'voluntarys', whose equipment was meagre in comparison.

Stroud General Hospital, built in 1875, received its income from church collections, businesses, financial institutions and donations, along with sundry other items, including toys, books, fruit, and cigarettes. All donations were listed in the *Stroud News and Journal* for everyone to read.

Patients on incomes of £6 or less could receive free treatment, but a hospital insurance fund, where for a few pence weekly, contributors could receive free treatment for themselves and their family, was also in operation. There were also 'panel' patients, who were working-class men registered with a doctor who received a state capitation fee in recompense for their care.

It seems that the only problem with the hospital contribution system was the fact that it only covered the hospital to which the contribution was paid. One pregnant Stroud lady was required to attend Gloucester Hospital for an average of six weeks on each of her three confinements (which resulted in caesarian section deliveries), and was very worried about the resulting bill. Luckily her former employer, who donated substantially to both Stroud and Gloucester Hospitals, was able to assure her that her contributions would adequately cover the cost.

Later the same lady was again worried over costs when kidney trouble necessitated doctor's visits for the better part of three weeks, including a

Sunday visit, which cost more. She says, 'Doctor Newton said I looked worried, and I told him I was worried about paying. He said, "We'll meet the problem when we come to it", and when it did come, he just charged me £2 for all those visits'.

Local Authority hospitals, twice as many in number as voluntarys, had operated since 1929, treating mainly infectious diseases and maternity cases. Their buildings, in both sombreness and appearance, originated from the old poor law hospitals.

A revised health service, 'A General Medical Service for the Nation', inaugurated by The British Medical Association in 1939, did not materialize because of the war. Proof that it was needed soon appeared, as hospitals were swiftly equipped with more beds, accommodation, and operating theatres. Future plans heralded the amalgamation of hospitals, an end of buying and selling practices, and group health centres.

Initially, the British Medical Association was keen to back the improved medical structure planned for the future. However, when Aneurin Bevan, the Minister of Health, arrived on the scene in 1942, and politics became involved, their attitude changed. The members, professional independent status became their concern, instead of the overall sweeping plans previously considered. Although assured by Bevan that, all would be treated fairly and well rewarded, the medical profession felt their liberty would be infringed, and the end of private practices would take away their choice. Moreover, the nationalization of voluntary hospitals worried practitioners, who felt their profession would be completely taken over, and governed by the State.

Bevan, endeavouring to win the consultants over, assured the surgeons, physicians, and obstetricians that they would, as before, be allowed to continue in private practice, retain their hospital pay beds, the doctor capitation system, and merit points for those on committees. But they were not convinced and, throughout the three-day debate in April 1946, representatives of the BMA strongly opposed the scheme, with objections of ninety per cent, and many refusals to join.

Much discussion followed during the next year, but with little compromise. A conference at Gloucester's Guildhall, packed with sceptical doctors announced the proposed system was, 'grossly at variance with the essential principles of our profession, and should be rejected absolutely by all practices'. A few words were said in its favour, by a Stroud doctor who suffered unmerciful heckling in consequence. Another doctor, latching on to cost, thought a further service added to the National Assistance scheme (issuing grants to people in need) would add to production in industry costs, pointing out, 'Look how coal prices have increased since the mines have been nationalized!' A vote of 170–2 showed the meeting's general feelings.

Debates, and yet another vote of no confidence, continued until six months

The old-fashioned dispensary at Smiths the Chemists, in the High Street, Stroud prior 1963. Note the DDA (Dangerous Drugs) Cupboard, the array of bottles with which to make up medicines, and the stack of wrapping paper which was sealed with wax. Mrs Sheila Waters, (the owner) recalls prescriptions were a shilling per item during the 1950s.

before the National Health Services was due to commence, causing Bevan, with scarcity of time, to amend the Act, and abandon full-time salaries. However, at the same time he launched into a public publicity campaign, wherein application forms and registering with a doctor was advised. This was an obvious move against doctors, as those not complying could end up with no patients at all to treat.

Consequently, when midnight arrived on 5 July 1948, ninety per cent of doctors were pratically forced to assume involvement in the new National Health Service, along with dentists, opticians, and pharmacists.

Not everyone registered overnight. Committing oneself to a doctor was a gradual process spanning many months, the patients often not bothering until they were ill and needing his services. Soon, any doctor who had opted out realized they were losing patients, along with their regular annual payment, which through the scheme had yielded so much per patient per year.

There was a glut of doctors requiring work after the war. Most desired to set up in practice in regular, secure, financially sound positions. The end of buying practices, together with the basic and capitation fees system, and the country

The interior of Smiths before modernisation in 1963, with shelves packed with goods and Same Day Film Developing Service done by themselves.

divisions, which avoided over-doctoring in compact areas, enabled joining a practice to become possible. Those doctors who settled in remote districts obtained extra to cover the extra travelling.

To the man and woman in the street, the NHS was an overwhelming success, once its full implications were realized. It was a provision which removed the expense of illness, health care, and old age. Many could not understand that it was actually free (some still tried to pay the doctor), the long-standing tradition of undemanding expectation was difficult to cast off overnight. People had learned to put up with their ailments, most only resorting to consulting the doctor in dire emergencies. As most doctors worked in single practices on twenty-four hour call this was just as well, although many were called out three or four times each week, some several times in one night. Often a call would be awaiting them when they returned following a night out, and wives were even known to ring local businesses, requesting they 'stop the doctor's car' to prevent a return trip later. As patient numbers increased due to the National Health Scheme, arrangements were sometimes made between doctors to enable a regular night off.

For England's citizens, the chance to have health care throughout their lives into old age (the Willows at Eastington opened within four years), a free ambulance service (people had to carry their sick to hospital previously rather than call on one), dental treatment, false teeth, proper eye tests and proper lenses, seemed untrue. It was an impossible dream.

People with low incomes had rarely received eye care before, although eye examinations, tests for glasses, tooth extractions and minor operations were conducted when paid for. Previously, referral to an optician incurred expense, not just once for the consultation, but again on purchasing their spectacles. This situation resulted in sufferers simply going along to Woolworths, where numerous types of spectacles were on show, to test their own eyes on the glasses there and buying the ones which felt right, for about 2s a pair.

Dentistry fell into the same category, many working-class people only having visited a dentist when racked with pain, or through an insurance scheme, a visit to the Lady Almoner at Stroud Hospital, together with payment of 5s. Now they could attend their chosen dentist, confident in the knowledge that they could be rid of all their teeth, and within the week be the smiling owner of a perfect set of false ones, without spending a penny.

A visiting dental service was available for schools, where inspections, with relevant treatment, were conducted in a classroom especially set aside for the purpose. When Kingscourt Primary School's pupils endured these visits, a certain tension prevailed all day as the children yet to be inspected listened to the low, steady grind of the drill through the thin partition wall. Would they soon also be receiving the same torture?

We were fortunate at our school to have Mr James as our visiting dentist. He

The Stroud Mutual Benefit Approved Society.

(266).   **Men and Women.**

Head Office—9, LANSDOWN, STROUD.

TEL.: 120.

Date _____

Member's No. _943_ _9316_

M _rs_ _OM Iles_

Address _____

Dear Sir (or Madam),

    In reply to your application for Dental Treatment I am to inform you that the Committee have agreed to your obtaining same at the expense of the Society to the extent of £ _3 : 15 : 0_ , the balance to be paid by yourself to the Dentist, is £ _2 : 12 : 6_ .

Yours faithfully,

BWBolwer

Secretary.

Stroud Mutual Benefit Society Dental Treatment application form.

Receipt from GB Limbrick for examination and spectacles in 1939.

realized the unpleasantness of it all and tried to put us at our ease. He succeeded admirably with me who, having undergone one bad experience under gas with another dentist at when only five years old, was nervous it might happen again. But Mr James did not use gas, preferring to deaden all feeling with the needle, and back up the anaesthetic with his calm one-sided conversation on interesting subjects. This detracted from the investigative lights, picks, drills, and all other dentistry paraphernalia. Through Mr James my confidence returned, and he was my only dentist until he retired. Even my husband, a bad experience similar to mine having determined his twenty-odd years of tooth decay, sought pain relief in the sanctuary of his chair, where several months of repair work ensured the James family a good meal or two, and determined no further work on Keith's teeth for several years.

The new NHS paid the dentists differently from the doctors. Basically, the doctors were paid to do the minimum work, the length of their patient list providing their income, while the dentists needed to do the maximum, their payment coming from the quantity of work achieved. Consequently, hard work and long hours could make dentists a fortune, a situation which brought an influx of dentists from Ireland, Australia, and New Zealand into this country during the late forties and early fifties.

The new system produced full waiting rooms and a massive work-load. A Stroud doctor remembers, 'Everyone came in the beginning. A waiting room of thirty people would greet you, and you wondered how you would get through them all'. The patient, of course, had no trouble remembering his lengthy wait if he had not ensured early arrival.

There was an increase in surgical operations. Some were a consequence of wartime injuries, but many were from the long backlog of hernias and prolapses, some grossly enlarged because of the wait. Shortly, minor operations boomed in a wave of popularity. Tonsils and adenoids which were thought to be diseased were removed as a natural occurrence. Both had 'bottle display' potential as proof of the ordeal. My tonsils were taken out when I was six, during a three day spell in hospital, with the operation taking place under gas. I was told to watch for the balloon to burst when the time came to put me out. I suppose it did burst, for the next thing I knew I was back in bed, face down in a pillow of blood. I did not need to see my tonsils, my sore throat reminded me they had gone!

The sudden availability of nursing supplies were probably noticed by hospitals and nursing staff first. Vast quantities of bandages and dressings were readily available, unseen in such abundance before. District nurses had been accustomed to carry old sheets and cloth remnants along with them for dressings when visiting patients, and also relying on the people's natural thrift, causing them to habitually save old linen for cutting up.

The National Health Service offered a much improved maternity service.

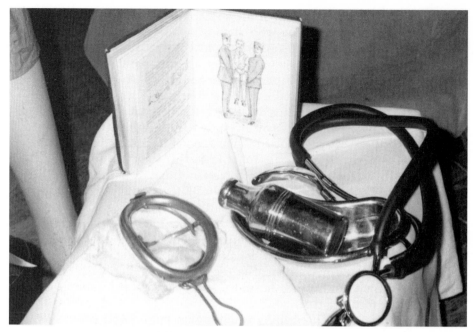

1930s Anaesthetic Kit using ether.

Districts were reorganized, and a relief system was introduced. District nurses now had one day off each week, and a free weekend each month, and with doctor's visits now free, patients could call them out, as they had previously summoned the nurse!

Moreover, it became routine for a doctor to drive round with the nurse, combining antenatal and general visits, a support for the nurse, and a saving on both time and mileage.

But the National Health Service did not yet produce Stroud's long-awaited Maternity hospital. This remained just a dream for another five years. Mothers still gave birth at home assisted by their District nurse, arriving now by car instead of on a bicycle. Emergency cases still travelled to Tetbury, Cirencester, or Cheltenham's Sunnyside, which was a long way when every minute counted.

The Council considered several alternatives when contemplating the site of the Maternity Hospital. Rodborough Manor, offered by Miss Lee Godfrey, with a capacity for thirty beds, was at one time the subject of many months of meetings. Eventually all other possibilities were discarded in preference to a

The Stanley Infant Welfare began in 1948 at Kings Stanley with Doctor O'Dowd (Senior). Previously because the County refused to pay for a village welfare, Doris Hale had kept the welfare foods in her home in a cupboard which was supplied by the authorities 'for on the spot allocation'. Once she and her husband Ernest were woken at 5.30 am by a father desperate to buy some powdered milk for his baby before leaving for work.

purpose-built new unit, to be built on hospital ground across from Stroud General, overlooking Rodborough Common.

Stroud's new maternity acquisition was a long, low, bright building, equipped with two five-bedded wards, a double ward, and several single rooms.

It opened in April 1953, under the control of Miss Haskins, the Matron, and staffed by three sisters, three midwives, and several orderlies. There, babies arrived to more peace than those poor souls nearly a decade before in January 1944, such as Ada and Leslie's second daughter Mary who was greeted with anti-aircraft fire from nearby Brockworth. 'I told everybody it wasn't only the Royalty who had a gun salute when their babies were born', joked Ada.

However, royalty did have some slight influence on Stroud's long-awaited maternity hospital, when the first baby born there was a girl, who was naturally christened Elizabeth, having being born in Coronation Year.

But for the average family, National Health meant free prescriptions, and their popularity led to the downfall of the free service. Within three years, prescriptions proved so costly, they became impossible to continue in their present unpaid form, and charges were introduced. This was one cause of Aneurin Bevan's resignation in 1951. Realistically, of course, nothing was free, funding came from a combination of National Insurance contributions, taxes and rates, and middle- and upper-class patients, who did not use the service. They instead paid twice, through extra contributions of eleven guineas a week to the continuing private service, obtaining slightly more comfort from a service which was already good.

CHAPTER FIFTEEN

LIVING AND MOVING IN THE FIFTIES

The general election in February 1950 had gained, by a mere twenty-eight votes, victory for the Conservative, Robert Perkins, over the existing Labour member, Ben Parkin, thus enabling him to become the first MP to represent the newly-formed Stroud and Tetbury division. The Labour party were returned to power nationally with just five seats. Their considerable post-war achievements of low unemployment, the Health Service, and outstanding industrial production, having pulled them through.

In just over a year, in October 1951, the Conservatives were to take away their power, through a seventeen seat majority in parliament, and Clement Attlee would give up his place to Churchill. Robert Perkins in Stroud increased his majority by 1,582, achieving his fifth success to date.

The year 1950 saw the end of the food points' system, and there was a predictable rush for biscuits, fruit, syrup, and tinned fish, although not salmon as it had still not reached the shops.

Clive Maton, having left Rodborough Secondary Modern, worked in George Mason's, the grocers, on a two year apprenticeship. He earned £1 17s 6d at the start, handing back 5s for his overalls. His first three months there were spent cutting up lard, and he was not allowed in the shop to serve customers for a month. Even then he was not entirely on his own. In 1954 meat rationing ended, but butter was still on ration. Each person was allowed two ounces one week and four ounces the next. Clive remembers customers would always ask, 'Have you got any extra butter?', to which he would reply, 'No, but we have got bags of fat and margarine'. About six months later, after rationing was finished and butter was available in plenty, he would ask them, 'Do you want any butter?', to which they would say, 'No thank you. But have you got any Spry?'

He says outwardly it seemed there was great rivalry between the traders, but it was not like that at all. If any of them were short the others chipped in to help out. After his apprenticeship was finished he left George Mason's. It was generally thought best to go out and gain experience in another place. The fifties was a workers' market, where it was possible to leave a job in the morning, and have another by the afternoon. Surprisingly, during his two years at George Mason's, prices did not change. Streaky bacon remained at 1s 8d a pound. Short back was still 3s 6d a pound, with gammon remaining at 5s a pound, and cheese at 1s 10d.

In Stroud during the fifties and sixties there were nine butchers and two fishmongers. The High Street was the centre for shopping where there was Revells and Milwards shoe shops, and Timothy Whites. Also Mac Fisheries, Liptons, George Isles, the leather shop, Coleys, the International Stores, Smith and Lees, and Bells. Bells, in combination with Batemans, had a marvellous money-changing device which whizzed down a wire from the upper sales floor to the cashier, whose office was on the ground floor. There was Alma House, Lewis the electricians, Balls the fruiterers, Bainbridges and Chapmans the butchers, George Mason the grocer and Smiths the chemist. And there were many more.

In Gloucester Street, there was an antique shop, where Peter Hickman is today, and Plesteds, which was a very up-market grocery store where morning suits were worn in the shop. Mr Anthony, at Anthony's shop in King Street, also wore a morning suit to work, and the women who worked there were each responsible for their own counter, behind which the goods were stocked, and had to be requested. There was a shop in London Road where people sat in the window mending stockings, and a fabric shop run by Mrs Longcrain. Also Sands, the gentleman's outfitters in Russell Street, which dates from the 1890s, becoming Sands in 1930 when Mr C.A. Sands took over. Mr Sands, despite being a batman to Captain Chatham in The Royal Marines during the war, still managed to do the buying throughout those years, while his wife ran the business.

Batemans began in 1893 as a tobacconist in Gloucester Street, their adjoining sports business opened in the 1920s. In 1930, they acquired their present Kendrick Street premises, and in 1940, Associated Warehouses in Johns Street, their main warehouse for the shop and school contracting business. Their wares during wartime were sports goods, toys, some of which were wooden and locally produced, tin railway sets, tobacco and cigarettes, which were manufactured locally, as well as utility clothing. Delivery was made by motorbike and sidecar. From the early fifties all goods were stored in their warehouse at John Street, and were priced and sorted there before being transported down to the Kendrick Street shop in a truck (custom-built to go through their door).

During their years in business, they also stocked sports equipment (Mr Bateman was a keen sportsman and played full back for Stroud), baby goods,

Bateman's corner in the 40s.

Bateman's first father Christmas arriving at his grotto at Batemans shop during the early 60s. The Landau is driven by and belonged to Ben Ford. A young Phil Gardiner is in the doorway, and an equally youthful Peter Bateman is behind Father Christmas.

including coach built prams, camping equipment, and ladies clothes, which involved them in fashion shows.

During the early days, all goods had their brand name stamped on them. The stamping process was done by an oil lamp, which gave them a black mark. 'County Star' was used for tennis racquets and 'County Driver' on cricket bats. Items were priced with a Kimball pricing machine or a Masseeley Machine which issued yellow tickets, and black lettering for window displays. Phil Gardener, who has worked at Batemans since 1953, feels the Matchbox toys

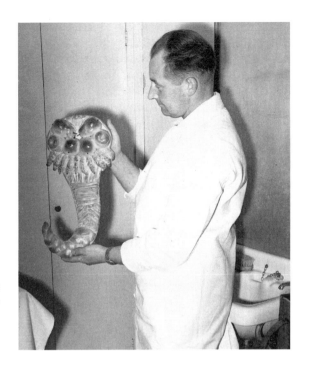

Winstone Tuck displaying a Goat's Horn, which was usually made for Harvest Festival. It was the Christian symbol of Plenty, and a Pagan symbol of Fertility.

which appeared in the 1950s made a big impact (the first was a little road roller), and the valve bladder took the hard work out of inflating footballs.

Hales the butcher began in 1935. By 1952, although theoretically still under rationing restrictions (two ounces of meat and two ounces of corned Argentine beef per head weekly), people were able to have more or less what they wanted, and queues stretched around the corner on to George Street. Apart from Hales, there was Blanch's, Pritchards, Bainbridges, the Co-op, Eastmans, Dewhursts, Baxters, LCM, the Excelsior Meat Company, and Whitehalls Provisions in George Street, run by George and Arthur Poole, where a doggy sat on the counter. There were three more butchers in Painswick and many more in other villages.

Tuck's bakers and confectionery business was founded in the 1860s by William T. Tuck at 20 Gloucester Street. On his death it was taken over by his son, Wilfred, who branched out setting up in Kings Street and Bath Street. The latter premises was the former Chew Iron Works, which was converted in 1921 into the Premier Hall, Headquarters of Stroud Rotary Club and venue of countless public gatherings. One son, Winstone Oliver, later married Peggy Chew. Another son, Lionel, ran the Tuckery Cafe.

At the outbreak of war, the Premier Hall supplied cooked breakfasts of eggs and bacon and Hales' sausages, to 160 Territorials for several days. Sixty eggs could be all cooked at one time if broken on to a baking tray. Before the war, a jam doughnut cost 1*d*, cream buns were 2*d*, and baked beans on toast were 6*d*. During the wartime shortages, Tucks developed a farmhouse cake, which included dripping and the ration of fruit and breadcrumbs, which sold well. Once a man came in and bought the whole batch of freshly baked bread outright, before going off to sell it at double the price elsewhere. In 1953 a Coronation cake was produced, which cost 6*d* a pound, and was a bit like madeira.

The relaxation of petrol control came quite suddenly over the Whitsun holiday, and sent people scurrying to book at hotels and boarding houses, unable to believe they were free to travel at last. The Waste Paper Campaign was abandoned when prices dropped from £6 7*s* to £2 10*s*, which scarcely covered the bailing costs. A ten-minute visit in March by Princess Elizabeth delighted the town.

On the other side, there were practically non-existent coal stocks, industry was threatened by electricity cuts, and the country was fraught through the Korean and Iranian conflicts.

Stroud suffered many electricity cuts throughout the year, which caused the factories, who were worried over their production level, to devise a hooter warning system. As electricity levels dropped dangerously low, it let out a long blast. On this signal all domestic and non-industrial users were to turn off appliances at home. 'A Switch in Time Saves Power Cuts'. The 'Big Four' were the power gobblers: electric fires, cookers, water heaters, and washing boilers. Many ideas were considered in order to reduce power usage even more. Someone thought street lighting should be stopped one month earlier. Mr Daniels remarked that he would like street lighting put out all together, and every electric fire put away.

With freedom to travel at last and holidays in view, the increasing affluent car-owning society turned their thoughts to caravans, revelling in a new kind of flexible holiday, with every necessity on tow. Caravan clubs offered facilities on site, and farmers allowed the use of their land, not needed so urgently for crops now war was over. Within no time at all caravan production became big business, and the once modest living 'van' became grander, nearly approximating to a small house. While these retained an outward appearance of mobility, it was obvious moving would not be easy, surrounded as the caravan was with all aspects of homely trappings, sheds, paths, and laid-on water and electricity. Steels in Stroud sold caravans. The Karen Cottage 'de luxe' living van cost £586, or the touring, four berth Sprite, £199.

The new mobility also prompted coach tours, which provided country viewing in comfort, a far flung contrast to 'Holidays at Home'. Seven days on

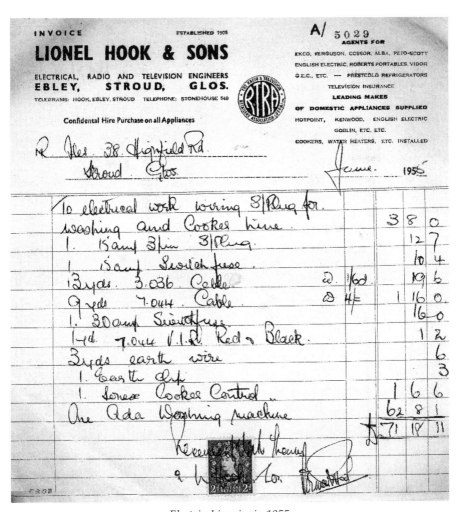

Electrical invoice in 1955.

the Co-op Luxury Coach Tour of the Scottish Lochs cost eighteen guineas, and for a holiday in The English Lakes, Yorkshire Moors, or Scarborough and Southport, it was twenty pounds. However, the seaside resorts, their beaches eventually cleared of wartime deterrents, now reached their holiday potential, and boarding houses were flooded with weekend and holiday visitors, most arriving by train for comfortable, easy travel. A return to Weston was 7s 3d, while a cheap Sunday trip to Bristol was only 4s 6d.

Brian Beavis began his driving career on February 3rd 1933, from which time he extended his garage and gained an impressive fleet of cars and coaches. This photograph which was taken before his extension shows: Back, L–R: Coaches - Bedford, AEC, Commer and AEC. Front: Armstrong Siddley 7-seater Limosine with Richard Selwyn, a Mercedes 1900 with Brian Beavis, an Austin 1100 with Bob Stinchcombe.

Beavis coach holidays, which started in 1920 with hackney carriages, progressed on to coach tours in 1949, after Brian had returned from the Forces. He already knew his way around abroad from having driven service vehicles. So when a lady asked him to chauffeur her to Rome in the Chrysler he had sold her, he realized that holidaying abroad was the thing for the future, and his successful business began. During the early days of coach travelling, everything, including a full lunch, was organized in advance. Brian was pleased to drop this arrangement when eating establishments appeared in plenty along with the motorways, as it had made one more time pressure in the days of a tight schedule.

The increasing trend to travel, and increased industrial haulage, demanded wider, better, and more roads. The M6, Britain's first motorway, was opened in the late fifties and was swiftly followed by the M1. Motor-producing factories at Cowley and Coventry became big businesses, and a host of associated industries grew up to support their product.

Workers in the motor industry received good pay, much higher than the farm worker, who was still the lowest paid of all industry, the adult wage being just £6 15s a week. 'A measly pittance', said Mr J. Paul at the 78th Gloucestershire County Conference of the National Union of Agricultural Workers, who were working to get it raised to £8 a week. Not surprisingly, hundreds left farm work every year. A total of thirty-five thousand left between 1955 and 1966.

At this time, Stroud Creamery opened their new modern pasteurizing plant at Lansdown. It was clean, safe, and efficient, fully equipped with lights, a carefully timed heating and cooling system, and mechanically bottled the milk, which was delivered by motor.

Some farmers continued in the old style of milk production, their simple filtering, cooling, and bottling by hand procedure was still adequate to get the milk to the customer.

Boney Webb at Knapp Farm, and W.W. Hawkes at the Riflemans, both began with horse and cart, although the Hawkes switched to motor cycle and side car, and then a former Co-op bread van, following the war. As petrol became in short supply, the Hawkes dispensed with their petrol-reliant transport, returning to the bicycle and two-gallon bucket system in which all the family had a part to play.

At this time milk distributors were allocated block areas, in which one sole milk distributor supplied everyone within, so the Hawkes' method was not too irksome. The Hawkes' allocated area was Upper Summer Street, Parliament Street, Chapel Street, and Nelson Street, which was reasonably compact, although problems arose when former far-flung customers pleaded for delivery, and Mike dashed here and there, to satisfy the demand. The Hawkes' milk came from different sources: Johnny Horn at Stroud Slad Farm; and

A sample of the variety of tours offered by Beavis's in 1955.

Continental Holidays

BY LUXURY MOTOR COACH

PROGRAMME **1955** PROGRAMME

By permission of G.T.B.

7 TO 15 DAYS FROM 23 GNS. INCLUSIVE

Cable Car, Beavis.

B. E. W. BEAVIS

BUSSAGE · NR. STROUD

GLOUCESTERSHIRE

Telephone: BRIMSCOMBE 2297

TOUR No. 2

BRUSSELS · LUXEMBOURG & PARIS

7 DAYS ★ 24 GNS. fully inclusive

Two { departures : Good Friday, April 8th
Monday, August 29th

1st Day. To Dover. Ferry to Ostend. Dinner on boat. Night in OSTEND.

2nd Day. To BRUGES (sightseeing) then to BRUSSELS. Lunch and rest of day free. Sightseeing, dinner and night.

3rd Day. Via NAMUR, DINANT, to GROTTOES OF HAN (visit and lunch), BASTOGNE to LUXEMBOURG for dinner and night.

4th Day. Via VERDUN, CHALONS (lunch), to PARIS for dinner and night.

5th Day. All day free in PARIS. Tour of the city, Notre Dame, the Louvre, Place de la Concorde, Champs Elysees, Arc de Triomphe, Eiffel Tower, Sacre Coeur, etc. Lunch, dinner and night in PARIS.

6th Day. Via PERONNE, CAMBRAI (lunch), LILLE to OSTEND for dinner and night.

7th Day. Ferry to Dover. Return.

This tour offers sightseeing and shopping in three North European capitals, visits to old-world Bruges, "Venice of the North", the magnificent caves "Grottoes of Han" and the battlefields of the 1914-18 war, and embracing the Ardennes forests.

Supplement for Single Rooms (see Booking Form)

V FORM amount £14

TOUR No. 3

BELGIUM, LUXEMBOURG FRANCE, GERMANY, AUSTRIA

10 DAYS ★ 30 GNS. fully inclusive

One departure : Friday, May 13th

1st Day. To Dover. Ferry to Ostend. Dinner on boat. Night in GHENT.

2nd Day. Via BRUSSELS (sightseeing), NAMUR, BASTOGNE to LUXEMBOURG, for sightseeing, dinner and night.

3rd Day. Via METZ, SAVERNE (lunch), STRASBOURG (sightseeing) to the BLACK FOREST resort of TRIBERG for dinner and night.

4th Day. Morning free in TRIBERG. Visit waterfalls, museum, etc. After lunch via LAKE CONSTANCE into AUSTRIA. Dinner and night in BREGENZ.

5th Day. Morning free in BREGENZ. Cable car, shopping, etc. After lunch, over the ARLBERG PASS 5,912 ft., through magnificent mountain scenery to LANDECK and then TELFS in Tyrol for dinner and night.

6th Day. Short journey into INNSBRUCK for day. Optional visit to Court Castle, Silver Chapel and Church, Cable Car to 7,000 ft. Excellent shopping centre. Return to TELFS for dinner and night.

7th Day. Via MITTENWALD to MUNICH for lunch. Then on the "autobahn" to STUTTGART for dinner and night.

8th Day. Via the "autobahn" to MAINZ for lunch, then via the RHINE road through ST. GOAR (visit), COBLENCE to BONN for dinner and night.

9th Day. to COLOGNE (visit), AACHEN, LIEGE (lunch), and GHENT for dinner and night.

10th Day. To Dover. Ferry to Dover. Return.

Embracing 5 Countries, this tour offers a diversity of landscape—the rolling Ardennes forests, Black Forest heights, a lakeside journey, majestic Austrian and Bavarian mountains and the mighty Rhine.

Supplement for single rooms (see Booking Form)

V FORM amount £20

TOUR No. 4

BLACK FOREST and RHINELAND

including STEAMER down the RHINE

10 DAYS ★ 32 GNS. fully inclusive

One departure : Sunday, August 14th

1st Day. To Dover. Ferry to Ostend. Dinner on boat. Night in GHENT.

2nd Day. Via BRUSSELS (sightseeing), NAMUR, BASTOGNE to LUXEMBOURG for dinner and night.

3rd Day. Via METZ, SAVERNE (lunch), STRASBOURG (sightseeing), to the BLACK FOREST resort of TRIBERG for dinner and night.

4th Day. All day free in TRIBERG. Visits to waterfalls, museum, church, etc.

5th Day. All day excursion to SCHAFFHAUSEN (Switzerland), visiting RHINE FALLS. Return to TRIBERG for dinner and night.

6th Day. Through the BLACK FOREST to FREUDENSTADT. Free until lunch. Afterwards via HERRENBERG to STUTTGART for dinner and night.

7th Day. Morning free in STUTTGART. Large city with excellent shopping facilities. After lunch via the "autobahn" to FRANKFURT for dinner and night.

8th Day. Short drive to MAINZ. Board Rhine Steamer, and travel down river, arriving BONN in early evening. Lunch on boat. Dinner and night in BONN.

9th Day. To COLOGNE (visit), AACHEN, LIEGE (lunch), and to GHENT for dinner and night.

10th Day. To Ostend. Ferry to Dover. Return.

Designed for those who prefer a more leisurely tour but still wish to visit several countries, this tour embraces Belgium, Luxembourg, France, Switzerland and Germany, and offers the unique attraction of a full day on the Rhine. Triberg, our Black Forest centre, is a charming spot, noted for its cuckoo clocks.

Supplement for Single Rooms (see Booking Form)

V FORM amount £20

Nance and Will Hawkes in 1958 with their cat Nina. When Mike went shooting Nina usually followed him to glean some spoils. Once when it was cold and snow was on the ground she was missing for three weeks. Eventually she was found, still alive in a rabbit snare. She had completely worn the snow away where she had repeatedly walked around.

Jimmy Dean at the long-gone Hope Inn in Merrywalks, near the Stroud Brewery. Mike, delivering milk before school, remembers watching the Brewery signwriters while waiting for his refill, little thinking he too would be painting pub signs at that very spot in later years.

When I said to him, 'It must have been difficult carrying buckets of milk and measures on the handle bars of a bike', Mike laughed, and related his meeting with a lorry on the narrow corner at the bottom of the Vatch, which sent him careering up the bank, and lost him the two buckets of milk.

The Hawkes family did not only transport milk in this way. Rabbits and flowers had their place on the frame too. Mike's mother, known locally as the 'Rabbit Queen', obtained her rabbits from the Ayres at Snows Farm, and

The Signwriters at Stroud Brewery before leaving Stroud for Cheltenham in 1966–7. The signwriters department was down towards Merrywalks on the left, and the Hope Inn was next door to the Wines and Spirits Department. Pictured L–R: Bob Simmonds, John Cook, Mike Hawkes, Graham Watkins, John Print, Colin Furley, Margaret Iles, Penny Burcombe.

wallflowers from Slad Stroud Farm. A good memory was essential on the Hawkes' milk round, as mother did not fill in the order book until after the round.

Nancy sometimes picked mushrooms from Camp for the market at the Painswick Inn, before school or, later, at work at Ham Mill. Once when working for Philip Ford, the well known Stroud builders and undertakers who had operated in Slad Road from 1875, she was shut in the mortuary. At the time it was packed with six bodies, one had his eyes open, and the 'smell from the brook was awful'. Suddenly the door accidentally slammed shut and she could not get out. Her merciful release only arrived after someone jokingly asked, 'Where is Nancy? Perhaps she has climbed into one of the coffins'. This comment caused laughter as they had often teasingly threatened to put her in one, but caused several broken nights sleep for Nancy.

Jack Timbrell in about 1946. He was a carter for 50 years from 1895–1945, firstly to Mr Trotman, and then to the Dickenson family.

A team of Brown horses pulling a timber carriage at the turn of the century. Denis Brown and Son originating from a family timber business established in 1890 at Leyburn, North Yorkshire, have operated from the late 30's in Stroud district, hauling for Henry Workman from Cirencester and Badminton Estates. One yard was in Cossack Square Nailsworth and another at Broadmead Yard Woodchester. Within time Denis had added to his vehicles, and increased his workforce to a dozen. Today, Peter and Anita Brown have changed timber tactics from round timber haulage to sawn products at their Broadmead yard at Woodchester.

The business of death followed Nancy into 1950, when she witnessed what was possibly the last funeral in the area to use a horse and cart. The deceased was Mrs Brookes from Slad.

Mrs Hawkes was a wonderful organizer and arranged trips after the war to Severn Beach, Wainloads, and Weston. Milk round customers and neighbours usually participated and The Red and White Service was booked, 'Because they had double-decker coaches and were more modern than the Western's which had got a bit tatty'. In pre-war days, when the children were smaller, the entire Hawkes family packed into their motorbike and side car for a day out at Weston.

Some horses and carts were still used around Stroud District during the fifties. Some people will remember the team of horses which pulled the timber

Dennis Brown hauling with steam.

wagons up the Slad valley, and the way they were reprimanded if they hung on the back. The wagons required five or six horses to pull them, had rubber wheels and a proper braking system, which was operated by turning a wheel. The lead and shaft horses needed to be quiet-tempered, any horses liable to get excited were put in the middle to calm them down.

The horses at Down Farm were Punch and Johnny, and Duke, who was the trace horse. Of the three, Punch was the quietest, albeit a bit lazy, but Johnny and Duke had plenty of 'go'. Once, when Jim was riding home from Timmins, the blacksmiths at Miserden, a group of Americans banged some tins and shouted, 'Ride him, cowboy'. This caused Duke to throw Jim off and bolt for home. Trudging back on foot, Jim met up with Jack Timbrell, who was looking to see what had happened to him.

Some might also recall the Dainty brothers from Rodborough, who were both unable to communicate easily through their handicaps, although father always managed to talk with them all right.

There were also the road men, who tarmacked the narrow country lanes, with their wonderful shire horse. Sometimes they took their dinner break in grandfather's yard, the men round the brazier, while their horse, deep in his nose-bag, sneezed and snuffled as the chaff tickled his nostrils.

Driver Ernest Preston in a pre-1947 Latil Timber Tractor which was able to haul twice as fast as a steam engine. It is in the process of restoration by his son Peter today.

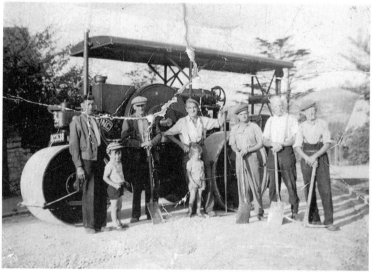

Stroud District Council's Steam Roller and workmen. Wilfred Steele is 2nd from the left.

Only one heavy horse, Blossom, remained from early delivery days, in the paddock below our house. Occasionally he was hitched up to the two-wheel coal cart, so that he and grandfather could deliver a basket or two at their leisure. As a child I assumed Blossom was old, and so had died when his sturdy magnificent dark body did not grace our field any more. But I was apparently wrong. A few years ago I learned that he was a youngster, his

Workmans Saw Mill at Woodchester with a steam crane (left) and an unloaded elm tree.

Workmans workforce. Date and Ada's brother Ralph undetermined. 'He wore a cap!' said Ada. Henry Workman began his sawmill at Woodchester about 1800 on the Piano Works site, before the move to their present premises at South Woodchester in 1870 to be near the railway line. Wood from as far as Wiltshire and Herefordshire could now conveniently enter and leave the yard. Despite a disasterous fire in 1911 which destroyed everything, 150 men were employed at Workman's during the Second World War, making ammunition boxes and items valuable for the war effort. Mr John Workman O.B.E. recalls the use of one of the earliest electric chain saws, the Teles from Czechoslovakia, in pre-war days, in about 1937. However following its selling in 1949 it was closed down within five years.

Workman's Fire.

sudden absence not due to death, but to enter a fuller active life, as befitted an animal in his prime.

Horses would have found difficulty coping with an increasingly congested vehicle-bound Stroud, which traders in the fifties thought would drive their customers to shop elsewhere. Some traders wanted to exclude bus-stops from the town completely, and have a bus terminal instead, while others wished to be rid of street parking. Was there a need to squash into parking gaps in town, they asked, when Merrywalks offered two hours parking for 6*d*, and a season ticket was only thirty shillings.

Although car ownership had increased, owners rarely used them then on a daily basis, just exhibiting their prized acquisition at weekends, and using public transport during the week. Therefore buses still remained the main mode of local transport, even though a fair amount of legwork was sometimes involved to get to the bus routes. It was two hills for us if we caught the 'bottom one' from Nailsworth to Stroud.

However, in May 1951 things began to look up. There were bus station promises for Merrywalks. When, a year later, nothing was forthcoming, permission was granted for a trial bus terminus on the old LMS yard, to alleviate the town's congestion. From the day it began, on Sunday 14 September, there were complaints. The road crossing was apparently too busy, the lighting down Rowcroft was inadequate, and the walk was too long! The 'marathon walk' grievance was dispelled when a timed test, conducted by a person in no hurry, clocked up three minutes and thirty seconds from town to bus-stop!

CHAPTER SIXTEEN

CORONATION YEAR

With the austerity of the war fast fading into past history, and a promising new future ahead, 1953 began with the anticipation of the Coronation of Queen Elizabeth II in June, and the festivities which would accompany it.

The nation needed cheering up following the news of the death of King George VI on Wednesday 5 February. Stroud heard the news at 1 a.m., and had immediately hung their flags at half mast, The Red Cross House flying The Crown of St George, while the Parish Church tolled their tenor bell to broadcast the news to the town. The cinemas closed for the day, the BBC broadcast only official announcements, and many schools held short impromptu services.

Thirteen-year-old Clive Maton heard it on the *Light Programme* following *Mrs Dale's Diary*. The announcer said, 'It is announced by Buckingham Palace, his Majesty George VI passed away during the night'. Then he remembers the radio going dead, and everything was a national service broadcast until the funeral.

The funeral on 15 February was at St George's Chapel, Windsor, although most churches held their own services. The nation was hushed throughout a two minutes silence, the shops were closed and their windows draped, and pubs stayed closed until 12.30 p.m.

More distress followed in Stroud District in May and June, when an epidemic of foot-and-mouth disease struck the area, and all cattle classes were eliminated from the Stroud Show because of it. Grazing became short when farmers were unable to send their stock to Gloucester market, and there was a worry that hay prices might rocket because of it. Furthermore Marking Day on the commons was delayed, and all cattle banned.

Things did cheer up in August. The Woodchester Roman Pavement opened in mid-August as a contribution towards the 1951 Festival of Britain. It attracted over 7,600 visitors, many from far-flung corners of the globe, who came to see their remarkable mosaic pavement. The profits, which were well in excess of £3,000, were due considerably to the work of the villagers, who served teas, and even three course dinners in the marquee.

Deavreaux Crescent Coronation Street Party.

As the shadow of the King's death faded into the past, and a Coronation with a new queen of only twenty-six was imminent, preparations began in Stroud for 'the most glorious and moving pageant in the world'.

Villages followed suit, as each individual committee sorted out their own events and funding for street parties, carnivals, school functions, whist drives, dances, band concerts, and bonfires. Decorations of red, white, and blue were at the top of everyone's list, and people planned for riots of flowers in town centres, window boxes, hanging baskets, municipal parks, and their own gardens. Gardeners, who ten years before had wielded forks and spades to feed stomachs, were now seizing trowels and flower seed packets with which to feast the eyes. Packets of alyssum, lobelia, and salvia were planted in abundance. Many schools, such as ours at Kingscourt, laboriously scratched out patches and borders, determined that their display would be better than the rest.

Stroud itself thought about the costly business of lighting up its town, and happily accepted offers from the Gas Board to fund the floodlighting of Stratford Park Mansion House, and the Midlands Electricity Board to contribute lamps for St. Laurence Church.

Soon, a programme was published for the celebratory week which was designed for 31 May to Saturday 6 June.

Smiths The Chemist. Note the crown in the centre of the right hand window.

Stratford Park was to host several major events throughout the week, commencing with an open air service and combined band concert on Sunday, and, on Coronation Day itself, a bonfire and firework display. A variety concert was planned for Wednesday, and choral singing on Thursday. Each was just a part of the variety of supporting activities which were to take place throughout the week.

Often, when an important occasion lies ahead, matters laid aside due to war, limited funds, or simply a lack of enthusiasm, can suddenly receive attention. There is a last minute momentum to get the job done.

Leonard Stanley needed a village hall, which was estimated to cost £800. To set the ball rolling villagers donated £1 each, this modest contribution amazingly raising £64. This was combined with a competition, and a mobile illuminated Christmas tree, trundled around the village on a trolley accompanied by thirty carol singers. So the village began to raise money towards their long-awaited village hall. But this new building enterprise was abandoned when Mrs Fisher offered the redundant village school building instead.

The Cotswold Players had been formed in 1912 after their successful performance of a *Historical Pageant of Progress* in Fromehall Park, organized by

Leonard Stanley collecting some stone from the burned down Vicarage cottage in readiness for their hall, which was not required when the old school was offered instead. Ernest Hale is wielding the pickaxe, Doris is behind him in the hat, and Arthur Savage is driving the tractor.

Constance Smedley and her husband Maxwell Armfield. Now, forty years later, they acquired their new permanent home at Slade Hall, the old Methodist Chapel at Parliament Street. In January, despite the austerity of their yet-to-be converted home, the chilling tale of 'Bluebeard' was produced for their pantomime, which matched venue and climate.

Others were on the move. The newly-built Stroud Technical College, designed by County Architect S.E. Urwin, had taken over some of the classes from Brimscombe Poly, which, as an early handicraft centre dating from 1888, was ready to retire.

The new college in Stratford Road already had some students, who were studying engineering, building, and textiles in the workshop and laboratory block, which had been completed in 1951. The two storey classroom wing, drawing offices, kitchen, and refectory had only just been completed, but the

A scene from Episode VIII, Corn Law Riots, A.D. 1846. One of around thirty photographs which appeared in the Souvenir Programme of the Mid-Gloucestershire Historical Pageant of Progress of 1911. The performances were held on Saturday September 2nd, Thursday September 7th and Saturday 9th. Constance Smedley was the brainchild, Frank Gwynne Evans from Butterow was the author and Honorary Secretary, Miss May E Cull was the director who kept order with a whistle, Sir Alfred Apperley JP was Chairman and Treasurer of Central Committee, Mr Charles A Apperley JP was the master of the Pageant Ground, John Jacob was Musical Director, and Miss Seymour Keay was Mistress of the Robes. Photo by Conway.

A scene from A Midsummer Night's Dream *by William Shakespeare which was officially opened by Sir Barry Jackson (the director of the Birmingham Repertory) on Saturday June 22nd 1957. The costumes were designed and made by the cast who included Tony Morgan, Philip Young, Kenneth Blair James, Don Barker, Herbert Lines, John Clark, Jack Marshall, Mirium Morgan, Hazel King, Rachael Blundell, Ann Buffham, June Dodsworth, Jeanette Luker, Deborah Pawson, Sally Streman, Alison Hemming, Moira Murray, James Gammans, Michael Bishop, Robert Bashford, Joan Burge, Elizabeth Jupp, Janet Bignell, and a host of Court Ladies and Gentlemen, Huntsmen, Amazons and Soldiers.*

During wartime the Cotswold Players managed to produce Dear Octopus *in 1941 which was produced by Harold Sydney, and following the war the comedy* Tony Draws a Horse *and* A School for Scandal *in 1949. When installed in their new Playhouse they hosted visiting members from the Royal Opera House Covent Garden, The Bristol Old Vic, The Winchester Cathedral Players, as well as local Youth Drama and One Act Festivals and Area Finals, also* Hiawatha's Photographing *and* The Proposal *which took them abroad to Duderstadt in West Germany in 1970.*

Before their purchase of the Slade Hall, The Stroud Boys Club of which Geoffrey Hoyland was chairman, and their leader Mr Macarthy used it. When it was de-commissioned by the church Bryan Durn can remember 'skulls and bones lined up against the wall'.

A scene from Love's a Luxury *which was performed in November 1964 in the Institute Hall by The County Players, who began life as The Painswick Players with Miss Lucy Hyett, the daughter of Sir Francis Hyett of Painswick House. On her death the Players changed their name to the County Players, until yet another change to the present Pads (The Painswick Amateur Dramatic Society). One renowned member who is fondly remembered by the County Players is May Jenkin, who was Aunty May from the early days of BBC Children's Hour. Pictured L–R: Margaret Hurrell (sitting), Les Lewis (standing) and Paul London. During their life The County Players took several of their plays down to Gloucester Prison where they were enjoyed greatly, and Colin Maclaurin-Jones designed and painted their wonderful posters.*

three storey block and hall, which was still in construction, would eventually house commercial, handicraft, science and gymnastic subjects, which currently took place in the School of Art building at Lansdown. Soon, this new spacious building would accommodate a range of school leavers who, free from uniform regulations, sported short or tight 'fashion clothes', while those still in dowdy Grammar School attire looked on with envy. However, it was the older students who probably enjoyed their new-found opportunities most, as they enrolled to pick up the threads of needlework, upholstery, cookery, typing, language classes and many more.

Stroud District Council reached its own landmark in May 1953 by completing its 1,000th council house, which was at Cashes Green. Shortly, road

The Stroud Brewery decked out for the Coronation.

naming for the estate had to be done; two of the new names were Princess Road and Queen's Drive, to suit the year. Also, Cotswold Road, Elm Road, Moor Place Hall, and Harper Road, as a tribute to Jack Harper, the retiring councillor. The Council had built 617 homes before the war, 383 since, and another 106 were undergoing current construction.

The real achievement of the year was the long-awaited Maternity Hospital which, although desired in 1939 and planned for in 1947, only opened during the first week of April 1953.

As Coronation week drew closer, a gradual buildup began. Strachans received a visit from the BBC as part of their factory visit programme, *Coronation Preparation*, and the nation learned that the scarlet cloth produced for the Grenadier Guards' uniform was dyed with cochineal.

The Painswick Amateur Operatic Society presented *Merrie England* at the Institute Hall, and Rodborough Fort hoisted a huge Union Jack over its battlements. The Stroud Brewery exhibited a large portrait of Her Majesty the Queen, with rows of guardsmen, and a gilded State Coach, with wheels which turned round, across their Rowcroft building, and they also produced a Coronation Ale. Mr Hale, the butcher, toyed with the idea of producing red, white and blue sausages, but practicality inhibited their appearance.

Lynton, Burdett Road Stonehouse, which was decorated for the Coronation by Mrs Vera Parrott.

The great day began with wind and rain, and people focused their eyes on London. Some were lucky enough to obtain tickets to viewpoints in London, but others were content to see the elaborate arrangements on television. The camera's prying eye had prompted a grand clean-up during the preceding weeks, when buildings were painted and streets freshly cleaned. There had been parade rehearsals in ungainly hours through London's streets, and Westminster Abbey had been closed for several months in order to install seating for seven thousand guests.

The day was one of glitter, of priceless gems, rich fabrics, and gold. The Regalia itself possesses some of the world's priceless gems. Among them being 'The Great Star of Africa', which is the largest cut diamond in the world, and the breathtaking St Edwards Crown, which is encrusted with 3,093 jewels. For the children it was the glorious golden great state coach which captured their attention. It is used only at Coronations, and many thousands of us had a replica (with the horses), out on our mantelpieces at home.

Stroud's festivities went ahead as planned. The beer flowed at Frocester, the Maypole rocked at Paganhill, there was dancing at Amberley, and teas, sports, and fancy dress at Box. Cranham opened their new children's playing field,

Sheepscombe children in fancy dress.

presented to the village by Mr Herbert Evans of Woodside, and Painswick held a parade, wherein Peggy Perrin's daughter Sheila was dressed as an English Rose in a white crinoline dress, while her brothers went as Poachers. They had a bonfire on the Beacon.

Slad had a large marquee with 'tea for all the kids', and Ada, now a resident of Leonard Stanley, partook of Mankley Road's street party fare. Orchard Road had a tree on the green with lights, and collected a shilling for every child, and Stroud pensioners enjoyed old-time dancing. Children everywhere received sweets, souvenir coins, and beakers, and everyone, everywhere, attended carnivals, fireworks, and bonfires.

Most people wanted to see the pomp on television, and the overwhelming demand to get a set in time prompted a rush. Bryan Durn, who was courting his future wife, was just one among thousands who bought a television especially for the day, many little realizing they would have to entertain half their village as well. Friendships with neighbours blossomed overnight for anyone who had a television, many visitors arrived for the day, equipped with sandwiches, tea, sweets, and cushions, to ensure uninterrupted viewing.

We had no set, so went with numerous others along the road to Granny

Sheepscombe schoolchildren with their Coronation Beakers. Back L–R: Ruth Allen, Maureen Beard. 5th row: Clifford Glover, Melvyn Young, Rachael Allum, Mary Beard. 4th row: Margaret Chadwick, Carol Spens, Elisabeth French, Eldwith Young, Pat Morey. 3rd row: Jack Weston, Pamela Twitchen. 2nd row: John Allum, Tom Holford, Robert Workman, David Halliday, Billy Teakle. Front: Mary Allum, Ricky Rogers, David Cowdrey, Gillian Glover, Ronnie Beard, Carol Teakle, Betty Mitchel, Pat Purcell, Mrs Hemming.

Hogg's. She accommodated us all admirably in her sitting room, even lacing our tea with whisky (not mine as a child), as the weather was so cold. A few months later, in company with thousands more, we acquired our own set. It was a nine-inch television in a large shiny case, and had numerous press knobs including one which said 'Sound Only', which seemed strange to me, when we had bought it especially for the picture!

People unable to claim friendship with the owner of a set could sometimes arrange to view in the Village Hall as at Miserden, the church as at Selsley, or school, as Allen Hale did with his friend, who was a pupil at Upfields, and about forty others.

Wilf Merrett did not have a television, having only married that April. He was busy with other things on Coronation day, putting the finishing touches to a coal-house he had built in the garden of his cottage at Selsley. However, having completed the job, he hoisted a flag on the top in a joint celebration of her Majesty's Coronation, and the completion of his masterpiece.

Ruth Parrott as Miss Britannia at the Old Folks Party in Stonehouse in 1953.

Ted Hewer had no television either. It would have been impossible at The Heavens, where there was no electricity. Instead the small group of houses there, which included the Forester's Arms pub run by Sylvia and Albert Pierce, celebrated in the field adjoining The Heavens with sports and teas for the youngsters in the afternoon, and a further party in the evening to take care of the adults. Camp had a cask of beer and a large bonfire on the 'Humpty Tumpty' field.

Keith Browne had just received his call-up papers, and was feeling quite excited. He and his mates went rabbiting at the top of the Weighhouse where, having caught their fare, they roasted it over a fire, and drank some Stroud Breweries' Coronation Ale.

Min was in Standish with a TB spine, but The Western National had supplied every ward with a television set so they could watch the Queen crowned from their beds. As it was difficult for Min to see lying down flat, hers was projected.

Clive Maton, then still at Rodborough Secondary Modern School, went to

The Butchers Arms at Sheepscombe in June 1953.

Marling School for a party. The boys were given a mug, with a bag full of Granny Ball's sweets inside, and the girls received fruit bowls. During the occasion, they all had to be silent while Councillor Mason, Chairman of Cainscross Parish Council and a Stroud Urban District Councillor, made a speech. An occasion Clive particularly remembers, as he holds that very title himself today. The Maton family had no television either, so he went with his mother and father to the Rose at Paganhill in the evening.

The planned events continued throughout the week, culminating on Saturday with a carnival through Stroud, which began at the Hospital and finished at the Park. Although it had been a miserable morning, the weather cheered by midday, the sun appearing shortly before the parade was due to start at 2 p.m.. The Stroud District, and the Cainscross County Girls Schools' Jazz Bands escorted the floats along the way. Many contributed to the floats, including one of 'The Conquest of Everest' by Ebley School, another 'The Queen and her People', compiled by the Technical School for Girls, and 'The Royal Throne', from the Thrupp and Brimscombe British Women's Legion.

At Stratford Park's ring, events took over. There were demonstrations of archery and weightlifting, a motor cycling exhibition, a comic football match, and acrobatic and gymnastic displays. There were sports finals for school children, an exemption dog show, pony rides, skittles, and a fun fair which lasted all week!

Stratford Park, the centre stage of Stroud's Coronation Festivities, received its own special reward, which was a set of new local craftsmen-made gates, presented by Mr Ben Johnson. The inscription over the top, 'Stratford Park, E II R, 1953', ensuring that Stroud's Coronation festivities would be remembered as long as they stood there.

Buildings emblazoned with E II R were common throughout the county during the Coronation, and the tiny hamlet of Camp was no different. One story tells of a passer-by cheekily shouting to Captain Simmonds (who was precariously balanced up a ladder in the act of embellishing his home similarly at the time) what the initials E.R. stood for. Back came the dry reply, 'Early Riser of course!'

Keen to see more elaborate decorations, Camp had collected enough money to enable a coach visit to London to view the post-Coronation decorations. This was achieved with enough money remaining to secure a concrete top on their well in Honeycombe Lane, and repair the bus shelter roof. The day of the visit saw the villagers travelling by coach to alight at the Houses of Parliament amid crowds of people doing likewise. Moving about was slow, and most sites could not be seen because of the protective boards. However, headed by Ivor and Beryl Gardiner with their street map, and six foot six Mr Davis, who provided a 'leading light' above the crowd, the little group visited Buckingham Palace and witnessed the changing of the Guard. Ivor bought some bananas off a barrow boy, and they were so delicious he purchased some pears on his return to enjoy on the journey home. His discovery of 'being conned' came later on the coach, when, instead a bag of anticipated juicy pears, he discovered he had bought just two pieces of fruit, among several balls of screwed up paper.

The Coronation television boom was assisted by hire purchase arrangements. The low unemployment in Stroud district (5 per cent unemployed, and 213 vacancies) meant a wide range of people could afford television in some form or another.

Electricians and aerial riggers became in constant demand, working all hours trying to keep everyone happy. Viewers became upset when the frame or line hold failed, or 'went fuzzy', or a neighbour roared down the road on a motorbike without a suppressor. Many frustrating hours were spent fiddling with knobs, or up ladders twisting aerials on cold wintry nights. Television viewing became addictive. Children rushed home from school to see *Children's Hour*, their homework suffering in consequence, and strained eyesight warnings doing little to ease the situation.

The Camp outing at Horse Guards Parade, London. L–R: Mrs Davis, Mrs Gladys Foster, Mr Tom Davis, Ivor Gardiner, Beryl Gardiner, June Workman, Gladys Workman and children. Ivor is giving a two finger salute with a couple of bananas.

Curry's in Stroud sold radiograms and televisions for 63 guineas, and Smith and Co in the High Street stocked Cine Cameras. The age of seeing without attending, and recording for later, had begun. Anyone who wanted to see the Coronation on film could see *Elizabeth is Queen* at the Ritz during 22 June week.

The news of the successful scaling of Mount Everest on 29 May, the 29,002 foot high Himalayan mountain, reached London on Coronation morning. Colonel John Hunt's expedition, and Edmund Hillary and Sherpa Tenzing's remarkable achievement, added an extra national pride to the day. The film of their struggle, *The Conquering of Everest*, was seen by every school in the district. Kingscourt Primary went in the morning, and walked excitedly in crocodile up Russell Street to wait with all the other primary school children who were due to see it that day.

The year of 1953 also held numerous sporting achievements. Roger Bannister ran the mile in 4 minute 5.2 seconds, Gordon Pirie covered six miles at the White City in 28 minutes 19.4 seconds, and Denis Compton and John Edrich played cricket for England and won the fifth Test Match and the Ashes. The Coronation Honours' list knighted Gordon Richards, and Stroud was proud as local rider, Pat Smythe, with her famous horses, Tosca and Prince Hal, represented Britain in America in the British Show Jumping Team.

Stroud staged a youth drama festival during Coronation year, and Rodborough Secondary school performed a play which was based on Drake's Drum, and came second. Clive Maton played a beefeater, and made his own costume, as did the rest of the cast. His cost little money, as the bloomers were his football shorts, the frill around his neck came from the tail of his father's shirt with a cord pulled through, and he made his pike in woodwork class. Clive stood behind the Queen. Other actors were Jeff Bartleman who played Sir Walter Raleigh, Rita Taylor and Dan Ball, but there were many more. Clive remembers the whole thing being so successful it later toured the villages.

In 1953, the refuse tip, which had been in existence for forty years by the canal in Chestnut Lane, closed. Its demise was generally thought to be because of the 3,665 ton load of waste which it was unable to accommodate. But my theory is it was probably when the council realized they were employing three men there simply to keep off the flies!

CHAPTER SEVENTEEN

BRANCHING OUT DURING THE FIFTIES AND SIXTIES

Wartime rationing ended in 1954, and with it came the opportunity to spend. A physically and mentally richer society, intoxicated with more money, no coupons, and now hire purchase, created a boon in working-class consumer spending.

Cars were available to most people's pockets, either through a savings nest egg, or by so many payments over several years for the less financially endowed. An upsurge of driving schools mushroomed everywhere to cope with the driving test, and were kept in business by a whole new generation of seventeen-year-olds learning to drive. Aston Down, hardly recognizable since the majority of the hut accommodation had been removed, became the perfect spot for driving practice on its remaining network of concrete roads. It was especially useful for reversing practice (from which I suffered a crick in the neck every Sunday afternoon).

Ferdinande Porsche's Volkswagen was 'the car for the people'. It was stocked at Steele's Garage in London Road, and cost £635 2s new, although alongside it stood the costlier convertible version at £1,006, or a new Sunbeam Rapier at £695. The Morris Oxford, whose boot capacity boasted 16 cu. feet, and which could manage The Bear Hill 'easily in third', appeared in May and cost around £789 inclusive of tax. But the newly qualified young driver usually opted for something like a second-hand 1953 Ford Popular at £345 from the 'Used Car' column in *The Stroud News and Journal*. This required more care after September 1960 when a vehicle testing scheme for cars over ten years old was introduced. A vehicle test cost 15s, while one for a motor bike was 10s 6d.

Father sold his prized Standard Ten during the fifties. A shiny but still second-hand, reliable Morris Eight pushed it out of the garage. He tried to foist it upon my newly married sister, but she and her husband soon returned it, so it sat dispiritedly outside for several months before someone bought it for a paltry ten pounds. Its temperamental behaviour had tired us, just as it had tired

Russell Street, Stroud. Steel's Garage entrance is on the left.

the person who had once tried to steal it during the night, but left it when it would not start. Yes, we had all endured enough pushing, towing and turning of starting handles.

Lambretta scooters also made their appearance during the fifties. A modern trendy machine to replace the moped, its achievement of 100 miles per gallon was especially welcomed, as it arrived towards the end of a petrol shortage. It was equipped with splash-free guards, which the advertisments suggested could protect even 'Sunday best' dress, and many women, who for years had queued and complained over the buses, were encouraged to take the plunge to buy one. Having mastered the driving technique, women paid £158 for an aggressive 150 cc scooter, or £71 17s for the gentler model, thus missing the opening on 3 July 1960 of the long-awaited Merrywalks Bus Station, and the complaints of the lack of queuing space. The passengers, said one traveller, 'were like sheep at a market'.

The new commercial television channel, which advertised consumer products to provide its funding, came on the scene to rival the BBC. The new channel was awaited with scepticism by some future watchers who feared their programmes would be disrupted, but most people actually liked it better than the BBC. The cartoons were fascinating, and most people stayed to watch them

213

instead of going to make tea or wash up, as they had said and thought they would. Many people particularly enjoyed the new types of programme which the richer commercial television could afford, particularly the soap operas, and the game shows with the numerous prizes, which advertising enabled contestants to win. Stroud received its new television station in 1956, and a modern thirteen channel set arrived in the shops to handle the change of programmes. It was possible to convert their existing sets, but usually people chose the new type, although they were assured of good reception either way once the Lichfield Station was opened in June. 'Their test card signals will be as good, if not better', announced the promoters, 'than those received from Sutton Coldfield when BBC transmissions first began'.

Therefore, by the close of the decade, three quarters of England's population possessed a television of some kind. The other, unconvinced, quarter bought theirs later in the sixties, when BBC 2, and then the Open University, made an appearance. These new owners remind everyone how their set was, 'not a waste of time, but a means of further education'.

Grandfather died in the fifties, and an era disappeared with him. There were no more jaunts in the cart, no more pigs, and no more bacon curing. His ducks disappeared from the field, and his cottage nearly vanished too, along with other homes 'unfit for human habitation' and demolished in Bowl Hill. Luckily, father bought the cottage instead, and modernized it according to Authority ruling. The old wash-house, which had seen so many cockerels drawn and dressed for Christmas Day, was converted into a bathroom, a modern hygienic convenience unnecessary and undesired by previous generations. When newly up-dated, his home was rented out to tenants, an income, father thought, would provide for his own retirement. But this simple action, and the system of letting during the mid-sixties, ensured that none of Grandfather's family could live in his home for over forty years.

Stroud changed dramatically through slum clearance, as the Council dealt in one way or another with 354 unfit houses, taking with them a large chunk of Church Street and Hill Street and a whole section more from the top of the town. It was all in the name of damp, out-of-date facilities, and car parks. The reporting of the trek up the main street and along an alley for two families just to reach their toilet was the knell of death for fourteen homes in Hill Street. Among these was a small workshop, The Orange Tree Inn, Granny Ball's shop, where everybody had bought sweets (and those within a hundred yards' vicinity knew when they were in the making), and her cottage, which Francis Dodsun rented once for 2s a week. Later, in 1964, 4, 5 and 6 Nelson Street, which dated from 1676, succumbed to the same fate. Rickety floorboards and cellars were the reason given this time. The council were determined to fulfil their 1960 New Year Resolution in which they had promised to, 'Press on with the clearance scheme and demolition of old properties, and resolve the traffic problem'.

Granny Ball's Sweet Shop, No 4 and 5 Hill Street during the early sixties, when it was owned by Stroud County Council and rented by Alan and Joan Tucker for their secondhand/antiquarian/catalogue bookshop: the latter was printed on a press which the Tuckers still possess. The property was doomed for demolition in preparation for the proposed ring road which did not materialise, so a short term lease ensured a move in 1966 to the former hairdressers shop in Station Road, which had once been a coal office situated between The Imperial Hotel and Boots. Here they sold new books and opened a children's bookshop across the road, before moving in 1983 to The Original Holloway Society's prestigious 1930s building where they remain a valuable asset to Stroud.

Ada and Leslie Webb, whose housing dilemma has been recorded through these pages, bought their own home around this time to join the increasing number of 'own home owners'. Their purchase was a modern convenient bungalow on the Gannicox Estate, which was neat and trim, built by G W Enoch and Sons, and sponsored by the Stroud Mutual Society. A prize of five guineas tempted contestants to, 'determine a suitable modern name' for the estate, but we still know it as Gannicox. Unfortunately, the new inhabitants for some time had to endure the Gannicox Refuse Tip, which opened in June 1960 to replace the completed one on Minchinhampton Common. They were protected from the tip by a high wooden fence.

Although the wartime civil defence was disbanded following the war,

Granny Ball's Sweet shop in the process of demolition.

Stroud still continued its own civil defence until the mid-sixties. It consisted of a Welfare Headquarters, a Warden Service, ambulances and the Auxiliary Fire Service which was affiliated to the Fire Service. There was also the little-known National Hospital Service Reserve, which was self-contained, but could have supported the main service until it was disbanded in the early sixties. Jim Gouge recalls the Fire Brigade being called to numerous flock mill fires years ago, at The Fleece and Crystal Fountain Mill, and a disastrous one at Eagle Mill in 1955. There were also numerous chimney fires, which could be tricky to extinguish if the old oak beam (which many cottages had, built into their structure) caught fire, but they coped with rick fires too. The ricks constructed of bales were the worst. The Brigade were also frequently called out by people who lived on common boundaries, to douse the fires which some 'old hands' (which included our family) lit to burn off the old stubble in the springtime, and probably still do. Later as more vehicles appeared on the roads they dealt with increasing road accidents. Jim says people used to think they had to pay to

216

Bisley Girls Club in about 1950. Back L–R: Phyllis Smith,Grace Clissold, Mary Trinder, Margaret Brunsdon, Audrey Skinner, Jean Trinder. Front: Kathleen Evans, Josephine Skinner, Marion Stevens, Pamela Ruck, Susan Williams, Cynthia Brown, Eileen Brunsdon, Joy Baynard, Mavis Brunsdon.

summon the Fire Brigade, but this was not so, and anyway it all changed when the Civil Defence Act in 1948 came along.

During the fifties 'teenagers' were a new influence, the result of the birth boom as men returned from war. They formed a band of young energy, who positively asserted their opinions and rights in a world so different from the one inhabited by their parents. A healthy, educated, product of the welfare state and increased education.

Their appearance apparently from nowhere fuelled instant complaint, and was received generally as was chickenpox, 'A nuisance while here, but would eventually get better'. But the contagious element had been overlooked, and soon the teenage influence was sweeping through the country like an epidemic.

They were labelled 'aggressive and rebellious', and their music was blamed because it 'aroused primitive instincts. Rock 'n' roll is at the root of it and should be stopped'.

The first most people heard of 'Rock 'n' roll' was in 1956, when Bill Hayley's film, *Rock around the Clock*, toured British cinemas and caused riots. Some cinemas refused to show it, Stroud itself banning it in August following trouble in Cheltenham a fortnight before. Therefore 'Rock 'n' Roll is not for Stroud' was the decision, and three hundred Stroud youngsters were left disappointed, with a determination to see it elsewhere.

Stroud's youth suffered a further blow in February, when the popular Teenager's Club at The Liberal Hall closed down. A simple notice posted on the door said so. It seems that an incessantly noisy juke box in early December was the reason, though the newly-formed Boys Club Headquarters at Church Street, which opened a few weeks later, was welcomed by all.

Music did appear to be the dominating factor, and the root of all disorder, 'which should be suppressed'. The expanded news network contributed towards the boom. I became aware of the change when in the dentist's waiting room awaiting the drill. Flicking through the pages of a glossy magazine, I hit upon a centre-fold spread of Tommy Steele, with quaffed fair hair and dazzling white teeth. He was Britain's first rock idol. During the evening, Tommy was on a television show, and on the news later. The next morning, he smiled from the newspaper, and the shops stocked his record, 'Singing The Blues'. Tommy was famous overnight.

Anyone could participate in the new beat music, as little skill or money was needed (skiffle proved that). It seemed that within no time a whole new industry, with an eye to business, had arrived to cater for the new youth's needs: records, clothes, entertainments, and coffee bars. Arriving in the music business at the right time, at a remarkably young age, was David Smith, owner of Stroud Music Centre in London Road, (formerly Miss Fyffes Sesome Bookshop). Stroud was in need of a music outlet following the death of Mr Grainger and the closure of his shop. David's Music Centre fitted the bill. The escalating record-buying teen market especially appreciated it, and arrived in vast numbers to buy the newly-produced 45 rpm records, which were preferable to their larger 78 rpm predecessor, which cracked. Queues of young record fans stretched well along the pavement, eager to spend their 2s 6d on the His Master's Voice records which David stocked. David said that record companies sometimes arranged promotional sessions in shops, when the singers came along to sign their autographs. His shop once hosted Max Bygraves, but larger towns like Gloucester were generally used.

With the circular skirts, which came into fashion when jive arrived, there was suddenly a demand for felt. A black off-the-shoulder top usually accompanied the skirt, together with several starched net petticoats which 'crackled when you sat down, scratched bare legs and were death to stockings'.

Even Sunday dress received criticism. The Church expressed sorrow at the demise of the, 'specialness of Sunday hitherto expressed through neat smart

218

Jack and the Beanstalk *performed by Thrupp Church Youth Fellowship, Dec. 1947–Jan. 1948. L–R: Maureen Halliday (herald), Maureen Savage (chorus), Bill Peters (Chips), Eunice Smith (Odorous Egg), Self (Mrs Egg), Eric Taylor (Widow Twanky), Enid Halliday (Jill), Phylis Savage (Jack), Graeme Neale, Mike Guy (Cows), Delphine Paterson (Daisy), Violet Ireland (Chorus), Dorothy Reeves (Chorus and Fairy Godmother), Doris Williams (Chorus).*

dress, and pride in dressing up. . . . Casualness, boredom and a cheap Sunday paper have taken over, with scruffy untidy flannel bags and slacks, and that ugly garment jeans!'

Things were to get worse. The skirts became shorter, trousers narrower, pink and green luminous socks peeped out from loafers, and flamboyant drapes replaced the conventional suit. Very soon, all boys wearing narrow trousers automatically became 'Teddy Boys', and every girl with long fair hair, and pale pink lipstick, was 'common'.

An influx of rock dances, youth clubs, and coffee bars, appeared throughout the district, and many villages formed a youth club, where they played records and put on dances. Coffee bars with juke boxes sprang up in towns, where, for the price of a cup of coffee or a milk shake, the teenager could spend all evening chatting to their friends. There was 'The Flamingo Bar' in Stroud's

Leonard Stanley Church Choir with Canon le Flemming.

Kendrick Street, Sarannes' and 'Roxy's' along London Road. Later came 'Flanigan's Bar' at The Union Inn, which was run by Neil Prenter, and the '61 Club', opposite Fowler's Cake Shop, which was run by Manns, and later burned down.

The drift towards a change in social habits became obvious to all when Stroud Co-operative opened on Good Friday, a day formally on a par with Sunday. The Church, upset at this liberty, strongly condemned what they saw as a weakening of the high ideals which the movement's founders had implemented since 1882, hoping 'the patrons of these shops will not hesitate to reprimand the executive officers for what is a retrograde step'. Time however saw that far from condemning Good Friday opening, this leap forward into modern consumerism was positively welcomed, and in successive years The Stroud Co-operative (which from 1959 became merged with the Cainscross and Ebley), was joined by a variety of other retailers who opened on Good Friday.

During 1959 the long-established strength of the Co-op received large-scale competition in the form of Burton's Supermarket which opened on the site of

Stroud Townswomens Guild 10th Anniversary Dinner. The Townswomens Guilds which were formed in 1929 spring from The Kensington Society and the National Union of Women's Suffragettes. They are predominently town based and aimed 'to advance education of women in the principles of good citizenship'. Stroud gained their Guild in April 1952, and have since contributed towards a children's clinic in Ghaka, India, planted five woods following the gales in the late 1980s and during their early days were involved in music, drama, social studies and visits at home and abroad. L–R: Mr Sanders of the Stroud News and Journal, *Mrs E Pope (Vice Chairman), Mrs Parker (Chairman of Stroud Council), Mrs M Baker (Chairman of the Guild), Mr Comben, Miss Maley (The Matron of Stroud Hospital), Mr T John (Dentist).*

the old Green Dragon Pub in Kings Street. Here, accompanied by 'soothing background music', 2,350 square feet of display space and a range of 'virtually unlimited products which Served you better – Saving you more' were displayed on shelves and in refrigerators. Johny, the famous T.V. Chimp of Brooke Bond Tea, opened the store under Alan Tucker's management on Wednesday 9 September. Two spin-driers were offered as prizes, and The Bell at Walbridge accommodated Johny.

Morality was still important during the fifties, as society struggled with its escape from the Victorian closet, although since the war divorce and marital problems were on the increase. This was the direct result of men arriving home from war to meet their growing families whom separation had determined they should not know. One result of this was that The Stroud Rotary Club hosted a

Fashion Show at the Subscription Rooms organised by Batemans. L–R: Pat Bath, Jane Holford, Betty Bingham, Brenda Elderkin, Ann Powell, Beryl Foster, Florrie Tyler, Maggie Combes, Josie Astley, ?.

talk by the General Secretary for the Unmarried Mother and her Child in 1957, where it was reported that thirty thousand illegitimate births had occurred in 1955. Little it seems had changed here yet, for adoption was still advocated as surely as it had been twenty years previously, as well as 'the use of the shorter birth certificate because it did not require a father's name'.

The Subscription Rooms, once host to numerous wartime dances, was eventually taken over by the Council during the early sixties, following negotiations dating from May 1927, and rented out. Wrestling and boxing, fashion shows, and Saturday and Wednesday night teen dances were held, with many rock bands and stars appearing. Clive Maton, who was engaged as a 'floor walker' for £2 a night, says the Jay Bee Club arranged the dances for stars such as Mike Sarne, The Barron Knights, Emile Ford and the Checkmates, and Marty Wilde, who arrived so late, because of a hold up, he could not appear, so had his money returned. The Beatles came twice, their appearance the second time meriting an increase on admission money from 5s to 7s 6d, because they were better known. Once Clinton Ford, who was renowned for revamping old songs, came, but Clive turned him away from the front door when he did not recognize him or believe he was who he said he was, and poor Clinton had to get in around the back.

The dances were extremely well-attended, and it was normal for the queues to stretch well down the street. Clive says it was nothing to have five hundred in the hall. Everyone received a rubber stamp as proof of their admission payment, whereupon the girls swarmed into the cloakroom to have their coats taken, and re-do, and re-do their hair.

Usually the ballroom was short on dancers for the first hour, although some girls danced with other girls while the boys watched. However, by ten o'clock, under the umbrella of dimness and engulfed with sound, the floor heaved with vibration, and soon there was scarcely room to move. Sometimes at going-home time trouble flared up, and the 'Gloucester Teds' who had come over for the dance had to be escorted by the police back on to the train. There were reports of torn railway seats and fights with flick-knives, but they may not all have been true.

Mother, having cooked for the young while they were at Primary school, carried on benefiting them nutritionally at their dances, when Miss Eggleston managed events. Her mass Friday morning baking sessions in the Subscription Rooms kitchen of treacle tarts, chocolate cake, and bread pudding by the trayful were eagerly consumed by perspiring youngsters, along with numerous cups of orange juice and coke. Mother says the first time she served at the Saturday night dance, Mrs Prior 'an old hand' had to 'practically push me out front', but she soon got acclimatized to the situation, and became accustomed to receiving praise for her bread pudding .

In 1960, National Service finally ended after twenty years, and an increased freedom entered society. *Lady Chatterley's Lover* and the Contraceptive Pill arrived in 1961, and Tommy Steele was a film star, practically on a par with royalty when his popular film *Tommy The Toreador* appeared in Stroud's cinema in the same week as the film of Princess Margaret's Royal Wedding.

The Ritz Cinema, home of so much happiness and glamour, along with the Cadena above it, burned down at 10.15 on 23 June 1961, caused through a fault in an extractor fan in the roof. Despite the fall in cinema attendance (the closure of the Regal at Stonehouse in October 1959 was another nail in the cinema coffin caused through television), Mother still remained loyal to her Friday cinema treat. She had been there that night, and was treading her familiar route up Rodborough Hill when the fire engines rushed along the Bath Road. Many others, on hearing the bells, had roused themselves too. Margaret Hawkes heard it from Highfield Road, 'popping and spurting', and Michael Carter, who

A Premier Cafe shop window exhibition in Festival year 1951, in which many of Stroud shops participated. The 'open Bible' in the left window has The Lord is my Shepherd *written clearly on it, and was given to Standish Hospital after the display.*

was in bed at Lightpill, walked into town with the rest of his family after the Nailworth fire engine had roared past their house. Clive Maton went down too, and stayed until two in the morning. 'Half of Stroud was there and the roads were all blocked off', he said, 'Orange lights were flashing and bells were ringing, but the cat escaped because it went into the gents' toilets, which was the only part not burned down.'

Although the building seated 1,250 people, there was no one hurt, and no cars in the car-park underneath which could accommodate a hundred cars. The Premier Hall, which was hosting a banquet, immediately cleared their building when the news was received. As everyone had already partaken of their buffet dinner, their guests stayed on, and went outside to watch. While the roof of the building was covered in burning cinders, William Tuck's house, which was next door, only suffered one cracked window due to the intense heat. Allen Hale, who was emerging from the Union Inn, saw this glow in the sky and immediately thought, 'Oh no, King Street's going up!' and rushed down to see the damage. 'The next morning, the remaining standing wall seemed very thin and reached up to the clouds', he said.

The fire had the same effect on mother, who had actually sat in her seat ten minutes before it became a raging inferno, as the Bristol Woolworths bomb had done on Pat Hawker. Her Friday night ritual lost some of its sparkle, and with only the Gaumont left and no choice of films, television and a warm fireside gradually took its place. A change in Stroud's life had begun.

BIBLIOGRAPHY

A.J.P. Taylor, *English History 1914–1945*, The Clarendon Press.
The Stroud News, 1939–1946.
The Stroud Journal, 1950–1960.
Jennifer Davies, *The Wartime Kitchen Garden*, B.B.C. Books.
W.Oliver Wicks, *Marling School, 1887–1987*, Oxford University Press.
Susan Harrison and Janet Maddocks, *High Old Times*, Stroud High School Old Girls Association.
Molly and Alfred Hoy, *They Met in a Barn: The Story of Congregationalism in Stroud, 1687–1987*.
Peter Hennessy, *Never Again*, Vintage 1993.
Area Eight, Captain Symonds, Stroud Urban & Rural & Nailsworth Defence Committee 1945
David Godwin and Ron Gardiner, *Chalford Blows a Century: the History of Chalford Band, 1885–1985*.

Housing Information supplied by Stroud District Council.
Statistics on Employment from Statistics Services Division.
Photograph of Stroud Brewery on cover courtesy of Whitbreads.